WORLD SEA POWER GUIDE

WORLD SEA POWER GUIDE

David Wragg

Pen & Sword
MARITIME

First published in Great Britain in 2012 by
Pen & Sword Maritime
an imprint of
Pen & Sword Books Ltd
47 Church Street
Barnsley
South Yorkshire
S70 2AS

Copyright © David Wragg 2012

ISBN 978-1-84884-879-5

Typeset in Palatino 10/12pt by
Concept, Huddersfield

Printed and bound by
CPI Group (UK) Ltd, Croydon, CRO 4YY

Pen & Sword Books Ltd incorporates the Imprints of Pen & Sword
Aviation, Pen & Sword Family History, Pen & Sword Maritime, Pen &
Sword Military, Pen & Sword Discovery, Wharncliffe Local History,
Wharncliffe True Crime, Wharncliffe Transport, Pen & Sword Select, Pen
& Sword Military Classics, Leo Cooper, The Praetorian Press, Remember
When, Seaforth Publishing and Frontline Publishing.

For a complete list of Pen & Sword titles please contact
PEN & SWORD BOOKS LIMITED
47 Church Street, Barnsley, South Yorkshire, S70 2AS, England
E-mail: enquiries@pen-and-sword.co.uk
Website: www.pen-and-sword.co.uk

Contents

Acknowledgements

In writing any book of reference, the author is always indebted to those who provide assistance, and especially those who provide good photographs. I am very grateful for their help to those in the many navies and coastguard services and, of course, those in the shipbuilders and their archivists, as well as the service attachés and advisers in the embassies and high commissions who have put me in touch with their headquarters.

David Wragg
Edinburgh, May 2012

INTRODUCTION

It is upon the navy under the Providence of God that the safety, honour, and welfare of this realm do chiefly attend.

Charles II, Preamble to the Articles of War

A ruler that has but an army has one hand, but he who has a navy has both.

Peter the Great

Without a decisive naval force we can do nothing definitive.

George Washington

We ought to begin a naval power, if we mean to carry on our commerce.

Thomas Jefferson

When a crisis confronts the nation, the first question often asked by policymakers is: 'What naval forces are available and how fast can they be on station?'

Admiral Carlisle A.H. Trost, USN

In any book such as this, the contents are a snapshot of the situation at a particular time, although it has also been the intention to provide a brief history whenever possible and relevant for the navies and paramilitary coastguard organisations that are covered. History is important, for the last century saw two global conflicts and many other more localised, but often serious, wars and campaigns. It is easy to forget those wars that don't directly affect us, but the lessons of, for example, the Falklands Campaign or the war between Iraq and Iran, or those between Pakistan and India, or between the Arab states and Israel, is that war happens all too easily. It is as well to be prepared. Deterrence is so often associated with massive nuclear retaliation that people forget that conventional forces have their part to play: Well balanced, well equipped and well trained armed forces are a deterrent against disagreements flaring up into war.

Yet, these lessons have been forgotten by politicians and their advisers, as well as by the mass of the general population. One can understand this to some extent in those countries where the day-to-day struggle to survive dominates all else, but in the well-educated and affluent democracies, such negligence is inexcusable. In the United Kingdom in 2010, just 0.28 per cent of the population was in the armed forces, and today that percentage is being reduced further. The situation is even worse in other countries, not only in Western Europe but in Canada and Australia as well. In the United States the figure is 0.5 per cent. This is the cost of having taken the so-called 'peace dividend' on the collapse of the Warsaw Pact and the break-up of the former Soviet Union. Too many have forgotten that a dividend is a return on an investment. Yet, there has been little investment in many of the armed forces covered in this survey. The dividend, if one is deserved at all, has been taken in advance before any benefits have accrued. The terrorist attacks on New York and Washington showed that the world is, if anything, more unstable and uncertain today than during the second half of the twentieth century. The threats are more varied. Democratic governments delude themselves and fail to provide leadership by burying their heads in the sand, claiming that there will be as much as ten years' notice of an emerging threat. No such period of warning existed before hi-jacked airliners, as devastating as any conventional bomb or missile, slammed into the twin towers of the World Trade Center and the Pentagon. Governments anxious to remain in office accord higher priorities to expenditure on social welfare than to defence, but without adequate defence, democracy itself is threatened and effectively taken hostage. There are other means of providing for education and health, but only governments can provide defence!

On our seas today, piracy has become a major problem. This has been most publicised in the Red Sea and Indian Ocean as Somali-based pirates become ever more ambitious and capable, but it is also a problem in the Gulf of Benin, especially off Nigeria, and in the Straits of Malacca and further east. Yet, the response of Western governments has been tepid. There has been none of that co-operation that enabled a combined British, American and Dutch naval squadron to finally resolve the problem of the Barbary pirates in 1816. In an age where longer distance travel is dominated by aviation, it is necessary to remind ourselves that 90 per cent of world trade is by sea.

Twice during the twentieth century, democracy was saved by the timely intervention of the United States. The new century has started with what has to be regarded as a *Pax Americana*. The lesson learnt should have been greater preparedness on the part of the democracies, but the United States had to take the lead in the Gulf War, in Iraq and in action over the former Yugoslavia. The question is not one of American leadership, since that would probably be a fact of life given the massive economic and military power of the United States. The problem is that the USA has had to provide more than the sum of its European allies in terms of effort, time and time again. Despite posturing by the European Union, too few European countries have the capability or inclination for operations outside of their own territory. New command structures, duplicating those of NATO, divert scarce funds and skilled and experienced staff officers. NATO is the longest lasting and most successful alliance in the whole of history, but it is undermined at great risk by European politics. In the late 1930s, the Dutch, Belgian and French governments knew, as did the British, that in the event of a major war, British intervention would be essential. Yet, there were no joint exercises, no attempts at collaboration. NATO has provided all of this, and a command structure as well, and no less important, it formally tied the USA and Canada into protecting Europe. Given current rates of defence expenditure, in terms of a percentage of GNP often half what they were a decade or so ago, lessons have been forgotten.

The British like to believe that they always 'punch above their weight,' but there are limits. They have gone from having only two out of three aircraft carriers operational to one, in which the remaining single carrier has been designated to only operate helicopters, with its fixed-wing aircraft withdrawn and sold. Earlier, in 2006, the Royal Navy lost its Sea Harriers with their Blue Vixen radar, leaving the fleet without an air defence fighter until the end of the present decade. How is it that the United States, with just five times the UK's population, can afford eleven large aircraft carriers, each more than four times the size of a British carrier, and keep a twelfth carrier in reserve? The French now maintain just one carrier, and would be embarrassed if the ship met with an unfortunate accident of the kind all too frequent at sea. Yet, the French, most of all amongst the Europeans, like to pretend that they can do without the United States. The malaise is global, but at least Australia is at last doing something about power projection, with two helicopter carriers entering service.

No intelligence agency and certainly no politician foresaw the so-called 'Arab Spring' of 2011. Having scrapped the Royal Navy's fixed-wing element a few months earlier, and severely reduced the capability of the Royal Air Force, including scrapping new maritime-reconnaissance aircraft before they could enter service, a British government immediately decided to use air power against the Libyan government forces and in support of a rebel uprising. The lack of naval air power and suitable ships meant that aircraft had to operate from land bases in Italy. When finally it was decided to use Army Air Corps Apache helicopters from the helicopter carrier HMS *Ocean*, these had to fire their missiles from offshore because they were vulnerable to Libyan surface-to-air missiles.

History repeats itself, but never exactly. The British idea of ten years to prepare in the 1930s seems to have returned. That was a politicians' and civil servants' ten years, not that of an airman, sailor or soldier. Given

3

the lengthy time taken to develop modern combat aircraft and get them into service, ten years is not enough. As events in the United States in September 2001 have shown, it does not even take three or four years for a major new threat to emerge. Given the situation in the states of the former USSR, where the populations are suffering a hangover from the old regime without feeling the benefits of a free society and market economy, a reversal of the new freedoms could have popular appeal. Where would that leave the democracies? In fact, Russia is using its oil and gas revenues to rebuild the country's armed forces and is commissioning new nuclear-powered submarines as well as having bought an assault ship from France, with a licence to build more. One has to ask why a continental nation needs such a capability. Perhaps plans revealed in late 2011 for a Eurasian Union to rival the United States, the European Union and Communist China hold a clue to future Russian intentions and what seems to be a desire to rebuild the USSR.

GLOSSARY

AAM	Air-to-air missile
AEW	Airborne early warning
AIP	Air-independent propulsion – a conventional submarine with sufficient battery capacity for extended operations without resort to diesel engines or snorkelling
AShM	Anti-shipping missile
ASROC	Anti-submarine rocket carrying a torpedo
ASTT	Anti-submarine torpedo tubes
ASW	Anti-submarine warfare
Blue water navy	A service capable of operating at long range in the open ocean
Brown water navy	A service for riverine, coastal and littoral use, but also often used for services confined to an enclosed sea such as the Baltic, Black Sea or Mediterranean
CIWS	Close-in weapon system used for defence against anti-ship missiles or low-flying aircraft
CV	Aircraft carrier
CVH	Helicopter carrier
CVL	Light, or light fleet, aircraft carrier
Displacement	Tonnage of a warship, sometimes given as light, meaning without weapons, aircraft or fuel, or full load or deep load, meaning fully armed, fuelled and equipped
EEZ	Exclusive economic zone, often known as territorial waters
GRT	Gross register tonnage (normally used for merchant vessels)
HWT	Heavyweight torpedo
ICBM	Intercontinental ballistic missile
LCT	Landing craft tank
LCM	Landing craft, medium
LCU	Landing craft, utility
LHA	Landing ship assault

LPD	Landing platform dock
LPH	Landing platform helicopter
LSL	Landing ship logistic
LSM	Landing ship medium
LST	Landing ship tank
MCMV	Mine counter measures vessel
MTB	Motor torpedo boat
RAM	Rolling airframe missile
RBU	Rocket bomb launchers – more usually armed with depth charges
SAM	Surface-to-air guided missiles
SAR	Search and rescue
SLBM	Submarine-launched ICBM
SSBN	Submarine capable of launching ballistic missiles
SSM	Surface-to-surface missile, now generally superseded by AShM
SSN	Nuclear-powered submarine, often capable of launching cruise or AShM missiles
Taken up from trade	The practice in wartime or an emergency of a navy commandeering or chartering merchant vessels to augment the standing fleet
UAV	Unmanned air vehicle
VLS	Vertical launch surface-to-air or anti-ship guided missiles

NATO DEFINITIONS FOR SOVIET-ERA SHIPBOARD MISSILES

Chinese-manufactured missiles of Soviet origin are usually prefixed with a 'C'.

NATO designations are set in parentheses, with official Russian names following when known.

Anti-Ship Missiles (AShM)
CSS-N-8 'Saccade'
SS-N-12 'Sandbox' or Bazalt
SS-N-14 'Stilex' or Rastrup
SS-N-19 'Shipwreck' or Granit
SS-N-22 'Sunburn' or Maskit
SS-N-25 'Switchblade'

Surface-to-Air Missiles (SAM)
SA-N-1 'Goa'
SA-N-3 'Goblet' or Shtorm
SA-N-4 'Geiko'
SA-N-6 'Grumble'
SA-N-7 'Gadfly'
SA-N-9 'Gauntlet' or Kindzhoz
SA-N-12 'Grizzly'
SA-N-20 'Gargoyle'

NATIONAL ENTRIES LISTING

Albania
Algeria
Angola
Antigua and Barbuda
Argentina
Australia
Azerbaijan
Bahamas
Bahrain
Bangladesh
Barbados
Belgium
Belize
Benin
Bolivia
Brazil
Brunei
Burundi
Bulgaria
Cambodia
Cameroon
Canada
Cape Verde
Chile
Chinese People's Republic
Colombia
Congo
Congo, Democratic Republic of
Costa Rica
Cote d'Ivoire
Croatia
Cuba

Cyprus
Denmark
Djibouti
Dominican Republic
East Timor
Ecuador
Egypt
El Salvador
Equatorial Guinea
Eritrea
Estonia
Fiji
Finland
France
Gabon
Gambia
Georgia
Germany
Ghana
Greece
Guatemala
Guinea
Guinea-Bissau
Guyana
Haiti
Honduras
Iceland
India
Indonesia
Iran
Iraq
Ireland

Israel
Italy
Jamaica
Japan
Jordan
Kazakhstan
Kenya
Korea, Democratic People's Republic of (North)
Korea, Republic of (South)
Kuwait
Laos
Latvia
Lebanon
Liberia
Libya
Lithuania
Macedonia
Madagascar
Malawi
Malaysia
Mali
Malta
Mauritania
Mauritius
Mexico
Montenegro
Morocco
Mozambique
Myanmar
Namibia
Netherlands
New Zealand
Nicaragua
Nigeria
Norway
Oman
Pakistan
Panama
Papua New Guinea
Paraguay

People's Republic of China – see China
Peru
Philippines
Poland
Portugal
Qatar
Romania
Russia
Saudi Arabia
Senegal
Seychelles
Sierra Leone
Singapore
Somali Republic
South Africa
Spain
Sri Lanka
Sudan
Surinam
Sweden
Syria
Taiwan
Tanzania
Thailand
Timor Leste – *see* East Timor
Togo
Trinidad & Tobago
Tunisia
Turkey
Turkmenistan
Uganda
Ukraine
United Arab Emirates
United Kingdom
United States of America
Uruguay
Venezuela
Vietnam
Yemen

NATIONAL ENTRIES

ALBANIA

Population: 3 million
Land Area: 11,097 square miles (28,741 sq.km.)
GDP: $9.23bn (£6.0bn), per capita $2,987 (£1,939)
Defence Exp: $434m (£282m)
Service Personnel: 48,570 active, plus 210,000 reserves

ALBANIAN NAVY BRIGADE

Although Albania became independent in 1912 after four centuries of Turkish rule, it was not until 1928 that a navy was formed, the Royal Albanian Navy, under the first, and last, monarch, King Zog. Initially it was commanded by an Italian captain, although it is not known whether he was still in command when Italy invaded in 1939, by which time there were just four patrol boats, all US-built.

After the Second World War, Albania became part of the Communist Bloc, but withdrew from the Warsaw pact in 1961 and the Soviet Navy withdrew from its base at Pashaliman. While the service had more than 100 craft by this time, most of them were small, Chinese-built, Huchuan-class torpedo boats, as well as some ASW patrol vessels, and the only vessels of any importance were four ex-Russian Whiskey-class submarines. The submarines remained in service until 1998, but their operational effectiveness was very low for most of the preceding twenty years.

In more recent years, the Albanian Navy Brigade has been part of the Albanian Joint Forces Command and is effectively subordinate to the army. The vessels operated are mainly patrol boats donated by Italy and the USA, while the status of the last of four Soviet-built minesweepers is uncertain.

Today the Albanian Navy Brigade has an unstated number of personnel but has its headquarters at Durres and a second base at Vlore, the latter being the former Soviet naval base of Pashaliman. There are four Dutch-built Damen Type 4207 patrol boats, while complementing the ANB is the Albanian Coast Guard, with as many as twenty-nine small patrol craft.

Unusually, the ANB is also responsible for lighthouses and other navigational aids.

ALGERIA

Population: 35.4 million
Land Area: 919,590 square miles (2,381,741 sq.km.)
GDP: $161bn (£104.5bn), per capita $4,553 (£2,956)
Defence Exp: $5.67bn (£3.68bn)
Service Personnel: 147,000 active, plus 150,000 reserves and 187,200 para-
  military

ALGERIAN NATIONAL NAVY

Algeria became independent from France in 1962 and immediately started to create its own armed forces out of the National Liberation Army, taking over former French bases, and initially received assistance from the Soviet Union, Czechoslovakia and Egypt. During its early years the service looked to the Eastern Bloc countries for assistance, and introduced Soviet Osa-class missile-armed boats to control its territorial waters. This meant that by the late 1970s, when the ANN had 3,800 personnel, it operated six Komar-class and six Osa-class boats with 'Styx' AShM, with a further sixteen smaller craft and three minesweepers.

In more recent years, procurement has been spread more widely and the country has been building smaller naval vessels itself. There have been exercises with NATO countries and visits by ships from these countries, including the NATO Rapid Reaction Mine Force. Aircraft have also been introduced, including Kamov helicopters, but again, in recent years there has been interest in Western products, especially from AgustaWestland.

Today the ANN has 6,000 personnel. It has three Soviet-built Mourad Rais-class (Soviet Koni-class) with 'Gecko' SAM, two RBU 6000 rocket launchers, two twin 76mm guns and one of these has two twin ASTT while the others are being modernised to the same standard. Augmenting these ships are three Soviet-built Rais Hamidou-class corvettes, with SS-N-2C AShM and 'Gecko' SAM; three Djebel Chenona-class corvettes with 'Saccade' AShM and a 76mm gun. There are still a few Osa-class vessels amongst the eighteen patrol craft. There are four Soviet-built submarines, two of which are 'Kilo'-class and two are Improved 'Kilo'-class, all with six torpedo tubes. There are just three logistics and support ships.

Reports that three British-built Nakhoda Ragami-class corvettes, rejected by the Royal Brunei Navy, were sold to Algeria in 2008 have so far been unsubstantiated.

The main bases are Mers el Kebir and Algiers, with additional bases at Annaba and Jijel.

There is also a small paramilitary coastguard with about 500 personnel and more than forty small patrol boats.

ANGOLA

Population: 19 million
Land Area: 481,226 square miles (1,246,369 sq.km.)
GDP: $85.1bn (£55.3bn), per capita $4,479 (£2,908)
Defence Exp: $2.74bn (£1.78bn)
Service Personnel: 107,000 active, plus 10,000 paramilitary

ANGOLAN NAVY

Angola became independent from Portugal in 1975 and a small navy, *Marinha de Guerra* (MdG), was formed with four ex-Portuguese patrol craft left behind by the colonial power. The country came under Cuban influence shortly afterwards and over the next fifteen years a number of Soviet minor warships were introduced, including Osa-class patrol boats with SS-N-2 AShM.

Today the MdG is the smallest of the country's armed forces with about 1,000 personnel, five patrol craft and a number of smaller patrol boats, mainly for riverine use. There are reports that a small number of fast attack craft will be delivered from Germany, although this is uncertain. Aircraft are manned by the air force. The main base is at Luanda.

ANTIGUA AND BARBUDA

Population: 88,550
Land Area: 170 square miles (449 sq.km.)
GDP: $1.1bn (£0.71bn), per capita $12,413 (£8,060)
Defence Exp: $33m (£21.4m)
Service Personnel: 170 active, plus 75 reserves

ANTIGUA AND BARBUDA DEFENCE FORCE

Since independence in 1967, Antigua and its dependency Barbuda have maintained a small defence force, with forty-five of its personnel in the small navy, which has two small patrol craft, *Dauntless* and *Swift*.

ARGENTINA

Population: 40.7 million
Land Area: 1,084,120 square miles (2,807, 857 sq.km.)
GDP: $382bn (£248.1bn), per capita $9,396 (£6,101)
Defence Exp: $2.60bn (£1.69bn)
Service Personnel: 73,100 active, with no formal reserves

ARGENTINE NAVY

The Argentine revolution that saw the country fight for its independence from Spain started in 1810 and a small navy was formed by the Irishman William Brown. On 17 May 1814, this small force defeated Spanish ships in the Battle of Montevideo.

Known officially as the *Armada de la República Argentina* (ARA), or 'Navy of the Argentine Republic', the service embarked on wholesale modernisation towards the end of the nineteenth century, by which time its largest vessels were five armoured cruisers. Two battleships were built in the United States and commissioned in 1915. The country remained neutral in both world wars, but in 1940 the ARA claimed to be the eighth largest navy in

The German-built MEKO 360 destroyer *La Argentina* is powerfully armed with a 127mm gun, Exocet AShM and anti-submarine torpedo tubes. Four of these ships provide the mainstay of the Argentine Navy. (Armada Argentina)

13

the world and the largest in Latin America. At this time, a new base had opened at Mar del Plata, and in addition to the two US-built battleships, which survived until the mid-1950s, there were five cruisers, including the British-built *La Argentina*, commissioned in 1938; sixteen destroyers, of which seven were new ships of the Buenos Aires-class; as well as three Italian-built submarines and two survey ships.

Post-war, Argentina joined the Organisation of American States in 1948, and became eligible for US military aid, including the transfer of two Brooklyn-class cruisers from the USN in 1951. Further changes took place in 1956, when ten F4U Corsair fighter-bombers arrived, joined in 1957 by Lockheed Neptune MR aircraft, Consolidated PBY-5A Catalina amphibians and Martin PBM-5 Mariner flying boats. Grumman F6F-5 Hellcat fighter-bombers, JRF Goose and J2F-2 amphibians followed, with North American T-6 Texan, Vultee 13T-13 and Beech AT-11 trainers. The fighter-bombers were for the aircraft carrier *Independencia*, formerly HMS *Warrior*, which arrived in 1958. The Royal Netherlands Navy carrier *Karel Doorman*, another former British carrier, was bought in 1969, renamed *Veinticinco de Mayo* and *Independencia* was withdrawn in 1970.

During the late 1970s, the ARA was operating the aircraft carrier *Veinticinco de Mayo*; two ex-US Brooklyn-class cruisers, known as the Belgrano-class; two British-built Type 42 anti-aircraft destroyers; while the rest of the destroyers were all ex-USN, including three Fletcher-class destroyers, three Allen M. Sumner-class and a Gearing 'FRAM II'-class; two King-class corvettes; two Salta-class (Type 209) submarines, built in sections in Germany and assembled in Argentina, and two ex-USN Guppy-class submarines. There were also five fast attack craft. Later, three French-built corvettes were added.

For some years, the Argentine Republic had claimed sovereignty over the Falkland Islands and South Georgia, although some distance from the mainland of Latin America and never occupied by Spain during the colonial era. Known to the Argentines as 'Las Malvinas', the islands were invaded on 2 April 1982, with an Argentine naval helicopter shot down by an anti-tank missile fired by a small detachment of Royal Marines, the sole defence for the islands. Although the ARA led the invasion, it played very little part afterwards when the British despatched a task force led by two aircraft carriers, other than joining the *Fuerza Aérea Argentina* in the air war, where the mistake was to concentrate on attacking British warships rather than gaining aerial superiority first against just twenty Fleet Air Arm and RAF Sea Harriers and Harriers. After the cruiser *General Belgrano* was sunk by a British nuclear-powered submarine, the ARA remained within a 12-mile limit from the coast of Argentina imposed by the British. Later, the submarine *Santa Fe* was disabled by a British helicopter off South Georgia. Argentine air attacks nevertheless sunk four British warships and a converted container ship carrying most of the British task force's troop-carrying helicopters.

Following the end of the Falklands Campaign on 15 June 1982, a new government in Buenos Aires started to rebuild and modernise the ARA. Second World War ex-USN destroyers were replaced by new MEKO 140 and 360 destroyers and frigates built in Germany, with the submarines replaced by TR-1700s, also built in Germany, although plans for additional boats to be built in Argentina were abandoned. The *Veinticinco de Mayo* was decommissioned in 2000 and not replaced, with her aircraft being based ashore. Nevertheless, the Tracker ASW aircraft, modernised to Turbo-Tracker standard, and Super Etendard jet fighters maintain carrier capability for their pilots by operating from the Brazilian carrier *Sao Paulo* and from USN carriers on passage through the South Atlantic in what have become known as the Gringo-Gaucho exercises.

An arms embargo imposed by the United States prevented updating of the maritime-reconnaissance force until the 1990s, when P-3B Orions were introduced.

Today, the ARA has 20,000 personnel, of whom 2,000 are engaged in naval aviation and another 2,000 are marines. There are four Almirante Brown-class (MEKO 360) destroyers, each with Exocet AShM, two triple ASTT, one 127mm gun and accommodation for a Fennec or Alouette III helicopter, while a fifth destroyer, the surviving Type 42, is used as a fast

Argentina's small submarine force is also German-built; this is the TR-1700 type boat *San Juan*. (Armada Argentina)

troop transport. There are six Espora-class (MEKO 140) frigates, also armed with Exocet AShM and two triple ASTT, a 76mm gun and accommodation for a Fennec or Alouette III helicopter; three French-built Drummond-class corvettes are also fitted with Exocet AShM and two triple ASTT, as well as a 100mm gun, and fourteen offshore patrol craft, one of which is an ex-US oilfield tug. The small force of three submarines includes a German-built Type 209, with eight torpedo tubes, and two German-built TR-1700s with six torpedo tubes, but there are plans to build a nuclear-powered submarine, possibly armed with AShM. There are eighteen amphibious landing craft of various types and a logistics force of twelve ships, of which the largest and most modern is the *Patagonia*, formerly the French *Durance*, a fleet oiler with a helicopter platform.

Some twenty-four aircraft are combat capable. All but two of the eleven Super Etendard are in storage, but there are five Turbo-Tracker and six P-3B Orion. Helicopters include four SH-3H Sea King and three Fennec, as well as six Alouette III.

AUSTRALIA

Population: 21.5 million
Land Area: 2,967,909 square miles (7,682,300 sq.km.)
GDP: $1.24tr (£0.81tr), per capita $57,686 (£37,458)
Defence Exp: $24.5bn (£15.9bn)
Service Personnel: 56,552 active, plus 20,440 reserves

Australia is one country that has been expanding and developing its navy in recent years. This is the Anzac-class frigate HMAS *Toowoomba*, a German MEKO 200 guided missile frigate with Harpoon AShM and Evolved Sea Sparrow SAM, and accommodation for two helicopters. (Royal Australian Navy)

For many years Australia looked to the UK and to the Royal Navy for support and a pattern of operations. Many in the UK felt that Australia did not take defence seriously enough. The limited capability of the UK to protect Australian interests was brutally exposed during the Second World War. Australia, and New Zealand, had been promised that in the event of war, a 'strong fleet would be sent' to the Pacific, but when Japan entered the war on 6 December 1941, the RN was engaged in a major war with Germany and Italy. Most of the naval action centred on the North Atlantic and the Mediterranean, but shipping had to be protected in the South Atlantic and Indian Ocean and, after the German invasion of the Soviet Union in 1942, on the Arctic convoy routes and the Persian Gulf as well.

Until the British Pacific Fleet could be established with the ending of Germany's ability to make war at sea, Australia's main ally was the United States and Australian warships operated in forces usually led by the USN. British influence returned with peace, enabling the Royal Australian Navy to establish its own Fleet Air Arm and a small submarine service, while the South East Asia Treaty Organisation was meant to enhance security in the region against the growing power of Soviet Russia and Communist China, but SEATO was not another NATO and did not last the course. The alliance that did matter, with successive UK governments anxious to abandon all commitments 'east of Suez' was once again with the USA.

Even so, once again Australia did not seem to attach the same importance to defence as the 'Mother Country' or its new ally, the USA. Fixed-wing naval aviation was lost when HMAS *Melbourne* was retired in 1982.

In recent years this has changed. Australian forces have become involved in Afghanistan, Iraq, East Timor and the Solomon Islands. A new government expected to reduce defence expenditure has instead increased it. The armed forces enjoyed a 6.4 per cent increase in the budget in 2008-2009, promised a 3 per cent increase in real terms until 2017 at least, and earmarked part of the tax windfall created by China's demand for Australian minerals for a special defence reserve fund. The money from this fund is covering Australia's existing overseas commitments.

Ambitious plans include the introduction of two Spanish-built 27,000-tonne amphibious landing ships, while other possibilities include a doubling of the submarine force using boats capable of firing conventionally-armed cruise missiles, and more surface vessels as well. There is also the possibility of buying the STOVL variant of the F-35 Joint Strike Fighter, the F-35B, if it can overcome its development problems as the Canberra-class landing ships may follow their Spanish counterparts in having a ski jump at the forward end of the flight deck.

The question will remain whether all of this, and the improvements to the capabilities of the RAAF and the Australian Army will be enough in a world where China is flexing its muscles and also increasing the capabilities of its armed forces and is set once again to become a maritime power with aircraft carriers and nuclear-powered submarines.

ROYAL AUSTRALIAN NAVY

Australia was granted dominion status on 1 January 1901, which meant that it became a self-governing member of the British Empire and with the right to its own foreign policy. The country regarded itself as a 'commonwealth' with the individual states each being self-governing except for the sparsely-populated Northern Territory, which was administered direct from the federal capital, Canberra. Locally-raised units formed the new Commonwealth Naval Forces, which formally came into existence on 1 March 1901. On 10 July 1911, King George V granted the right of the CNF to the title of the Royal Australian Navy.

The service saw action during the First World War, initially helping in the capture of German colonies in the Pacific and protecting merchant shipping from the German East Asia Squadron. It also escorted convoys as far as the Suez Canal carrying Australian and New Zealand troops to Europe. For the remainder of the war, with the German naval threat in the Pacific and Indian Ocean under control, the RAN operated alongside Royal Navy units in the Mediterranean. During the war years, the RAN was incorporated into the Royal Navy and under Admiralty control from London. Post-war, the service was considerably reduced in size during the 1920s, although during the late 1930s, as the threat from not only Germany but also Japan became apparent, the fleet started to be rebuilt. Nevertheless, on the outbreak of war in Europe in 1939, many of the ships dated from the previous conflict.

Despite Australia's dominion status, throughout the time from the inauguration of the RAN to the Second World War, like all of the Australian services, it was commanded by British officers on secondment. Uniforms for those serving in the RAN were identical to those of the Royal Navy other than that a shoulder flash with 'Australia' was worn and ratings' cap tallies carried 'HMAS' rather than 'HMS'. The British White Ensign was worn on the ensign staff with the Union Flag quartered rather than the Australian flag, in contrast to the practice today in which the Australian White Ensign is a variation of the national flag.

Essentially, the RAN shared the mission of the RN, with a high priority accorded to protecting trade and keeping the homeland safe from invasion. Between the two wars, a major naval base was built by the British at Singapore, and both Australia and New Zealand were both given assurances that, in the event of war breaking out in the East with Japan, a 'strong fleet' would be dispatched eastwards. This would be done by moving units in sequence from the Indian Ocean and then the Mediterranean.

The Armidale-class offshore patrol boats provide EEZ protection and are also used to intercept illegal immigration. They are usually organised into flotillas of four ships, each with six crews who are rotated during their tour of duty. This is HMAS *Maryborough*. (Royal Australian Navy)

During the first winter of war, with little sign of war with Japan, the RAN dispatched five First World War vintage V & W-class destroyers to the Mediterranean to help protect convoys from the German U-boats. Initially using Malta as a base, these ships remained for two years in the Mediterranean and saw action at Calabria and Matapan, as well as taking part in the evacuation of troops from first Greece and then Crete. In between, they also helped protect convoys and the British Mediterranean Fleet from U-boats.

With Japan's entry into the war with the surprise attack on the US Pacific Fleet at Pearl Harbor, the Australian ships were sent home to the war in the Pacific. Nevertheless, the rapid advance of Japanese forces culminating in the seizure of Hong Kong and the fall of Malaya and then Singapore saw the Royal Australian Navy suffer heavy losses. A new command was established to co-ordinate the remnants of British and Dutch forces in the area with those of the United States and Australia – ABDA (American, British, Dutch, Australian). This was improvised, under-resourced and untried, and at the Battle of the Java Sea, where the ABDA force was commanded by the Dutch Rear Admiral Karel Doorman, defeat ensued. Out of five cruisers and nine destroyers, just four destroyers, all US, escaped: the losses included the Australian light cruiser HMAS *Perth*.

After the Battle of the Java Sea, the RAN found itself operating globally, taking part in escorting convoys in the Mediterranean and the North

Atlantic while also operating alongside the United States Navy in the Pacific. It was present at many of the major battles, including the Battle of Savo Island, off Guadalcanal, August 1942, where the RAN suffered its largest single ship loss when the cruiser *Canberra* was lost on 9 August. Earlier in the war, the cruisers *Sydney* and *Perth* had been sunk, the former with the loss of the entire ship's company. The loss of *Canberra* attracted much international sympathy for the RAN, and to commemorate her loss, the United States President, Franklin Roosevelt, ordered that a heavy cruiser under construction be named the USS *Canberra*: the first time an American warship was named after a foreign city.

By the outbreak of war, the RAN was already largely self-sufficient in training with a Royal Australian Naval College at Jervis Bay, but in 1930 this was transferred to Flinders Naval Depot, HMAS *Cerberus*, near Melbourne in Victoria as the impact of the world economic recession took its toll on government funding. Flinders had originally opened in September 1920 to train ratings for the RAN. It became known as Flinders Naval Depot in 1921, and was commissioned on 1 April that year.

The transfer of warships under construction for or operated by the Royal Navy kept the RAN up to date and in line with British ideas on anti-submarine warfare, using ASDIC and depth charges, as well as depth charge throwers. When at Singapore on their way to the Mediterranean, the original Australian wartime destroyer flotilla exercised anti-submarine warfare with a Royal Navy submarine, HMS *Rover*. By the end of the war, the RAN had six frigates and fifty-three corvettes, both wartime types that had not existed in 1939.

Japanese submarine attacks on Australian shipping effectively started in late May and June 1942. Five Japanese submarines began a series of attacks on Sydney and the port of Newcastle, close by, including sending three midget submarines into Sydney Harbor on the night of 31 May/1 June. On 8 June, two Japanese submarines shelled Sydney and Newcastle, although they caused little damage. These attacks nevertheless persuaded the RAN to start coastal convoys along the east and south coasts, from Brisbane to Adelaide. In contrast to the Royal Navy, which did not make convoys compulsory, in Australian waters all ships of more than 1,200 tons and speeds of less than 12 knots were compelled to sail in convoy. That these measures were necessary can be judged from the fact that seventeen ships were sunk in Australian waters in 1942 and a further sixteen during the first half of 1943, before the Japanese campaign ended in July. Overall, Australian warships escorted more than 1,100 coastal convoys during the war years, although only one Japanese submarine was sunk in Australian waters. Nevertheless, the RAN's tally of Japanese submarines elsewhere in the Pacific was considerable.

The RAN ended the Second World War with three landing ships infantry, which was a wartime enhancement of its capabilities. It supported many of the landings as the Allies battled their way across the Pacific towards the Japanese Home Islands. Between the wars, the personnel strength of the RAN had fallen as low as 3,117 personnel with another 5,446 in the reserves, but during the Second World War, the RAN's strength grew rapidly to 39,650 personnel. The capability and experience of the service had also grown during the war years, but it was still without submarines or naval aviation other than seaplanes and amphibians operated from cruisers and the seaplane carrier *Albatross*.

A Fleet Air Arm was formed in 1948 using Nowra, near Sydney, as a naval air station, and equipped with two squadrons each of Hawker Sea Fury fighter-bombers and Fairey Firefly anti-submarine aircraft. The RN's 7XX and 8XX squadron numbers were used at first, although later, as US equipment arrived, the USN squadron numbering scheme was adopted. A light fleet carrier, HMAS *Sydney* (formerly HMS *Terrible*) was acquired from the UK and joined the British carriers in operations off Korea during the Korean war, 1950-1953. A second carrier, *Vengeance*, was leased in 1953 while delivery of the slightly larger *Melbourne* (formerly HMS *Majestic*) was awaited. The Australian FAA's first jets, de Havilland Sea Venom fighters and Vampire trainers, were received along with Fairey Gannet anti-submarine aircraft and Bristol Sycamore light helicopters. *Sydney* became a training carrier until the Vietnam War, in which Australia participated for some years, when the ship became a fast troop transport. *Melbourne*'s aircraft were updated with the Sea Venoms replaced by Douglas A-4G Skyhawk fighter-bombers and Grumman S-2E Tracker anti-submarine aircraft as well as Westland Wessex (S-58) ASW helicopters and Bell UH-1H Iroquois utility helicopters, while in 1970-71 the Vampires were replaced by Aermacchi MB326H trainers.

While Australia was a founding member of the South East Asia Treaty Organisation (SEATO), this organisation never became a true southern hemisphere version of NATO with a command structure and was eventually overtaken by a new alliance, Australia, New Zealand and United States (ANZUS). One factor in the weakening of SEATO and its eventual demise was the desire of successive British governments to be relieved of any commitments east of Suez.

Submarines were acquired with first British-built Porpoise-class and then Oberon-class boats joining the RAN in the 1970s. These were later replaced by the current fleet of six US-built Collins-class submarines.

Plans to replace *Melbourne* with the Royal Navy's *Invincible* were abandoned after the Falklands Campaign, which led the Royal Navy to retain the ship and Australian fixed-wing naval aviation ended with the withdrawal of *Melbourne* in 1982. Meanwhile, US-built Perry-class frigates were introduced, capable of handling helicopters and later augmented by German MEKO-200 frigates.

The older escorts in the RAN are updated US-built Oliver Hazard Perry-class frigates, known in Australia as the Adelaide-class. This is HMAS *Sydney*. (Royal Australian Navy)

The RAN today has 14,250 personnel and is re-equipping with greater emphasis on force projection and is introducing two Canberra-class amphibious ships, both capable of operating V/STOL or STOVL aircraft, built in Spain, and may order a third. The six Collins-class conventional submarines can launch torpedoes or Harpoon anti-shipping missiles, and may be joined in the future by another six submarines capable of launching cruise missiles. The current fleet includes four Adelaide-class frigates, each with Harpoon AShM, VLS Evolved Sea Sparrow SAM, two triple ASTT, a 76mm gun and accommodation for two S-70B Seahawk ASW helicopters; eight Anzac-class (German Meko 200) frigates each have Harpoon AShM, VLS Evolved Sea Sparrow SAM, two triple ASTT, a 127mm gun and accommodation for an S-70B Seahawk ASW helicopter. The coastal patrol force has been updated with the replacement of the Attack-class by the Armidale-class, of which there are fourteen, mainly in flotillas of four ships with six crews to maximise sea time. There are six Huon-class MCMV. Amphibious capability includes HMAS *Tobruk*, and two Kanimbla-class, at least one of which will be replaced by the new Canberra-class ships. The fleet train includes two oilers and four light oilers, while there are also ammunition carriers and survey ships. Helicopters include sixteen Sikorsky S-70B Seahawks. Six Westland Sea King (S-61) and Eurocopter NH-90s are also on order, while there are also thirteen Eurocopter AS-350BA Ecureuil light helicopters for training.

The main bases are the Fleet Base East, HMAS *Kuttabul*, near Sydney and Fleet Base West, HMAS *Stirling*, at Garden Island, near Perth, as well as HMAS *Coonawarra*, at Darwin and HMAS *Cairns*, at Cairns. Nowra remains the main air station and Flinders the training school. Overseas deployments include a frigate on patrol in the Arabian Sea with NATO forces.

In addition to the RAN, Australia also has a paramilitary Border Protection Command, which has operational co-ordination and control of naval and civil maritime enforcement within the country's EEZ. In addition to seconded naval personnel this also includes personnel from customs, fisheries and the quarantine service. It has ten small patrol craft and ten light aircraft as well as five DHC-8 patrol aircraft.

AZERBAIJAN

Population: 8.9 million
Land Area: 33,430 square miles (86,661 sq.km.)
GDP: $52.2bn (£33.9bn), per capita $5,846 (£3,796)
Defence Exp: $1.59bn (£1.03bn)
Service Personnel: 2,200 active, plus reserves

AZERBAIJANI NAVY

Azerbaijan seized independence in 1917 during the Russian Revolution, and the following year the government established a navy using six ships from the Russian Imperial Navy left in Azerbaijani ports. The Soviet Union absorbed the country in 1922 and the fleet was absorbed into the Soviet Navy. History repeated itself in 1991 when the Soviet Union collapsed and its ships in Azerbaijani ports were once again taken over and in 1992, the Azerbaijani Navy was re-established.

The service is confined to the Caspian Sea, the world's largest inland salt lake, which has no outlets. It claims to be the second largest naval force in the Caspian after the Russian Caspian fleet.

Today the Azerbaijani Navy largely consists of patrol craft and MCMV, although there are four amphibious landing ships. The largest ship is a former Soviet Petya II-class corvette armed with a 76mm gun and rockets, while there are two Petrushka and one Shelon-class patrol craft, and three patrol boats. There are four MCMV vessels and four landing ships. A Luga-class offshore patrol craft can accommodate a helicopter and has an additional training role. There are two replenishment ships. The entire fleet is based on Baku.

BAHAMAS

Population: 345,736
Land Area: 4,404 square miles (11,406 sq.km.)
GDP: $7.54bn (£4.9bn), per capita $21,803 (£14,157)
Defence Exp: $46m (£29.9m)
Service Personnel: 860 active

ROYAL BAHAMIAN DEFENCE FORCE

Part of a unified defence force, the maritime element has two Bahamas-class patrol craft and seven smaller boats, augmented by six light aircraft, including a Beech A350 King Air, a Cessna Caravan and a Cessna Titan. The main base is at Coral Harbour, New Providence Island.

It was formed in 1980, after independence. That same year it was involved in an incident when HMBS* *Flamingo* attempted to arrest two Cuban fishing vessels poaching in Bahamian waters. Two Cuban MiG-21s attacked and sank the ship with cannon fire and then fired upon the crew in the water, killing four men. The survivors were picked up by the Cuban fishing vessels and arrested. Cuba later admitted liability and paid compensation.

* HMBS – Her Majesty's Bahamian Ship

BAHRAIN

Population: 807,131
Land Area: 231 square miles (570 sq.km.)
GDP: $21.7bn (£14.1bn), per capita $26,931 (£15,539)
Defence Exp: $742 m (£481m)
Service Personnel: 8,200 active, plus 11,260 paramilitary

ROYAL BAHRAIN NAVAL FORCE

Bahrain has been developing small but well-equipped armed forces since the mid-1980s, with British and American assistance.

Today, the Royal Bahrain Naval Force has 700 personnel. There is a frigate, *Sabha*, an ex-USN Oliver Hazard Perry-class ship, with Harpoon AShM, SM-1MR SAM, two triple ASTT and a 76mm gun as well as accommodation for a small ASW helicopter, although currently one of the RBNF's two Bo-105s is kept aboard; two German-built Al Manama-class corvettes, each with Exocet AShM, a 76mm gun and a helicopter landing platform; four German-built guided missile fast patrol craft also have Exocet AShM and a 76mm gun; two US-built Al Jarim-class and two German-built Al Riffa-class patrol boats. There are nine landing craft and four auxiliaries. The main base is at Mina Salman.

There is a small coastguard service with about 260 personnel and some fifty small patrol craft.

BANGLADESH

Population: 164.4 million
Land Area: 55,126 square miles (142,766 sq.km.)
GDP: $105bn (£68.2bn), per capita $640 (£415)
Defence Exp: $1.32bn (£857m)
Service Personnel: 157,053 active, plus 63,900 paramilitary

BANGLADESH NAVY

Until 1972, Bangladesh was East Pakistan and participated in that country's armed forces. Independence was seized after the Indo-Pakistani War of 1971. Initially, the new Bangladesh Navy used coastal and riverine craft that had been deployed in the country by the Pakistan Navy, but in 1976 a British Salisbury-class frigate was transferred and this was followed in 1977 by a Leopard-class frigate and a second ship of this class followed later.

In recent years, a variety of sources have provided surplus warships, with modern vessels unaffordable due to the country's extreme poverty.

Today the Bangladesh Navy has 16,900 personnel. There are two guided missile frigates: the *Bangabandhu*, formerly a South Korean modified Ulsan-class, with Otomat AShM, two triple ASTT, a 76mm gun and accommodation for a light helicopter; the *Osman*, formerly a Communist Chinese Jianghu-class, with 'Silkworm' AShM, RBU 1200 rocket bomb launchers and two twin 100mm guns. The two Abu Bakr-class (ex-British Leopard-class) and the *Umar Faroq*, formerly HMS *Llandaff*, have doubtful serviceability, although the latter ship is officially used for training. There are forty patrol and coastal vessels, including five Kapatakhaya-class, which are former Royal Navy Island-class fishery protection vessels, while most of the remainder have come from Communist China. Another nine coastal patrol craft are in the 900-strong Coast Guard, which is not part of the Navy. There are five MCMV, of which four are Shapla-class, formerly Royal Navy River-class, minesweepers formerly used by the Royal Naval Reserve. There are ten landing craft and landing ships, essential for communications and rescue work during severe flooding in this low-lying country, while there are ten logistics and support ships, mainly for coastal and river work.

The Bangladesh Navy has its headquarters at Dhaka, with a major base at Chittagong and other bases at Kaptai, Khulna and Mangla.

BARBADOS

Population: 256,552
Land Area: 166 square miles (438 sq.km.)
GDP: $3.96bn (£2.57bn), per capita $15,445 (£10,029)
Defence Exp: $34m (22.1m)
Service Personnel: 610 active, plus 430 reserves

BARBADOS DEFENCE FORCE

Formed in 1979, the Barbados Defence Force consists of the Barbados Regiment and the Barbados Coast Guard, with the latter having 110 personnel and operates six small patrol boats from HMBS* Pelican at St Ann's Fort, Bridgetown. Although a light aircraft was obtained in 1980, currently neither branch of the service has any air power. Main duties are anti-smuggling and anti-poaching.

* Her Majesty's Barbadian Ship, in this case a 'stone frigate'.

BELIZE

Population: 312,928
Land Area: 8,867 square miles (22,965 sq.km.)
GDP: $1.43bn (£0.93bn), per capita $4,575 (£2,970)
Defence Exp: $19m (£12.34m)
Service Personnel: 1,050 active, plus 700 reserves

BELIZE DEFENCE FORCE

A small maritime wing operates small patrol boats. Most of the personnel are in the ground force. Two Britten-Norman BN-2A/B Defender aircraft provide maritime surveillance.

BELGIUM

Population: 10.7 million
Land Area: 11,778 square miles (30,445 sq.km.)
GDP: $426bn (£276.6bn), per capita $39,790 (£25,837)
Defence Exp: $3.64bn (£2.36bn)
Service Personnel: 37,882 active, plus 1,600 reserves

BELGIAN NAVAL COMPONENT

Belgium became independent from the Netherlands in 1830, after centuries of having been governed by a succession of other European states. The Netherlands initially refused to accept the country's independence and a Dutch naval squadron blocked the Scheldt estuary, causing the country's parliament to order two brigantines to form the *Marine Royale* in 1831. When a French army captured the citadel of Antwerp in 1832, captured Dutch gunboats augmented the two original ships. Despite additional ships being commissioned in 1840 and 1845, in 1865 the *Marine Royale* was disbanded and, on the outbreak of the First World War in 1914, Belgium was without a navy.

Although most of Belgium was overrun by German forces during the First World War, in 1917 a 'Corps of Destroyers and Sailors' was established, with its personnel either serving aboard French minesweepers or providing gunners for Belgian merchantmen. Under the Treaty of Versailles in 1918, Belgium was allocated eleven torpedo boats and twenty-six minesweepers. The years between the two world wars were ones of considerable economic difficulty and once again the navy was disbanded. It was not until 1939 that a Naval Corps was founded against the growing probability of a war with Germany. In little more than a year, the country was completely occupied by German forces, leaving members of the Corps, along with fishermen and merchant seamen, to escape to the UK and join the Royal Navy. During the war, the RN put the Belgians into ships that were entirely or almost entirely Belgian-manned, including two Flower-class corvettes, HMS *Buttercup* and *Godetia*, a squadron of inshore minesweepers and three

27

patrol boats. Post-war, the UK donated all of these ships to form the basis of a new Belgian navy.

During the Cold War years, the Belgian navy became primarily a mine-countermeasures force within NATO, although as many as four small frigates were operational at one stage. During the 1950s, US-built minesweepers were transferred as military aid and at one stage the mine-sweeping force amounted to almost thirty ships to enable Belgian and Dutch ports to remain open for US troop reinforcements arriving in Europe in an emergency.

In the early 1990s, with the break-up of the Soviet Union and the end of the Warsaw Pact, the Belgian government restructured and reduced the country's armed forces. The frigate force was reduced and three modern Tripartite-class MCMV were sold to France. In 2002, the armed forces were combined and once again the Belgian Navy ceased to exist, other than as the Belgian Naval Component of the Armed Forces, COMOPSNAV, although it is popularly known as the *Marine*.

Today, the Belgian Naval Component consists of 1,590 personnel. The two largest warships are two modernised ex-Dutch Kortenaer-class frigates each armed with a 76mm gun, Harpoon AShM, Sea Sparrow VLS SAM, torpedo tubes and accommodation for a single medium helicopter. A patrol boat is in reserve while there are five remaining Tripartite-class MCMV. There are nine support ships including three oceanographic research ships, one auxiliary and five tugs. The only base is at Zeebrugge.

BENIN

Population: 9.2 million
Land Area: 44,649 square miles (115,640 sq.km.)
GDP: $6.65bn (£4.3bn), per capita $722 (£468)
Defence Exp: $53m (£34.4m)
Service Personnel: 4,750 active, plus 2,500 paramilitary

PEOPLE'S ARMED FORCES OF BENIN/BENIN NAVY

Originally the French colony of Dahomey, Benin became independent in 1958. The Benin Navy, Forces Navales Beninois (FNB), is part of the People's Armed Forces of Benin, which is dominated by the army.

It has about 200 personnel and operates two lightly-armed patrol boats donated by Communist China in 2003, which are known locally as the Matelot Brice Kpomasse-class. The only base is at Cotonou.

BOLIVIA

Population: 10 million
Land Area: 424,160 square miles (1,119,782 sq.km.)
GDP: $19bn (£12.3bn), per capita $1,899 (£1,233)
Defence Exp: $357m (£231m)
Service Personnel: 46,100 active, plus 37,100 paramilitary

BOLIVIAN NAVAL FORCE

Landlocked since the 'War of the Pacific', between Chile and Peru, 1879, the country established a lake and river force in 1963 to patrol its many large rivers, tributaries of the Amazon, and Lake Titicaca, the highest navigable lake in the world. In 1966, it became known as the Bolivian Navy (*Armada Boliviana*), but in 2008 the current title was adopted.

During the late 1970s, it had 1,500 personnel and sixteen patrol craft, but today it has 4,800 men, of which 1,700 are marines or naval police, and six naval districts with a headquarters at Puerto Guayaramerin. There is a single patrol boat, but two auxiliaries and eleven river transports as well as eight support vessels.

BRAZIL

Population: 195.4 million
Land Area: 3,287,195 square miles (8,512,035 sq.km.)
GDP: $2.04tr (£1.3tr), per capita $10,435 (£6,775)
Defence Exp: $34.7bn (£22.5bn)
Service Personnel: 318,480 active, plus 1,340,000 reserves and
    395,000 paramilitary

BRAZILIAN NAVY

Brazil declared its independence from Portugal in 1822, and many of the Portuguese Navy's ships stationed in the country transferred their allegiance to the newly independent state, forming the Brazilian Navy (*Marinha do Brasil*). By 1860, it had eight paddle steamers, seven screw sloops, six frigates and fourteen smaller vessels. During the war with neighbouring Paraguay, 1864-1870, Brazil purchased several ironclads from the United Kingdom and France. There were also conflicts with other South American states, including Argentina. Development was interrupted by a mutiny in 1893, and it was not until 1910 that two Dreadnought battleships were acquired from the UK, the *Minas Gerais* and the *Sao Paulo*, the country's only battleships, as well as the cruisers *Bahia* and *Rio Grande do Sul*, also British-built.

During both world wars, the country supported the Allies. In 1939, the fleet included the two battleships and cruisers already mentioned, although the former were extensively refitted in the USA in 1931; eleven destroyers, of which only three could be regarded as modern; four Italian-built submarines and a depot ship, as well as two monitors and three minelayers. Brazilian operations against German U-boats in the Atlantic were reinforced by the construction of air bases in the country for US maritime-reconnaissance aircraft.

In 1948, Brazil joined the Organisation of American States and became eligible for US military aid. While this included warships, in the early 1950s it extended to the creation of a naval air arm with three Bell 47J helicopters, later joined by two Westland Widgeons. The country's first aircraft carrier, *Minas Gerais*, originally the Royal Navy's HMS *Vengeance*, was acquired in 1957, with the US suppling Grumman Tracker ASW aircraft and T-28C armed trainers. In 1965, naval fixed-wing aircraft were transferred to the air force, with aircraft and personnel stationed ashore except for exercises off the carrier.

One of the older ships in the Brazilian Navy is the Niteroi-class frigate *Constutuicao*, one of six, four of which were built in the UK, and much modernised in recent years. (Marinha do Brasil)

By the late 1970s, the MdB was operating the *Minas Gerais*; six Niteroi-class frigates based on the Vosper Mk 10, of which two had been built in Brazil and were the service's first escorts to be able to accommodate helicopters, with each ship having a Westland Lynx ASW machine; seven ex-USN Fletcher-class destroyers and five ex-USN Allen M Sumner destroyers as well as two Gearing 'FRAM I' destroyers. An extensive submarine force included three British-built Oberon-class boats as well as two ex-USN Guppy III and five Guppy II boats. These were augmented by six Piratini-class large patrol craft built in Brazil.

Brazil remained neutral during the Falklands Campaign between the UK and Argentina in 1982, although the country has since come to favour the Argentine position over the future of the islands.

In recent years, the MdB has resumed fixed-wing flying and the *Minas Gerais* has been replaced by the *Sao Paulo*, the former French *Foch*, which entered service in 2003.

Currently, the MdB has 59,000 personnel, of whom 15,000 are marines and another 2,500 are involved in naval aviation. The service is divided into nine naval districts with its HQ at Rio de Janeiro and the other districts

The largest ship in the Brazilian Navy is the former French aircraft carrier *Foch*, renamed *Sao Paulo*. She carries helicopters and Douglas A-4 Skyhawks bought from Kuwait. (Marinha do Brasil)

at Belem, Brasilia, Ladario, Manaus, Natal, Rio Grande, Salvador and Sao Paulo. The current fleet includes the aircraft carrier *Sao Paulo*, with up to eighteen A-4 Skyhawk strike aircraft, four to six S-61 Sea King ASW aircraft, plus Ecureil and Cougar helicopters, with the latter for SAR. There are three Greenhaigh-class destroyers, formerly Royal Navy Type 22 Broadsword-class frigates, each capable of carrying two Super Lynx ASW helicopters, and fitted with Exocet AShM, Sea Wolf SAM, and two triple ASTT, but no gun main armament. The six Niteroi-class frigates remain in service and each has a 115mm gun, Exocet AShM, Aspide SAM and twin A/S mortar, while another five frigates include four Inhauma-class and a Barrosa-class, all of which carry a Super Lynx helicopter and have Exocet AShM, two triple ASTT and a 115mm gun. A substantial patrol and coastal force of forty-two ships includes four Bracui-class (ex-RN minesweepers), two Imperial Marinheiro-class and one Parnaiba, as well as another thirty-five smaller craft, of which the latest is the Macae-class, (two are in service and additional vessels are under construction), while three British-built patrol craft intended for Trinidad and Tobago were commissioned in 2012, with additional vessels likely to be built in Brazil. The submarine force is much reduced and consists of four Tupi-class (German T-209/1400) with eight single torpedo tubes, and *Tikuna*, which

Tapajo is one of the Brazilian Navy's German-built T-209 conventional submarines, with eight torpedo tubes and normally-uses Tigerfish heavyweight torpedoes.
(Marinha do Brasil)

The *Ceara* is one of two ex-USN Thomaston-class LSDs in Brazilian service and can carry up to twenty-one landing craft and 345 troops. (Marinha do Brasil)

also has eight torpedo tubes, but plans exist for the construction of a nuclear-powered submarine, possibly armed with AShM, and there have been reports, unconfirmed, that the People's Republic of China is helping in the design of this craft in return for help with carrier operation of aircraft. The amphibious warfare fleet is headed by two Ceara-class, formerly USN Thomaston-class, LSDs, as well as a former USN LST and two ex-RN LSLH, while there are forty-six landing craft. There are thirty-nine logistics and support ships, including fleet oilers and two troop carriers, and four training ships.

Naval aviation continues to use the Skyhawk, while ASW helicopters include 12 Super Lynx and 4 Sea King, while transport is provided by 7 Super Puma and a variety of light helicopters.

BRUNEI

Population: 407,045
Land Area: 2,226 square miles (5,765 sq.km.)
GDP: $12bn (£7.8bn), per capita $29,478 (£19,142)
Defence Exp: $372m (£241.6m)
Service Personnel: 7,000 active, plus 700 reserves and 2,250 paramilitary

ROYAL BRUNEI NAVY

Originally a protectorate and part of the British Empire, the Sultanate of Brunei refused to become part of the Federation of Malaysia in 1963. The country founded its own armed forces in 1961, with the Royal Brunei Navy (*Tentera Laut Diraja Brunei*, TLDB) formed in 1965 as the Boat Section of the Royal Brunei Armed Forces to provide EEZ protection and search and rescue duties. With just eighteen personnel at the outset, it was equipped with a number of light patrol craft and fast assault boats. In 1966, with expansion, it was renamed the Boat Company and introduced three river patrol boats and an SR.N5 hovercraft, joined by an SR.N6 and the service's first fast patrol craft in 1968.

Fundamentally still part of the army-oriented Royal Brunei Armed Forces, it later became the First Sea Battalion, Royal Brunei Malay Regiment. Two more fast patrol craft were commissioned in 1971. It was not until October 1991 that it acquired its current title and autonomous status.

Today, the TLDB has 1,000 personnel and is based at Maura. The mainstay of the service is three Darussalam-class patrol craft, essentially corvettes with a 76mm gun and accommodation for a helicopter, which have replaced the older Waspada-class. There are also another seven patrol craft for coastal and riverine use, as well as four landing craft. Maritime patrols are provided by a Royal Brunei Air Force CN-235M, while the RBAF mans the helicopters used aboard the corvettes.

The TLDB is involved in an annual series of bilateral maritime training exercises, Co-operation Afloat Readiness and Training (CARAT), between the US Navy and the armed forces of Singapore, Thailand, Malaysia, Indonesia, Brunei and Philippines.

BULGARIA

Population: 7.5 million
Land Area: 42,818 square miles (110,911 sq.km.)
GDP: $46.7bn (£30.2bn), per capita $6,227 (£4,043)
Defence Exp: $609m (£395m)
Service Personnel: 31,315 active, plus 303,000 reserves

BULGARIAN NAVY

Located on the Black Sea, maritime power has not featured prominently in Bulgaria's priorities and by 1939, the country had only a handful of minor warships. Although King Boris III attempted neutrality, the country was closely linked to Germany economically and in effect became a part of the Axis, although operations were confined to the Balkans. For the most part, naval operations against the USSR in the Black Sea were conducted by German warships under the command of the German Admiral, Black Sea.

At the end of the Second World War, Bulgaria was firmly within the Soviet sphere of influence and a member of the Warsaw Pact. The service remained small, especially compared to the country's other services and typically at any one time consisted of two small Riga-class frigates of about 1,200 tons each and two Romeo-class submarines, although this force eventually grew to four. In addition there were six fast patrol boats with torpedoes, and up to twenty MCMV, as well as landing craft.

Today, Bulgaria is part of NATO but there have been delays in bringing the fleet up to NATO standards because once again sea power comes behind land and air power. Naval personnel have shrunk by more than two-thirds to 3,471. The sole remaining submarine is in reserve and may be scrapped. There are four frigates, of which three are Draki-class, ex-Belgian Wielingen-class, each with a 100mm gun, Exocet AShM and Sea Sparrow SAM and two single torpedo tubes. A fourth frigate is the Russian-built *Smeli*, with two twin 76mm guns and rockets. Six Russian-built patrol craft are operated and there are nine small MCMV. Just two landing ships remain. There are seventeen support ships, including replenishment vessels, survey ships and tugs.

There are six Panther helicopters, which have replaced six Warsaw Pact-era Mi-14 'Haze' helicopters, of which only three were operational.

There are two bases, one near Varna and the other at Ativa, near Burgas.

BURUNDI

Population: 8.5 million
Land Area: 10,747 square miles (27,834 sq.km.)
GDP: $1.5bn (£974m), per capita $176 (£114)
Defence Exp: $7m (£4.54m)
Service Personnel: 20,000 active, plus 31,500 paramilitary

BURUNDI MARINE POLICE

Burundi has a small marine contingent in the paramilitary police, with three ex-Chinese patrol craft whose operational status is uncertain, and a landing craft as well as a support ship.

CAMBODIA

Population: 15.1 million
Land Area: 71,000 square miles (181,300 sq.km.)
GDP: $11.3bn (£7.3bn), per capita $748 (£485)
Defence Exp: $274m (£178m)
Service Personnel: 124,300 active, plus 67,000 paramilitary

ROYAL CAMBODIAN NAVY

Cambodia was originally part of French Indo-China, during which time it was defended by the French armed forces although occupied by Japan during the Second World War. The Royal Cambodian Navy was formed in 1953. Its early history was seriously affected by both the war in Vietnam and internal unrest. In 1970, the monarchy was overthrown and a republic declared, but this was followed by a civil war that lasted until 1975, after which the country became isolated as international opinion turned against the Khmer regime, which in turn was overthrown in 1979 by Vietnamese forces and in 1981, the country became known for a while as Kampuchea, until the restoration of the monarchy.

Today, the Royal Cambodian Navy has some 2,800 personnel, of whom 1,500 are naval infantry or marines. It has eleven patrol or coastal craft, mainly from Communist China, with two bases at Ream for sea-going craft and Phnom Penh for riverine operations.

CAMEROON

Population: 19.9 million
Land Area: 183,000 square miles (475,500 sq.km.)
GDP: $22.4bn (£14.5bn), per capita $1,123 (£729)
Defence Exp: $346m (£223)
Service Personnel: 14,100 active, plus 9,000 paramilitary

CAMEROON NAVY

Originally a French protectorate, Cameroon established a small navy after independence from France in 1960, and continued to receive assistance from France for some years before turning to Communist China. There are long-standing border disputes with neighbouring Nigeria, but none of the services has combat experience. Known locally as the *Marine Nationale*

Republique, the service had 300 personnel in the late 1970s, but has since grown to 1,300 personnel. Current equipment includes two ex-French patrol craft, nine smaller patrol boats, some of which are Chinese in origin, and two ex-French landing craft. The main base is at Doula, with smaller bases at Limbe and Kribi.

CANADA

Population: 33.9 million
Land Area: 3,851,809 square miles (9,976,185 sq.km.)
GDP: $1.57tr (£1.02tr), per capita $46,331 (£30,085)
Defence Exp: $19.9bn (£12.9bn)
Service Personnel: 65,722 active, plus 33,967 reserves

Canada has often in the past been accused of not taking defence seriously, and indeed between the two world wars its air force and navy virtually disappeared. Proposals for a British Empire naval force were rejected and a strongly independent line taken. Currently, Canada is increasing its defence expenditure and plans to increase the number of personnel in

Three Canadian Halifax-class frigates. Six of these ships are deployed on the Pacific Coast and another six on the Atlantic Coast. (Canadian Armed Forces)

its nominally unified armed forces to about 70,000, although this will still be only slightly more than 0.2 per cent of the population.

In more recent years, defence was cut drastically due to severe economic problems, and many believe the economic policies and cuts imposed by the Canadian Federal Government at that time have strongly influenced the current UK government, ignoring the fact that Canada, ultimately, rests under the overwhelming superiority of the United States and its armed forces, so that any territorial incursion would be severely dealt with by the country's southern ally.

Canada has the dual problems of having a vast land area, much of it in the Arctic and underpopulated, and of having to maintain an air and naval presence in both the Pacific and the Atlantic. Fisheries protection is obviously of prime importance, and during the Second World War the then Royal Canadian Navy became a significant convoy escort force, and post-war received submarines and started a fleet air arm, maintaining a light fleet carrier for a number of years. While force projection might not seem to be a priority, the Canadian Federal Government has been to the fore in providing support for United Nations and NATO operations.

CANADIAN ARMED FORCES (*FORCES ARMÉES CANADIENNES*)

Officially, Canada has a unified defence force, but more recently many of the changes made when the Royal Canadian Navy was merged with the other two services in 1967 have been reversed, so that Maritime Command is usually known as the Canadian Navy and distinctive naval uniforms have returned.

At the beginning of the twentieth century, there was much debate within the British Empire over the role of locally-raised forces in defending the Empire. Canada was effectively presented with the choice of providing ships and manpower for the Royal Navy, or of creating its own naval service after the Royal Navy left its bases in Canada in 1906. The two main bases, at Esquimalt in British Columbia and Halifax in Nova Scotia, were acquired by the Canadian government. A Naval Service Act received the Royal Assent on 4 May 1910, creating the Naval Service of Canada, or Canadian Naval Forces, sponsored by the then Ministry of Marine and Fisheries and headed by a retired British admiral. The first ship was the British cruiser *Rainbow*, commissioned on 4 August 1910 in the UK at Portsmouth. She arrived at Esquimalt, British Columbia, on 7 November 1910 for training duties, helped by a number of her ship's company who opted to transfer from the RN to the RCN. The title of the Canadian Navy was adopted on 30 January 1911, but it was not until 29 August that

King George V granted the right for the service to use the title of Royal Canadian Navy.

Despite Canada's dominion status, throughout the time from the inauguration of the RCN, uniforms for those serving in the RAN were identical to those of the Royal Navy other than that a shoulder flash with 'Canada' was worn and ratings' cap tallies carried 'HMCS' rather than 'HMS'. The RCN used the same White Ensign used by the Royal Navy, but eventually a blue version of the Canadian flag was also used, and the custom eventually emerged of painting a maple leaf on the funnels of Canadian ships.

Immediately before the First World War, the province of British Columbia presented the Royal Canadian Navy with two submarines, commissioned as *CC1* and *CC2*, bought from a shipyard in Washington State, USA, which had built them for the Chilean Navy, but the order had been cancelled. At this time, the Royal Canadian Naval Volunteer Reserve was created, with an initial recruiting target of 1,200 men spread over three areas, the Atlantic, Pacific and Lakes, with the latter covering Canada's interior. Wartime expansion of the RCN and its reserves was hindered by an agreement that Canadian recruits could either join the RCN or the Royal Navy, and many chose the latter. HMCS *Rainbow* remained on the west coast and patrolled as far south as Panama, but this became less important after the German East Asiatic Squadron's defeat in the Battle of the Falklands. With most of her ship's company posted to the east coast, *Rainbow*, by now elderly, was retired in 1917. The two submarines, HMCS *C1* and *C2*, also patrolled the Pacific at first before being transferred east to Halifax in 1917, and in so doing they, and their tender HMCS *Shearwater*, became the first ships to pass through the Panama Canal wearing the White Ensign. On arrival at Halifax they were also deemed unfit for further service and withdrawn.

A significant event before the war ended was the formation in September 1918 of the Royal Canadian Naval Air Service for anti-submarine patrols using flying boats. By this time the USN had an air station in Canada at Halifax, which was transferred to the RCNAS, but shortly after the armistice in November, the RCNAS was stood down.

Between the two world wars, the RCN suddenly found itself struggling to find a mission, and at first started to take over many of the civil duties of the Ministry of Marine and Fisheries, so for a while it looked as if the RCN would become a coastguard service. It was not until 1931 that it received its first new ships, two destroyers that were delivered from the UK, but when the Second World War broke out in Europe in September 1939, the RCN still had only six destroyers and a handful of smaller ships, with manpower to fewer than 2,000 men. At this time, no clear mission had been defined other than fisheries protection, mainly for the substantial cod fishing off Newfoundland, and the RCN was viewed by the Royal Navy as an adjunct that would provide support and bases for ships escorting the North Atlantic convoys. It was, in fact, what became a massive need for convoy escorts that created a mission for the RCN during the war years, during which the service underwent huge expansion so that by August 1945, it was the world's third largest navy, after the USN and RN, with 365 warships and 95,750 personnel. The Royal Canadian Naval Air Service was re-established, but operated solely from shore bases using Consolidated PBY Catalina flying boats on anti-submarine warfare, which became the predominant role of the RCN. The warships used were mainly corvettes and frigates, but the RCN also manned two escort carriers for the Royal Navy, whose personnel continued to operate the aircraft, HMS *Nabob* and *Puncher*.

As a consequence, the RCN was not involved in any of the major naval engagements of the Second World War. Post-war, with Canada a founding member of NATO, a role soon became clear with the RCN not only responsible for its littoral protection with Pacific and Atlantic bases, it also assumed a wartime role that would include protecting reinforcements being moved from North America to Europe in a time of international tension. The RCN acquired cruisers and submarines and its first aircraft carriers, forming its own Fleet Air Arm with RN assistance. The first ship was HMCS *Warrior*, which was obtained from the UK in 1946 on loan and retained her original name. This Colossus-class aircraft carrier carried a squadron of Supermarine Seafire fighters and one of Fairey Firefly ASW aircraft. In 1948, she was replaced by the slightly larger Majestic-class carrier, HMCS *Magnificent*, while Hawker Sea Fury fighters replaced the Seafires and 100 Grumman TBM-3E Avengers replaced the Fireflies, with many of the Avengers shore-based, augmenting the RCAF's long-range maritime-reconnaissance. *Magnificent* was returned to the RN in 1957 and replaced by HMCS *Bonaventure*, formerly HMS *Powerful*, which served until 1968, operating McDonnell F2H-3 Banshee jet fighters and Grumman S2F-1 Tracker ASW aircraft. Exercises with NATO saw *Bonaventure* operate in the Mediterranean in the late 1950s. From 1961, she lost her fixed-wing aircraft and became an ASW helicopter carrier with Sikorsky S-61 Sea King helicopters.

Even though losing the aircraft carrier and concentrating on ships of destroyer and frigate size as well as submarines, including Oberon-class submarines from the UK, the RCN was amongst the leaders in deploying helicopters aboard frigates, designing ships that could accommodate two S-61 helicopters rather than the single small helicopter favoured by most navies. Plans for a small force of nuclear-powered submarines were abandoned due to budget constraints.

Today, the Canadian Navy has 11,025 personnel and 4,167 reservists. The backbone of the fleet is a force of twelve Halifax-class guided missile frigates with Harpoon AShM and Sea Sparrow SAM, each of which carries

A port quarter view of HMCS *Halifax*, with her helicopter hangar clearly visible. (Canadian Armed Forces)

HMCS *Cornerbrook* is one of four Upholder-class conventional submarines bought from the Royal Navy. Known in Canada as the Victoria-class, only two are operational and used mainly for anti-submarine training. (Canadian Armed Forces)

a gun main armament of just 50mm but each carries a Sea King helicopter, designated CH-124 in Canadian service. There are also three modified Iroquois-class guided missile destroyers, each with a single 76mm main armament, anti-submarine torpedo tubs and two CH-124s. There are twelve Kingston-class ocean MCMVs, ten of which are manned by reservists, and a force of four conventional submarines, the Victoria-class, originally built by the Royal Navy as the Upholder-class, of which two are operational and used mainly for training in anti-submarine warfare. There are a number of harbour defence vessels. The fleet train includes two Protector-class fleet replenishment ships, each of which carries up to three CH-124s, as well as diving tenders and an ocean research vessel. The two main bases are at Esquimalt on the Pacific for MARPAC or Maritime Command Pacific, and Halifax on the Atlantic for MARLANT, while headquarters are at Ottawa. Maritime-reconnaissance remains with Air Command or, as it is more usually known, the Canadian Air Force.

A paramilitary Canadian Coast Guard has 4,554 personnel and is maintained by the Department of Fisheries and Oceans, which classifies its personnel as civilian and the vessels and aircraft as non-combatant. A total of seventy-three small patrol craft are operated, supported by logistics and support vessels, while there are twenty-two transport and utility helicopters.

Augmenting the larger warships in the Canadian Armed Forces Maritime Command, as in so many other navies, are twelve coastal defence vessels, one of which is HMCS *Glace Bay*, seen here. (Canadian Armed Forces)

CAPE VERDE

Population: 512,582
Land Area: 1,580 square miles (4,040 sq.km.)
GDP: $1.6bn (£1.04bn), per capita $3,126 (£2,029)
Defence Exp: $8m (£5.2m)
Service Personnel: 1,200 active

CAPE VERDE COAST GUARD

A former Portuguese colony in the Atlantic off the coast of West Africa, Cape Verde has a small army that includes the Coast Guard with about 100 personnel. It has a patrol craft and two small patrol boats, with one of Chinese origin.

CHILE

Population: 17.1 million
Land Area: 286,397 square miles (738,494 sq.km.)
GDP: $204bn (£132.5bn), per capita $11,907 (£7,731)
Defence Exp: $2.07bn (£1.34bn)
Service Personnel: 59,059 active, plus 40,000 reserves and 44,712 paramilitary

CHILEAN NAVY

The Chilean Navy (*Armada de Chile*, AdC) traces its history to the war of independence in 1817. Although formed by an army officer, General Bernardo O'Higgins, he recruited a British naval officer, Lord Cochrane, to develop the new service and in its early years it was largely led by former British and American naval officers. During this period, the new service continued to fight against Spanish Royalist forces not only in Chile and its offshore islands, but also in Peru, until eventual victory for rebel forces in both nations in 1830.

A naval training school was opened in 1868, while the largely uncharted territories to the south around the Straits of Magellan led to the formation of a hydrographic office as early as 1874. Nevertheless, the 'War of the Pacific' soon broke out with Peru and Bolivia, with a naval battle at Iquique on 21 May 1879, with Chile gaining territory to the north and Bolivia losing its coastal territories to become a landlocked country. Easter Island was annexed by Chile in 1888. For the rest of the nineteenth century, Chile was the dominant naval power at the southern end of South America, with the Argentina Navy of the day being a 'brown water' service. A modernisation

43

plan prompted by an arms race with neighbouring Argentina saw two armoured ships updated and two cruisers and two torpedo-boat destroyers ordered during the 1890s. In 1902, two battleships were ordered from British yards, but these were soon rendered obsolete by the emergence of the Dreadnought-pattern all-big-gun battleship within a couple of years. Nevertheless, this was an unsettled period with civil war in Chile, with the navy siding with the national parliament against the president, who was largely supported by the army. The navy organised a new army of 40,000 men and in August 1891, this won a battle against the army and ended the civil war.

A pact with Argentina in 1902 was supposed to end the arms race, but in 1904, Brazil ordered two new battleships and to maintain the balance of power, the Argentine ordered two battleships from the UK and a third from the United States. Chile tried to respond by ordering further ships, but a collapse in the nitrate market in 1907 brought about an economic depression, worsened by a serious earthquake in 1908.

Chile was not involved in the First World War, but during the inter-war years, the impact of the Great Depression meant that the government had to make economies and in 1931, pay was cut. This resulted in a mutiny that affected twenty-six ships, mainly based at Coquimbo and Talcahuano. The government ordered the air force to bomb the ships at Coquimbo while the army made an assault on Talcahuano. The mutiny was suppressed and afterwards the officer ranks were purged, even though the lower deck had been responsible for the mutiny.

A Naval Aviation Service was formed in 1919, mainly to operate seaplanes and flying boats, but in 1930 this was merged with the Military Aviation Service to form the Chilean Air Force.

By 1939, the AdC had a single battleship, the *Almirante Latorre*, a ship originally ordered before the First World War but taken up by the Royal Navy as HMS *Canada* and not released to Chile until 1920. A sister ship had been converted post-war and became the aircraft carrier HMS *Eagle*. The fleet also included an elderly French-built coast defence ship, *Capitan Prat*, dating from 1890 but rebuilt in 1909. There were three cruisers, all dating from about 1900, but of eight destroyers, six dated from 1928. In addition there were nine submarines and a depot ship. Again, Chile was not involved in the Second World War, during which attention turned to the Antarctic, with a race developing between the three armed services as to which would establish the first base on the continent. The navy won, establishing the Captain Arturo Prat Base in 1947.

Chile became a member of the Organisation of American States in 1948 and became eligible for US military aid, although also continued to buy equipment from other sources. Friction between Chile and Argentina arose during the 1950s, with Argentine fishing vessels poaching in Chilean waters and in 1958, the Argentine Navy shelled a Chilean lighthouse. The Argentine laid a claim to the islands of Picton, Lennox and Nueva, as

Chile has been a regular customer for former Royal Navy frigates and destroyers. This is a Type 23 Duke-class frigate leaving Portsmouth *en passage* to Chile, where she will be one of the Chilean Navy's Almirante Cochrane-class ships. (BAE Systems)

well as Cape Horn, but in 1978, an invasion plan was abandoned. This led Chile to support the UK during the Falklands campaign of 1982, reasoning that if Argentina won, it would be encouraged to invade the islands and Cape Horn.

By this time, the AdC had two cruisers, with one, the *Latorre*, being the former Swedish *Gota Lejon*, and the other was the *Prat*, formerly the USN's *Nashville*. There were two British-built Almirante-class destroyers, both modernised with Exocet AShM and Sea Cat SAM, as well as four ex-USN destroyers, with two being Fletcher-class ships and the other two Allen M Summer FRAM II ships. Other escort vessels included two Leander-class frigates, bought new from the UK and modified to include Exocet AShM as well as Sea Cat missiles, and three ex-USN Charles Lawrence-class frigates, as well as two Sotoyomo-class corvettes. There were two Oberon-class submarines, bought new from the UK, and an ex-USN submarine, the *Simpson,* formerly the USS *Spot.* The fleet was completed with a handful of patrol craft, and the *Buque Escuela Esmeralda*, a sail training ship introduced in 1952, which sailed to many parts of the world.

Modernisation of this fleet occurred during the closing years of the twentieth century, including ex-Royal Navy County-class guided missile destroyers and Leander-class frigates, but further updating has followed in recent years, again based largely on ships surplus to the requirements of the British and Dutch navies, although a joint venture with a German company sees the first two, the *Piloto Pardo* and the *Comandante Toro*, of a new class of EEZ patrol ships being built in Chile. The Leander-class frigates were sold to Ecuador.

Currently, the AdC has 16,299 personnel, of whom 807 are conscripts on twenty-two months' voluntary training, 600 of the total being involved with naval aviation and 3,616 are marines. There is one destroyer, the *Almirante Williams*, an ex-RN Type 22 frigate, which has had its Exocet missiles replaced with Harpoon AShM, Barak SAM instead of Sea Wolf, a 76mm gun and two triple ASTT, while a Cougar helicopter can be accommodated; three Almirante Cochrane-class guided missile frigates are former RN Type 23s, each with Harpoon AShM, VLS Sea Wolf SAM, two twin ASTT, a 114mm gun and accommodation for a Cougar helicopter; two Lattore-class frigates are ex-Royal Netherlands Navy Jacob Van Heemskerck-class, with Harpoon AShM, Sea Sparrow SAM, and two twin ASTT. In addition to the two Piloto Pardo-class vessels, there are three Israeli-built Casma-class patrol craft with Gabriel AShM and a 76mm gun and four German-built Tiger-class patrol craft with Exocet AShM and a 76mm gun, which may be replaced by additional Piloto Pardo-class ships in the future. Submarines include two O'Higgins-class with six torpedo tubes and two German-built Thompson-class with eight torpedo tubes. There are five amphibious landing ships and nine support ships, including two replenishment vessels.

Naval aviation includes three shore-based P-3A Orion; three C-295 MPA Persuader and three EMB-111 Bandeirante, as well as five AS-532SC Cougar and eight Dauphin helicopters. There are also a number of light aircraft for training and communications duties.

The Coast Guard is part of the AdC, and has forty-seven small patrol and rescue craft.

The main base is at Valparaiso, with other bases at Talcahuano, Puerto Montt, Puerto Williams, Iquique and Punta Arenas. The coastline is divided into three naval zones, of which the first, the most northerly, is at Valparaiso.

CHINA, PEOPLE'S REPUBLIC OF

Population: 1,354.1 million
Land Area: 3,768,000 square miles (9,595,961 sq.km.)
GDP: $10.1*tr (£6.56tr), per capita $4,234 (£2,749)
Defence Exp: $76.4bn (£49.6bn)
Service Personnel: 2,285,000 active, plus 510,000 reserves and 660,000 paramilitary

* estimated

Passing one of the piers of the new Hangchow Bay Bridge while the bridge was still under construction is the People's Liberation Army, PLAN, Navy Type 052C destroyer, *Lanzhou*.

Once considered the 'sleeping giant', after the Communist takeover, China became Asia's most heavily-armed nation, initially using Soviet equipment but after relations soured with the USSR, the country steadily became self-sufficient in defence equipment production and today has export customers that include Pakistan. In recent years, very strong economic growth has also provided a platform for investment in the armed forces to the extent that China is now seen as the next superpower and poses a threat to the stability of the Pacific Region. In addition to border disputes with India, the country also influences North Korea, which may emerge as a 'client state', and has been undermining Nepal, as well as claiming the South Spratly Islands and, of course, the territory of Taiwan, officially the Republic of China (ROC). Having bought an uncompleted aircraft carrier from Russia, China is now planning her own carrier force as the country believes that this gives it credibility, status and, of course, power projection.

THE PEOPLE'S LIBERATION ARMY NAVY

A Chinese Imperial Navy is claimed to have emerged after 1132 during the Song Dynasty and survived to the end of the Qing Dynasty in 1912, when a republic was declared and the Republic of China Navy formed, which survives to this day as the naval service for Taiwan. While the Chinese

Imperial Navy for most of its existence depended on war junks, after the First Opium War, 1839-1842, in which China ceded Hong Kong to the United Kingdom, more modern warships were bought from Europe.

The main base for the Chinese Imperial Navy was at Shanghai, while another base and home to the naval academy was at Tainjing, and the Admiralty was at Dinghai.

The Republic of China Navy was overwhelmed by the Imperial Japanese Navy between the two world wars as the country was invaded by Japanese forces and the Chinese forces were divided between Communist and Nationalist forces. References to the Republic of China Navy's strength in 1939 made it clear that many of the ships might 'no longer be afloat'. On paper, the service had nine cruisers, of which only two were reasonably modern while the others dated from the late nineteenth century, supported by more than twenty sloops and gunboats plus six torpedo boats. They had to face a Japanese fleet with battleships and aircraft carriers. After the Japanese lost the Second World War, China descended into civil war, which the Communists won in 1949, with the Nationalists (*Kuomintang*), being forced onto the offshore islands of Formosa and Quemoy.

The new People's Republic of China inherited a few ships as some naval personnel defected to the People's Liberation Army (PLA) towards the end of the civil war, when it established a new navy in 1950, which, like the air force, is regarded as a branch of the army, being known as the People's Liberation Army Navy (PLAN). During the closing stages of the civil war, the PLA had been forced to use junks armed with machine guns for the landings on Hainan Island.

A naval academy was established at Dalian in late November 1949, staffed by Soviet instructors, and, by 1954, it is estimated that 2,500 Soviet instructors and advisers were working with the PLAN. PLAN was formed in 1950 by combining the regional naval forces of the PLA. Naval aviation was founded in 1952. Reorganisation in 1954-55 saw the PLAN establish a North Sea Fleet, East Sea Fleet and a South Sea Fleet, with members of the PLA used to create a strong cadre of officers for the new service, which adopted distinctive naval uniforms and ranks. Although some Russian ships were provided, the Soviet advisors preferred to supervise construction of ships to Soviet designs in Chinese shipyards before the Chinese themselves were able to work to Soviet designs, and later started to develop their own designs. At first the relationship between the two largest Communist states was good, even to the point of planning a joint Sino-Soviet Pacific Fleet, but relations cooled later as ideological differences arose.

The PLAN was relatively undisturbed by developments within the country during the 1950s and 1960s, although a number of senior officers were purged during the years of the Cultural Revolution. Naval forces were used to suppress an uprising in Wuhan in July 1967. By the 1970s, the PLAN was receiving about a fifth of the overall national defence budget

The PLAN Luda-class guided missile frigate *Zhuhai*, seen from the air.

and had developed a conventional submarine force of about 100 boats, as well as 200 missile-carrying ships. Development of nuclear-powered submarines began, along with ballistic missiles.

By the late 1970s, the PLAN had seven Luta-class destroyers, the first indigenous Chinese design for this type of vessel, as well as four ex-Soviet Gordy-class guided missile destroyers. There was also a force of nine frigates of the Kiang Hu, Kiang Tung and Kiang Nan-classes. The service's first ballistic missile submarine was a Russian Golf-class, built under licence, powered by diesel engines and with just three missile tubes, but no missiles. Most of the submarines were of the Russian Romeo and Whiskey-classes, of which there were seventy-two in total, but there were also two Chinese-designed Ming-class boats. Copying Soviet practice, this fleet was augmented by more than 400 fast attack craft, many of which were fitted with AShM.

This was a fleet that could be described as a brown water navy, but that was to change over the next two decades. China started to become first a regional naval power, and then set her sights on global naval ambitions. Even during the late 1980s, with just 12 per cent of the total PLA man-power, the PLAN was estimated to be the world's third largest navy. In 1988, for the first time, the service was commanded by a career naval officer rather an army officer on secondment. By 1986, the service had two Xia-class SSBNs, each with twelve CSS-N-3 ballistic missiles, and three Han-class SSNs, each armed with six SY-2 cruise missiles. Deficiencies remained, however, especially in naval aviation, anti-submarine and mine warfare, electronics and electronic countermeasures. Under its new com-mand, the PLAN started to build fewer but more sophisticated and capable ships, able to undertake longer-range operations. In the mid-1980s, extended

The People's Republic of China believes that the aircraft carrier will be an essen
part of any significant naval fleet in the future. This is the ex-Soviet Navy's Vary
bought from the Ukraine and completed in China. Another four or five carriers .
planned.

operations were undertaken in the South China Sea and there were vis
to three Asian nations. This policy of making courtesy visits and circu
navigations of first the Pacific and then the globe seems to have becon
a means of showing how far the PLAN has come, using warships to ga
influence. Between 1985 and 2006, Chinese warships visited thirty-s
nations, including eight in Europe.

Part of the rationale behind this has been the continuing claim
sovereignty over Taiwan, while another has been the growing interest i
Africa and especially that continent's natural resources for China's rapidl
growing economy. There are also frictions between China and Japan. Chin
has a growing merchant fleet and after a number of attempted hijackings o
Chinese vessels by Somali pirates, PLAN deployed two destroyers and
an auxiliary to escort shipping in the Gulf of Aden from late December
2008. PLAN has recently gone further, seeking leadership of the 'Shared
Awareness and Deconfliction' organisation, SHADE, even though this
would mean increasing the number of ships deployed.

From 1985 onwards, China bought no fewer than four aircraft carriers,
starting with HMS *Melbourne* from Australia, and followed by the ex-
Russian *Minsk* and *Kiev*, both of which became tourist attractions, while the
Admiral Kuznetsov-class *Varyag* was bought from the Ukraine, ostensibly

to become a casino, but was refitted, including installing engines, and has now joined the fleet. Together, all four ships gave the Chinese an insight into carrier technology, and while attempts to purchase a carrier from Spain came to nothing, it is believed that some technology was transferred. There are reports, unconfirmed, that help in carrier operation of aircraft is being provided by Brazil in return for Chinese assistance in the construction of Brazil's first nuclear-powered submarine.

Some analysts believe that the break-up of the Soviet Union has allowed the Chinese government to increase the proportion of resources devoted to PLAN, while relations between Russia and China are better than for many years. An idea of the service's ambitions can be gained from reports that an underground base is being built for nuclear submarines that would allow up to twenty boats to be stored under hillsides near Sanya in Hainan province. In addition, the completed ex-Soviet aircraft carrier *Varyag* put to sea in September 2011 for trials, while work continues on establishing a small fleet of aircraft carriers and developing V/STOL aircraft. Ultimately, it seems that China intends to be able to compete with the United States in the exercise of sea power.

Today, PLAN is the world's second largest navy and has 255,000 personnel, of whom 40,000 are conscripts on two years' selective national service, with 26,000 of the total engaged in naval aviation and another 10,000 are marines. The service is organised into five arms: submarine, surface, naval aviation, coastal defence and marine corps, while there are three fleets: the Beihai or North Sea, based on Qingdao in Shandong; Donghai, or East Sea, based on Ningbo; and Nanhai, or South Sea, based on Zhanjiang, Guangdong. Overall, there are some 2,000 naval vessels. Major fleet units include an aircraft carrier, the steam turbine-powered *Varyag*, and up to five other ships are planned. There are thirteen destroyers, of which eleven have guided missiles and helicopters, including four Hangzhou-class (based on the Russian Sovremenny-class), each with 'Sunburn' AShM, 'Grizzly' SAM, two twin ASTT and two twin 130mm guns as well as accommodation for an AS-565S Panther or Ka-28 'Helix' helicopter; two Luyang-class, both with YJ-83 AShM, 'Grizzly' SAM, two triple ASTT and a 100mm gun as well as accommodation for a Ka-28 'Helix' helicopter; two Luyang II-class, both with YJ-62 AShM, 'Grizzly' SAM, two triple ASTT and a 100mm gun as well as accommodation for two Ka-28 'Helix' helicopters; one Luhai-class, with YJ-62 AShM, HQ-7 (licence-built Crotale) SAM, two triple ASTT and a twin 100mm gun as well as accommodation for two Ka-28 'Helix' helicopters; two Luhu-class, both with YJ-83 AShM, HQ-7 SAM, two triple ASTT and a twin 100mm gun as well as accommodation for two Ka-28 'Helix' helicopters. In addition, two Luzhou-class destroyers both have YJ-83 AShM, VLS SA-20-N SAM and a 100mm gun as well as a helicopter landing platform. There are sixty-five frigates. These include two Jiangkai-class, both with YJ-83 AShM, HQ-7 SAM, two triple

ASTT, RBU 1200 anti-submarine rocket launchers and a 100mm gun as well as accommodation for a Ka-28 'Helix' helicopter; seven Jiangkai II-class, each with YJ-83 AShM, VLS HQ-16 SAM, two triple ASTT, RBU 1200 anti-submarine rocket launchers and a 76mm gun as well as accommodation for a Ka-28 'Helix' helicopter; four Jiangwei I-class, each with YJ-83 AShM, VLS HQ-16 SAM, RBU 1200 anti-submarine rocket launchers and a twin 100mm gun as well as accommodation for two Ka-28 'Helix' helicopters; ten Jiangwei II-class, each with YJ-83 AShM, HQ-7 SAM, RBU 1200 anti-submarine rocket launchers and two 100mm guns as well as accommodation for two Z-9C (licence-built Panther) helicopters; one Jianghu I-class is used for training with 'Scrubbrush' AShM, RBU 1200 anti-submarine rocket launchers, a 100mm gun and a Z-9C helicopter; two Luda-class have 'Styx' AShM, HQ-7 SAM, two twin 130mm guns and can lay mines; eleven Jianghu I-class each have 'Styx' AShM, RBU 1200 anti-submarine rocket launchers, and two 100mm guns; eight Jianghu II-class each have 'Styx' AShM, RBU 1200 anti-submarine rocket launchers and a twin 100mm gun as well as accommodation for a Z-9C helicopter; three Jianghu III-class each have 'Styx' AShM, RBU 1200 anti-submarine rocket launchers and two twin 100mm guns; six Jianghu V-class each have 'Scrubbrush' AShM, RBU 1200 anti-submarine rocket launchers and a twin 100mm gun; eleven Luda, Luda II and Luda III-class each have two triple ASTT, two FGF 2500 anti-submarine rocket launchers and two twin 130mm guns. There are several hundred patrol and coastal combatants with the intention being that any warships approaching the coasts would be swamped by a massive attack by missile-armed fast craft, as well as almost 100 MCMV. Amphibious warfare includes just one LPD, but there are about ninety landing ships and 150 landing craft.

The fleet of more than seventy submarines has surprisingly few nuclear-powered or missile-armed boats. There is the *Xia*, with twelve CSS-N-3 SLBM and four Jin with similar armament. Tactical submarines include four Han-class and three Shang-class, each with six single torpedo tubes, while a modified Romeo-class, conventionally powered, has eight torpedo tubes and six 'Styx' missiles. Another sixty conventional submarines include twelve Kilo-class with 'Sizzler' anti-ship missiles and six torpedo tubes; twenty Ming-class with eight torpedo tubes, as have eight Romeo-class; sixteen Song-class with YJ-82 anti-ship missiles and six torpedo tubes; while the most recent arrivals are six Yuan-class with six torpedo tubes. The solitary Golf-class used for SLBM trials remains.

There are more than 200 logistics and support ships, including five replenishment ships with helicopter accommodation and fifty other tankers.

Naval aviation is organised on the old Soviet lines with regiments rather than squadrons. Two regiments have H-6G bombers, based on the Tu-16 'Badger', and another has a mix of H-5, H-6G/DU and Y-8X. Four fighter regiments include one each with J-7, J-7E, both developments of the MiG-19,

J-8F and J-8H, developments of the MiG-21. All of these aircraft types are obsolete, although the H-6 series can carry cruise missiles, but there is also a squadron of Su-30 Mk2s. None of these aircraft are carrier types. There are also electronic intelligence and countermeasures units, as well as those for transport and training. Helicopters include two regiments with Ka-28 Helix A, Mi-8, Z-8 and Z-9. The *Varyag* will operate Shenyang J-15s, a copy of the Russian Sukhoi Su-33 'Flanker'.

COLOMBIA

Population: 46.3 million
Land Area: 462,000 square miles (1,139,592 sq.km.)
GDP: $278bn (£180.5bn), per capita $6,003 (£3,898)
Defence Exp: $6.2bn (£4.0bn)
Service Personnel: 283,004 active, plus 61,900 reserves

COLOMBIAN NAVY

The Colombian Navy is known locally as the *Armada Nacional de la República de Colombia* (ANRC), also known as the *Armada Nacional*, and is the only South American Navy to operate in two oceans, maintaining a presence in both the Pacific and the Caribbean, usually regarded as a branch of the Atlantic.

As with the other Latin American navies, the service emerged on the country gaining independence, in this case from Spain in 1810. Although a naval training establishment was founded in 1822, this had a short existence before being closed until 1907, when it re-opened, but only for two years.

Colombian naval history started effectively as a result of war with Peru in 1932, when new ships were acquired and separate training establishments for ratings and officers were founded in 1934 and 1935 respectively. Nevertheless, by 1939 the ARC had just two destroyers, both built in the UK for Portugal in 1932, but bought by Colombia in 1934, and three British-built gunboats also from the early 1930s.

While Colombia was neutral during the Second World War, the country leant towards the Allies and the ARC mounted patrols to counter German U-boats preying on Allied shipping sailing to and from the Panama Canal. The only engagement recorded was with a German U-boat that managed to escape, although sunk later by US ships.

In 1948, Colombia joined the Organisation of American States and became eligible for US military aid. The fleet grew, mainly using ex-USN warships, but in 1958, two destroyers were bought new from Sweden similar to that country's Halland-class but modified to meet the ARC's specifications. The rest of the fleet in the late 1970s consisted of an ex-USN Allen M Sumner-class destroyer and two ex-USN frigates, as well as two German-built Type 209 submarines, new to the ARC in 1975, as well as four Type SX-506 submarines built in Italy but assembled in Colombia.

Towards the end of the twentieth century, a small naval air arm was established, while US aid came to concentrate on anti-drug smuggling operations.

Today, the ARC has 33,138 personnel, of whom 7,200 are conscripts, and while just 146 are engaged in naval aviation, there are 14,000 marines. Of the six submarines mentioned above, four remain in service as the Pijao and Intrepido-classes respectively, with the former having eight torpedo tubes and the latter used for special forces. There are four Almirante Padilla-class frigates, each armed with Exocet AShM, Mistral SAM and two triple ASTT as well as a 76mm gun and capable of handling a light helicopter such as a Fennec or a Bo-105. The main force consists of coastal and riverine vessels, of which there are forty-eight, mainly small, but the *Reliance* and six vessels of the Nodriza-class have helicopter landing platforms. There are eight amphibious warfare ships. There are just seven logistics and support ships, including two ex-German Luneburg-class depot ships for patrol vessels.

Colombian and US marines exercise on an inland waterway, almost certainly training in anti-drug smuggling operations. (United States Navy)

Aircraft include three maritime patrol CN-235MPA Persuader, while helicopters include two Fennex and four Bell 412 as well as a Bell 212, a BK117 and two Bo-105. There are also a number of light aircraft for training and communications duties.

The main HQ is at Catagena, while there is a Pacific base at Buenaventura and a number of smaller bases on the coast and in major estuaries.

CONGO

Population: 3.8 million
Land Area: 132,000 square miles (341,880 sq.km.)
GDP: $12bn (£7.7bn), per capita $3,200 (£2,077)
Defence Exp: $218m (£141.6m)
Service Personnel: 10,000 active, plus 2,000 paramilitary

CONGOLESE NAVY

The former French Congo became independent in 1958 and was at one time under Soviet influence. Today, the Congolese navy has some 800 personnel and has three Zhuk-class patrol boats, although it is not clear if these are operational. The only base is at Pointe Noire.

CONGO, DEMOCRATIC REPUBLIC OF THE

Population: 67.8 million
Land Area: 895,000 square miles (2,345,457 sq.km.)
GDP: $13.4bn (£8.7bn), per capita $197 (£128)
Defence Exp: $218m (£141.5m)
Service Personnel: 10,000 active, plus 2,000 paramilitary

DEMOCRATIC REPUBLIC OF THE CONGO NAVY

Even by African standards, the Democratic Republic of the Congo has had a turbulent post-colonial existence since the country was granted independence by Belgium in 1960. Five days after independence, the army

55

mutinied and this was followed by an attempt by the wealthiest region, Katanga, to become independent. Between 1971 and 1997, the country was known as Zaire. Civil war once again wracked the country until 2003, with the situation made worse by both sides inviting the armed forces of other African states to participate.

Since 2003, the armed forces are being rebuilt, but all have serious problems with discipline and training, especially technical training. While the service is supposed to have about 6,700 personnel, including infantry and marines, it is believed that the true figure is nearer 1,000. There are claimed to be as many as twenty-three patrol craft, of which only eight are of any size with the rest being less than 50ft in length, but the only vessel known to be operational is a Shanghai II-class patrol craft. Nevertheless, there are riverine bases at Kinshasa and Boma, a base on Lake Tanganyika, another at Goma on Lake Kivu, and a coastal base at Matadi.

COSTA RICA

Population: 4.6 million
Land Area: 19,653 square miles (50,909 sq.km.)
GDP: $34.8bn (£22.6bn), per capita $7,502 (£4,871)
Defence Exp: $215m (£139.6m)
Service Personnel: 9,800 paramilitary active

CIVIL GUARD COAST GUARD

The Civil Guard was formed in 1949, primarily with an internal security role, and its functions included those of the police, coastguard, army, navy and air force. Initially equipped with light weapons, an attempted invasion by Nicaragua in 1955 led to a more military role, although it was not until the 1970s that personnel numbers rose from 1,200 to 2,000.

The original equipment for the Coast Guard was a 90ft launch on the Pacific Coast and another on the Caribbean Coast, plus a tug. During the 1950s, three small boats were added. By the mid-1980s, the Caribbean had a launch, five small boats and a rescue tug, while the Pacific had three small launches.

Today there are 400 personnel and eight patrol boats or launches, of which the largest is 32 metres. Bases are at Golfito, Punta Arenas, Cuajiniquil, Quepos, Limbe and Moin. There is a 400-strong Air Surveillance Unit, which is also part of the Civil Guard, but separate from the Coast Guard, and which has ten light aircraft and two helicopters.

COTE D'IVOIRE

Population: 21.6 million
Land Area: 124,510 square miles (322,481 sq.km.)
GDP: $22.9bn (£14.9bn), per capita $1,063 (£690)
Defence Exp: $340m (£220.7m)
Service Personnel: 17,050 active, plus 10,000 reserves and 1,500 paramilitary

IVORY COAST NAVY

Formerly part of French West Africa, the Ivory Coast became independent in 1960 and suffered from internal unrest in the years that followed, despite having French naval forces and marines stationed in the country. By the late 1970s, the country had a small brown water navy with 250 personnel, two patrol craft and seven small boats as well as landing craft.

Today, there are about 900 personnel, but just three patrol craft, the largest of which is an ex-French Patra-class, and the other two are used for fisheries protection. The main base is at Locodo, near Abidjan.

CROATIA

Population: 4.4 million
Land Area: 21,824 square miles (56,524 sq.km.)
GDP: $60.9bn (£39.3bn), per capita $13,811 (£9,045)
Defence Exp: $863m (£560.4m)
Service Personnel: 18,600 active, plus 21,000 reserves

CROATIAN NAVY

Formerly part of Yugoslavia, having earlier been part of the Austro-Hungarian Empire, Croatia seized its independence in 1991, when the present Croatian Navy was formed using ships of the former Yugoslavian Navy.

Today, the Croatian Navy has 1,850 personnel, of whom 250 are conscripts. Most of its vessels are patrol craft armed with RBS-15B AShM: there are two Finnish-built Helsinki-class with Mistral SAM; 2-Kralj and a Korcula-class without missiles, while there is also a single MCMV. There are three swimmer delivery vessels, but no submarines as such. Six landing craft, an auxiliary and a number of tugs complete the fleet. It is complemented by six Coast Guard patrol craft. The main bases are at Dubrovnik, Ploce, Pula, Sibenik and Split, where the HQ is based.

CUBA

Population: 11.2 million
Land Area: 44,206 square miles (114,494 sq.km.)
GDP: $61.1bn (£39.4bn), per capita $5,336 (£3,442)
Defence Exp: $1.96bn (£1.2bn)
Service Personnel: 49,000 active, plus 39,000 reserves, with 26,500 para-
   military, also having 1,120,000 reserves

CUBAN REVOLUTIONARY NAVY

Cuba did not gain independence from Spain until the Spanish American
War of 1898, after which the island was occupied by US forces until 1902,
but unlike many other territories seized during the conflict, became
independent. The country remained strongly influenced by the United
States for many decades afterwards.

A small navy, effectively a coastguard service, was formed and by 1911 it
had at least four gunboats, while a naval academy was founded in 1916.
Nevertheless, the navy did not rank high amongst Cuban priorities, even
military, and by 1939, there were just about a dozen warships, with nothing
larger than a destroyer and most of the rest being sloops, gunboats or
patrol craft.

Neutral during both world wars, although a Cuban ship is claimed to
have sunk a German U-boat that intruded into its territorial waters, post-
war the country slipped into civil unrest with a civil war fought between
the authorities and Communist insurgents during the 1950s, ending with
Communist victory in 1959. The old relationship with the USA was broken,
although the USN maintained its base at Guantanamo Bay, ceded by
Cuba in 1902, and a close relationship with the USSR began. The Soviet
Navy transferred patrol craft and submarines to Cuba, but the Cuban
Revolutionary Navy played little part when the USN blockaded the island
during the Cuban Missile Crisis of 1962.

By the late 1970s, the fleet included eighteen ex-Soviet patrol craft,
mainly of the SO-1-class, used as submarine chasers, as well as eight Osa-
class submarines, and a substantial number of lightly-armed patrol craft,
and a small fleet of landing craft. Personnel peaked at about 9,000 at this
time.

The collapse of the Soviet Union left Cuba isolated, and especially badly
affected by the end of supplies of cheap Russian fuel. Today, the personnel
strength is believed to be about 3,000. Few of the ships are fully operational
and reports indicate that two trawlers have been converted into patrol
craft. There are seven offshore patrol craft with one having 'Grail' SAM,

four single ASTT and a 76mm gun, while the remaining six have had their AShM missiles moved to shore batteries at 'invasion sites'. There are five MCMV and three support ships.

There have been reports of assistance from Pakistan, but these are unconfirmed, and today most of the emphasis is on coastal artillery, possibly due to fuel shortages, which makes sustaining a sea-going fleet difficult, while the personnel total also includes about more than 550 naval infantry. The main base is at Havana, but there are a number of smaller bases around the island.

CYPRUS

Population: 879,723
Land Area: 3,572 square miles (9,251 sq.km.)
GDP: $23bn (£14.9bn), per capita $26,178 (£16,998)
Defence Exp: $498m (£323.4m)
National Guard Personnel: 10,000 active, plus 50,000 reserves

NATIONAL GUARD MARITIME WING

Formed in 1964 after a breakdown in relationships between the Greek and Turkish communities in Cyprus, which had become independent in 1960, as a consequence the force is often referred to as the 'Greek Cypriot National Guard'. While the National Guard is predominantly a land force with conscripts accounting for more than 90 per cent of its personnel, it includes air and maritime wings, with the latter often referred to as the 'Cyprus Navy'.

No figures are available for the numbers actually serving with the Maritime Wing, but it includes two Rodman-class and two Vittoria-class fast patrol boats and two fast assault boats, as well as three landing craft, all in the Warships Command. A Coastal Battery Command deploys Exocet AShM. There is also a Special Forces Command that includes an Underwater Demolitions Unit, and a Base Command at Evangelos Florakis Navy Base.

DENMARK

Population: 5.5 million
Land Area: 16,611 square miles (42,192 sq.km.)
GDP: $309bn (£200.1bn), per capita $56,365 (£36,600)
Defence Exp: $3.66bn (£2.38bn)
Service Personnel: 18,707 active, plus 53,507 reserves

ROYAL DANISH NAVY

Although records exist of a Danish Navy in the fourteenth century, the Royal Danish Navy traces its origins from the formation of a 'Common Fleet' in 1509 by King Hans, with its first vessel commissioned the following year. At the time, Denmark was in a political and defensive union with Norway, Sweden, parts of Germany and Finland, Iceland, Greenland, the Faeroe Islands, Orkney and Shetland as protection against the Hanseatic League. The ships were owned by the monarch, who also provided core members of the ships' companies such as masters, but the rest were provided by the nobility from their farmhands and other estate workers. Sweden became independent and dominated much of the Baltic, and this led to two Nordic Wars, with Denmark forced to cede territory, but during the Scanian War, 1675-1679, it won the battle of Koge Bay. The Danes also enjoyed a number of victories during the eighteenth century, especially during the Great Nordic War, 1709-1720. Peace followed, and attention turned to acquiring colonies in Africa and the Caribbean. A Danish Mediterranean Squadron was established to counter the activities of the Barbary pirates, with notable actions including the bombardment of Algiers in 1770 and an engagement at Tripoli in 1797. The three Scandinavian countries agreed to respect each other's neutrality in a pact.

The beginning of the nineteenth century saw Denmark at war with the UK, which wished to stop Napoleonic France from benefitting from Danish trade that bypassed the British blockade of French trade. This resulted in two battles at Copenhagen, with the first, in 1801, being the second of Nelson's three great victories, while the third, in 1807, saw the first use in Europe of artillery rockets.

The modern history of the Royal Danish Navy dates from the separation from Norway in 1814, with the then fleet divided between the two countries. Reconstruction followed, but the RDN could never reach its former size and long reach. Wars continued over the fate of Schleswig-Holstein, which was annexed by Prussia in 1866.

Modernisation in the late nineteenth and early twentieth centuries resulted in a modern fleet by the outbreak of the First World War, although Denmark and the other Scandinavian countries remained neutral. Possibly because of this, the RDN was neglected between the two world wars, and during the Second World War, Denmark was overrun by German forces in a surprise attack in April 1940. The first year of occupation saw some co-operation with the German *Kriegsmarine* on minesweeping due to the need to keep the ferry routes to Norway and Sweden open but, in late August 1943, the Danes scuttled most of their ships following an order to either flee to the nearest neutral or 'Nazi-opposed' port, but fourteen ships were captured by the Germans. A 'flotilla in exile' was established in Sweden.

Denmark was liberated in 1945, and in 1949 joined NATO. US economic and military aid followed and a number of former German warships were transferred to Denmark while additional vessels were bought from the UK. Within NATO, the RDN was allocated the role of blocking the exit from the Baltic to Warsaw Pact invasion forces and a major role became minelaying, with the Falster-class minelayers, at 2,000grt, being the world's largest at the time and capable of each laying up to 280 900kg mines. An additional role was the use of fast attack craft to harass enemy ship movements, with typical craft being the Soloven-class torpedo boats, capable of 54 knots, and the Willemoes-class missile torpedo boats, while a mobile shore-based Harpoon AShM battery was also established. A submarine force skilled in shallow water operations also operated. During the 1950s, NATO funds enabled bases to be built at Frederikshavn and Korsor, as well as fortresses at Langeland and Stevns.

Post Cold War, the RDN has restructured itself with fewer but larger ships capable of participating in operations in distant waters. In 2006, a further restriction saw the end of the RDN's submarine capability, while the service was divided into two squadrons, with the 1st Squadron, based at Frederikshavn, being assigned to 'domestic affairs' and the 2nd Squadron, based at Korsor, assigned to 'foreign affairs'. The former's operational area extends to the Faeroes and Greenland, and includes EEZ, ice-breaking and pollution control activities. The latter includes disaster relief and evacuations, and provides Denmark's contribution to NATO standing maritime forces.

Today, the RDN has 2,959 personnel, of which just 153 are conscripts. Typical of the vessels now in service are the four Thetis-class frigates that date from the early 1990s, while the older Niels Juel-class frigates are being retired, and being commissioned between 2010 and 2013 are three Ivar Huitfeldt guided missile ships variously described as destroyers or frigates. The Thetis-class is fitted with a Stinger SAM and a 76mm gun, as well as accommodation for a Super Lynx ASW helicopter. The *Ivar Huitfeldt* has not got all of its weapons fitted. There are eleven patrol craft, of which the two Knud Rasmussen-class have helicopter landing platforms, while the two Flyvefisken-class have VLS Sea Sparrow SAM. There are eight MCMV. For the size of the combat fleet, there is a substantial logistics and support fleet of twenty-one vessels, including two multi-role auxiliaries of the Absalon-class with Harpoon VLS AShM, Stinger and Sea Sparrow SAM, a 127mm gun and capable of carrying up to 130 troops or forty vehicles. There are also ice-breakers and survey vessels. Eight ASW Super Lynx helicopters are operated, while Merlin ASW helicopters are operated by the Royal Danish Air Force.

The main bases are at Frederickshavn and Korsor, while the helicopters' shore base is at Karup on Jutland.

DJIBOUTI

Population: 979,053
Land Area: 8,958 square miles (23,200 sq.km.)
GDP: $1.14bn (£740m), per capita $1,296 (£841)
Defence Exp: $10m (£6.5m)
Service Personnel: 10,450 active

DJIBOUTI NATIONAL ARMY COASTAL NAVY

Djibouti became independent of France in 1977, but since that time there have been both internal unrest, including a civil war, and clashes with neighbouring Eritrea over the Ras Doumeira peninsula, claimed by both countries, with the most recent being in 2008. Both France and the United States have a substantial presence in the country.

The military are referred to collectively as Djibouti Armed Forces (*Forces Armées Djiboutiennes*, FAD), and include the Djibouti National Army, which consists of the Coastal Navy, the Djiboutian Air Force (*Force Aérienne Djiboutienne*, FAD), and the *National Gendarmerie* (GN).

The Coastal Navy has about 200 personnel with two Battalion-17 patrol boats and eight smaller craft. Its sole base is at Djibouti.

DOMINICAN REPUBLIC

Population: 10.2 million
Land Area: 18,699 square miles (48,430 sq.km.)
GDP: $51.2bn (£33.2bn), per capita $5,012 (£3,255)
Defence Exp: $335m (£217.5m)
Service Personnel: 24,500 active, plus 15,000 paramilitary

NAVY OF THE DOMINICAN REPUBLIC

The Navy of the Dominican Republic (*Marina de Guerra Dominicana*, MdeG) traces its history to the country's independence in 1844, when the government immediately established a small fleet using three schooners. The country was occupied briefly by Spain between 1861 and 1863, but an idea of how unsettled the country was is the fact that there were no fewer than fifty-six revolutions between 1844 and 1930. Later, additional ships were acquired, including a gunboat from Scotland in 1873. The country was occupied by the United States from 1916 to 1924, when the navy was disbanded, although its small fleet of two gunboats and four small launches was incorporated into the Dominican Constabulary in 1917 to provide a small coastguard. The service remained a part of the army until 1943, when it was reformed.

Civil war broke out in 1965, by which time the navy had enjoyed a period of expansion acquiring warships from the USN and the Royal Canadian Navy. During the four-month civil war, the navy bombarded Santo Domingo. Afterwards, the service went into a decline with its warships not kept up to date. Even by the late 1970s, when it had 4,050 personnel, its largest ships, two ex-USN Tacoma-class frigates and two ex-RCN corvettes, dated from the Second World War. The only modern warship was a PGM patrol craft dating from 1966, but displacing just 145 tons.

Today, the MdeG has 4,000 personnel and its two largest ships are two ex-US Coast Guard buoy tenders donated by the US in 2001 and used for coastal patrols, while there are also four patrol craft and eight small patrol boats. There is also an ex-USN landing craft and a tug. There are two Bell 206A JetRanger helicopters. The main bases are at Santo Domingo and Las Calderas.

There are plans to build a multi-role vessel, albeit of less than 200ft in length.

EAST TIMOR

Population: 1.04 million
Land Area: 5,743 square miles (14,874 sq.km.)
GDP: No figures available
Defence Exp: No figures available
Service Personnel: 1,332 active

EAST TIMOR ARMY NAVAL ELEMENT

The Portuguese colony of East Timor, often known as Timor Leste, was seized by Indonesia but became independent in 2000 due to United Nations intervention with the backing of Australian armed forces. The core of the armed forces is the army, which has a naval element with eighty-two personnel and four small patrol craft.

ECUADOR

Population: 13.8 million
Land Area: 104,505 square miles (265,443 sq.km.)
GDP: $61.5bn (£39.94bn), per capita $4,464 (£2,898)
Defence Exp: $1.47bn (£0.95bn)
Service Personnel: 58,483 active, plus 118,000 reserves and 500 paramilitary

ECUADORIAN NAVY

Although Ecuador became independent from Spain in 1820, for the next few years the country was part of 'Gran Colombia' and did not become completely independent until 1832, the date to which the Ecuadorian Navy (*Armada de Ecuatoriana*, AdE) traces its origins.

Throughout its history, the country has been involved in territorial disputes with its neighbours, and while many of these have not involved the navy directly, a brief and inconclusive naval engagement did ensue in July 1941 between an Ecuadorian gunboat and a Peruvian destroyer during the Ecuadorian-Peruvian War.

During the post-war years, the AdE was updated using surplus British and US warships, so that by the later 1970s it had an ex-USN Gearing-class destroyer; two ex-RN Hunt-class and one ex-USN Charles Lawrence-class frigate; as well as a number of patrol craft and two German-built Type 209 submarines, plus auxiliaries and amphibious forces, the latter being useful in maintaining supplies of military equipment to the Galapagos Islands. It later acquired ex-British Leander-class frigates in 1999, and this led to the establishment of a small naval air arm.

Today, the AdE has 7,283 personnel, of whom 375 are involved with naval aviation and 2,160 are marines, while the total also includes coast-guard personnel. There are two ex-RN Leander-class frigates, both with Exocet AShM and a twin 114mm gun, while one has a Mistral SAM and the other two triple ASTT. Both can operate Bell JetRanger helicopters. In addition there are six Esmeralda corvettes, each with a 76mm gun, Exocet AShM, Aspide SAM, two triple ASTT and a helicopter landing platform, and three German-built Quito-class corvettes, each with a single 76mm gun and Exocet AShM. Logistics and support are provided by eight ships, including a training vessel.

Aircraft include a single CN-235–300M and four Beech King Airs, as well as light aircraft for training and communications, and six Bell JetRanger and two Bell 230 helicopters.

The main base is at Guayaquil, but there is also a base on the Galapagos Islands.

EGYPT

Population: 84.5 million
Land Area: 386,198 square miles (999,740 sq.km.)
GDP: $215bn (£139bn), per capita $2,549 (£1,655)
Defence Exp: $6.24bn (£4.05bn)
Service Personnel: 468,500 active, plus 479,000 reserves and 397,000 para-
  military

EGYPTIAN NAVY

The Egyptian Navy dates back more than 100 years, but for much of the first half of the twentieth century it was effectively run by the Royal Navy with a British senior officer in command. Throughout this period it was known as the Royal Egyptian Navy and was effectively a brown water navy with coastal vessels and patrol ships. The relationship came to an end with the Egyptian invasion of Israel in 1948, while in 1954, the monarchy was overthrown, a republic declared and the current title adopted.

After the Anglo-French Suez Campaign of 1956, following the country's nationalisation of the Suez Canal, Egypt turned to the Soviet Union for support, and the next two decades saw substantial assistance given, effectively creating the Egyptian Navy, so that by the late 1970s, it had 20,000 men. The fleet comprised two ex-Soviet Skory-class destroyers and three ex-Royal Navy frigates, as well as twelve ex-Soviet 'Romeo' and 'Whiskey'-class submarines. A substantial coastal and patrol force of about eighty craft was mainly Soviet in origin and included Osa-class fast missile boats. By this time, the Egyptian Navy had gained the distinction of being the first navy to sink another warship using anti-ship missiles when, in October 1967, a Komar-class fast attack craft sank the Israeli destroyer *Eilat* with two direct hits. That apart, the service had relatively little involvement in the wars between Egypt and Israel.

Peace with Israel saw the reopening of the frontier between the two states in 1980, and in the years that followed, Egypt started to move away from Soviet equipment and with renewed links with the West came equipment from the US, France and the UK.

Today, the Egyptian Navy has 18,500 personnel, of whom 10,000 are conscripts while 2,000 of the total are in the Egyptian Coast Guard. Naval aircraft are crewed and operated by the Egyptian Air Force. Frigates include four Mubarak-class (ex-US Oliver Hazard Perry-class), each with Harpoon AShM and SM-1P SAM, a 76mm gun and accommodation for two SH-2 Super Seasprite helicopters; two Damyat-class (ex-US Knox-class), each with Harpoon AShM, ASROC, two twin ASTT, a 127mm gun and accommodation for a Super Seasprite helicopter; two Najim Al Zaffer (Chinese Jianghu-class), each with 'Silkworm' AShM and RBU 1200 rockets. Corvettes include two Abu Qir-class (Spanish Descubierta-class), each with Harpoon AShM, Aspide SAM, two triple ASTT, ASW mortar and a 76mm gun. There are also eleven Ramadan and Tiger-class missile-armed attack craft armed with Otomat AShM, and nine Komar-class with SY-1 AShM, plus twelve Osa-class with 'Styx' AShM and four Shershen-class with 'Grail' SAM; five ex-Chinese torpedo boats, each with two triple tubes, and six other fast patrol craft. The conventional submarine force includes four Chinese-built Romeo-class boats with eight torpedo tubes each and able to fire Harpoon AShM. A fleet of fourteen MCMV includes seven ex-US and seven ex-Soviet ships. There are three LSM and nine landing craft. The are twenty-five auxiliaries, including seven tankers.

Naval aviation includes ten Super Seasprite and four Sea King helicopters for ASW, as well as Gazelles for communications and training.

Coastal defence is provided by army troops under naval command.

The Egyptian Navy operates as two fleets, with the Mediterranean Fleet based on Alexandria and the Red Sea Fleet based on Safaga. Other bases are at Mersa Matruh, Port Tewfig, Hurghada, Suez and Al Ghardaqah.

The 2,000-strong Coast Guard has seventy-four small patrol boats.

EL SALVADOR

Population: 6.2 million
Land Area: 8,236 square miles (21,414 sq.km.)
GDP: $21.8bn (£12.14bn), per capita $3,519 (£2,270)
Defence Exp: $1.13bn (£729m)
Service Personnel: 15,500 active, plus 9,900 reserves and 17,000 para-
    military

NAVY OF EL SALVADOR

Although the Navy of El Salvador dates from 1842, shortly before the First World War it was disbanded and its duties performed by a coastguard service. It was revived in 1952, initially taking over the coastguard patrol boats. By the late 1970s, it was operating four patrol boats and had 170 men.

Today it has 700 personnel, of whom ninety are rated as commandos or special forces. There are eleven patrol craft and three landing craft. Duties are mainly fisheries protection and coastal patrols. The main base is at La Union, but there are a number of smaller facilities as well.

EQUATORIAL GUINEA

Population: 693,385
Land Area: 10,830 square miles (28,051 sq.km.)
GDP: $14.7bn (£9.5bn), per capita $21,238 (£13,790)
Defence Exp: estimated at about $8m (£5.2m)
Service Personnel: 1,320 active

EQUATOGUINEAN NAVY

This former Spanish colony has a National Guard and the Equatoguinean Navy, which has as recently as 1988 been granted US aid with the donation of a patrol boat for EEZ duties, but by 1997 this vessel was no longer operational. Today, there are about 120 personnel and six small patrol boats. Bases are at Bata and Malabo.

A report that two corvettes are being built in an Israeli shipyard seems unlikely and it is doubtful that anything of more than offshore patrol boat size could be operated. The country has substantial oil reserves but the uncertain political situation is inhibiting exploitation.

ERITREA

Population: 5.2 million
Land Area: 45,754 square miles (118,503 sq.km.)
GDP: $2.25bn (£1.46bn), per capita $432 (£280)
Defence Exp: estimated at $78m (£50.6m)
Service Personnel: 201,750 active, plus 120,000 reserves

ERITREAN DEFENCE FORCE NAVY

Although formerly part of the Ottoman Empire, Eritrea was occupied by Italy in 1890 until invaded by British forces in 1941, after which it became part of Ethiopia until after many years of internal unrest the country became independent in 1993. Border disputes continue and the bulk of the Eritrean Defence Force consists of the army, one of the largest in Africa despite the relatively small population.

There are currently about 1,400 personnel in the Eritrean Defence Force Navy. It is a brown water navy with twelve small patrol boats, while there is doubt over the serviceability of the two landing ships. The headquarters is at Massawa, with further bases at Assab and Dahlak.

ESTONIA

Population: 1.34 million
Land Area: 17,410 square miles (45,610 sq.km.)
GDP: $18.7bn (£12.14bn), per capita $13,930 (£9,045)
Defence Exp: $330m (£214.3m)
Service Personnel: 5,450 active, plus 30,000 reserves

ESTONIAN NAVY

Estonia was annexed by Russia after the Great Northern War of 1721, and only regained its independence after the Russian Revolution and Civil War in 1918. It inherited coastal batteries and a naval base at Tallinn. The coastal batteries were developed further between the two world wars, but in 1940, Estonia was occupied by Soviet forces.

Although Estonia regained its independence in 1991, the navy was not re-established until 1993. The departing Soviet Navy effectively destroyed the dockyard at Tallinn and left ten ships scuttled in the port, making operations difficult. In 1998, the Baltic States created the Baltic Naval Squadron, BALTRON, to enhance co-operation in naval matters and contribute towards NATO's naval presence. Initially, the service is concentrating on mine countermeasures, but expects to introduce more potent warships from 2015.

Currently, the Estonian Navy has 400 personnel. It operates a single Finnish-built patrol craft, a diving support vessel and three ex-UK Sandown-class MCMV, known as the Admiral Cowan-class locally.

The Estonian Border Guard, controlled by the Ministry of the Interior, includes a strong maritime element with nine patrol craft and another eleven river craft.

FIJI

Population: 854,098
Land Area: 7,055 square miles (18,272 sq.km.)
GDP: $3.2bn (£2.1bn), per capita $3,746 (£2,432)
Defence Exp: $55m (£35.7m)
Service Personnel: 3,500 active, plus 6,000 reserves

FIJIAN NAVY

Fiji gained independence from the UK in 1970. The Fijian Navy dates from 1975, since when it has avoided involvement in the military coups that have affected the country. Assistance has been provided by Australia, Communist China and the United Kingdom, although the latter was suspended after the latest coup in 2006 against the civilian government. Initially the service used ex-minesweepers for offshore patrols and throughout its history has effectively been under the overall control of the Fijian Military Forces.

Currently, the Fijian Navy has 300 personnel and has seven patrol boats as well as a presidential yacht, which is also officially claimed to be used for training. Training is at Viti, while the main base is at Walu Bay.

FINLAND

Population: 5.3 million
Land Area: 130,120 square miles (330,505 sq.km.)
GDP: $235bn (£152.6bn), per capita $43,926 (£28,524)
Defence Exp: $3.59bn (£2.3bn)
Service Personnel: 22,250 active, plus 350,000 reserves

FINNISH NAVY

In the past, Finland has been part of, first, Sweden and then, from 1809 to 1917, part of Russia, seizing independence after the Russian Revolution. Under Russia, a Finnish fleet operated within the Imperial Russian Navy's Baltic Fleet, and this participated in the Crimean War, mainly ashore.

After independence, a new Finnish Navy was created, based on old warships left behind by the Russians, mainly gunboats, motor torpedo boats and minesweepers. It was not until 1927 that two coastal defence ships and four submarines were built, while four gunboats were bought from the UK. Further ships followed, so that by 1939, the Finnish Navy had two coastal defence ships (roughly destroyer-sized), five submarines, four gunboats, seven motor torpedo boats, a minelayer and six minesweepers as well as a training ship. There were also a number of auxiliaries and icebreakers as well as the Finnish Coast Guard's small patrol boats.

The Soviet Union attacked Finland on 30 October 1939, at the start of what became known as the Winter War, intended to force the country into allowing the USSR to use its bases. At the outset, the FN moved quickly to occupy the demilitarised Aland Island to protect merchant shipping. During November, Finnish coastal artillery batteries engaged Soviet warships at Hanko, Uto and Koivisto, and in the latter engagement forced Soviet battleships to withdraw damaged. The two coastal defence ships were moved to the harbour in Turku and used to augment the city's AA defences. By December, the Gulf of Finland was icebound. The war continued into early 1940, and Finland was forced to cede some territory to the USSR, including the base at Hanko, but the latter had failed to retake Finland in its entirety despite deploying vastly stronger forces.

Finland found herself at war with the USSR once again after the collapse of the pact between Germany and the USSR following the German invasion of the Soviet Union in June 1941. This became known to the Finns as the 'Continuation War'. Before the war restarted, five additional motor torpedo boars arrived from Italy. Finnish and German forces laid minefields and the base at Hanko was bombarded by the coastal defence ships until evacuated by Soviet forces in December 1941. Both sides engaged in extensive use of minelaying and the setting of minesweeping obstacles, with the FN laying more than 6,000 mines while the USSR laid more than 16,000 and the German *Kriegsmarine* laid about 45,000 mines, of which 3,000 were magnetic.

The FN also deployed its submarines against Soviet shipping and contributed to the loss of twelve Soviet submarines. On 13 September 1941, the FN suffered its greatest loss with the sinking of the coastal defence ship *Ilmarinen* after she struck a mine, with the loss of 271 out of her ship's company of 403. Germany supplied the FN with fourteen new torpedo boats during 1943.

Despite Soviet forces forcing back German forces during 1944, in September Germany attacked Finland in what became known as the Lapland War as the Germans tried to secure the northern front against the advancing Russian armies. While, as the name suggests, most of the action was in the north, in repulsing an attempt by German forces to capture Suursaari, Finnish MTBs sank several German ships. Later, the FN hunted German U-boats in the Baltic.

Post-war, the FN embarked on a major mine-clearing operation that lasted until 1950, suffering high casualties in the process. Even after this major operation, seasonal mine clearance continued until the late 1950s but on a less intensive scale.

Finland adopted neutrality post-war, but at the Paris Peace Treaty negotiations in 1947, the USSR also demanded limitations on the country's armed forces, using the alliance with Germany as an excuse. Throughout the 1950s and 1960s, the wartime ships were phased out and replaced by new ships, with smaller craft built in Finland while larger ship orders were divided between NATO and Warsaw Pact countries. A Bay-class frigate, two Dark-class patrol boats and four minesweepers were bought from the UK, while two Riga-class frigates and four Osa II-class fast attack craft came from the USSR. Until the 1960s, the FN was not allowed missiles and mines.

All remaining restrictions ended with the collapse of the Soviet Union. Plans for a fast missile striking force including hovercraft were abandoned in 2003.

Currently, the Finnish Navy has 3,500 personnel, of whom 1,900 are conscripts. Equipment includes ten patrol craft, of which four are Ruama-class and four Hamina-class, all of which have RBS-15/15SF3 AShM and SAM, while there are also two Kiisla-class. There are two Hämeenmaa-class, with SAM, and three Pansio-class minelayers as well as the Pohjanmaa. MCMVs include three Katanpaa-class mine-hunters, which replaced the seven Kiiski-class and four Kuha-class minesweepers in 2011-2012. There are forty-three landing craft of various types as well as twenty-nine logistics and support ships, including an oceanographic research ship, a pollution-control ship and oilers and supply ships. Apart from Border Guard aircraft, all other air support is provided by the Finnish Air Force.

The main base and headquarters is at Turku, while there is another base at Upinniemi, near Helsinki. The main command has two subordinate commands, one for the Gulf of Finland and one for the Archipelago Sea, as well as a naval brigade. Coastal defence gun batteries remain important and include 100mm and 130mm guns as well as AShM. The force can be expanded to more than 30,000 personnel on mobilisation.

Augmenting the FN is a Border Guard with 2,800 personnel and more than sixty small patrol craft, a couple of Do-228 patrol aircraft and a dozen helicopters.

FRANCE

Population: 62.6 million
Land Area: 212,919 square miles (550,634 sq.km.)
GDP: $2.59tr (£1.68tr), per capita $41,297 (£26,816)
Defence Exp: $42.6bn (£27.6bn)
Service Personnel: 238,591 active, plus 33,686 reserves

The French *Marine Nationale*'s nuclear-powered aircraft carrier *Charles de Gaulle* at sea with a support vessel in the background. Note the Grumman E-2 Hawkeye AEW aircraft on the flight deck forward of the bridge. (*Marine Nationale*)

71

FRENCH NAVY

Known officially as the *Marine Nationale*, but colloquially more often as the *'Marine'* or *La Royale*, the French Navy can trace its history back to the Hundred Years' War, 1337-1453. It is not clear why the name *La Royale* is used, although some maintain that it referred to supposed royalist sympathies, but in contrast to other European navies, the French never described the service as the 'Royal Navy'. At the time, the French Navy consisted mainly of merchantmen armed and taken up from trade, as with most navies of the day, and in 1338, these included Genoese galleys hired by Philip VI of France to clear the English Channel of English ships, when two large English ships were captured. The following year, while English ships were deployed against Flanders and Scotland, the French took the opportunity to burn Hastings, Plymouth and Bristol.

Under King Louis XIV, the 'Sun King', the French Navy was given the support of the sovereign and became well-equipped and in the Nine Years' War, 1688-1697, also known as the War of the League of Augsburg, there were several victories in engagements with the Royal Navy and the Dutch Navy, including at Beachy Head (or Beveziers) in 1690, but the situation was reversed in 1692 at La Hogue (or Barfleur). Throughout the eighteenth century, the Royal Navy became the dominant force, although French support for the colonists in the American Revolutionary War resulted in the defeat of a British fleet at the Battle of Chesapeake Bay in 1781 and contributed to American victory at Yorktown.

Other achievements at this time included the first French circum-navigation of the globe in 1766 under the command of Bougainville.

An undeclared naval war with the United States followed between 1798 and 1800 over the resumption of American trade with Great Britain and the US refusal to repay war debts on the grounds that these were owed to the French crown and not the revolutionary government. As American ships were seized, a number of naval engagements followed in which the Americans triumphed.

The French Navy was badly affected by the revolution, not least because it not only lost royal patronage but also many of the senior officers belonging to the nobility. The Glorious First of June (or Battle of Ushant) on 28 May-1 June 1794 saw both the British and French fleets badly battered, but was a tactical defeat for France. The Battle of the Nile (or Aboukir Bay) in 1798 was the first of Nelson's three great victories and led to the British assisting the Maltese in ejecting French forces. After Napoleon Bonaparte seized power in 1799, a number of issues, including the status of Malta and what the British believed to be French preparations for a cross-Channel invasion, led to the Napoleonic Wars, 1803-1815. At the Battle of Cape Finisterre, July 1805, the French fleet was defeated but managed to seek refuge in Ferrol. The culmination of the attempts to gain supremacy by both fleets came on 21 October 1805 at the Battle of Trafalgar, where, despite the loss of the British admiral, Lord Nelson, to a French sniper's fire, the Royal Navy won a resounding victory and the French ships that escaped into Cadiz were blockaded and eventually seized by the Spanish when that country rose up against the French in 1808. This battle gave the Royal Navy command of the seas until the outbreak of the First World War in 1914. The French Navy recovered and was engaged in operations in the Far East and the Caribbean during the rest of the century.

The *MN* was amongst the first navies to experiment with the use of aircraft, and *La Foudre* was amongst the first seaplane carriers, with modifications including a launching ramp or deck for seaplanes to take-off when resting on wheeled trolleys.

The unification of Germany and its increasing military strength led to the *Entente Cordiale* between the UK and France in the early twentieth century, which saw the two countries as allies when war broke out, being supported by Italy and Japan, and eventually the United States, in due course. Nevertheless, the *Marine Nationale* was not heavily engaged during the war, and due to government neglect in the years preceding the war, had few modern vessels. The main operation was French participation in the Dardanelles campaign.

Post-war, a battleship, the *Bearn*, was converted to an aircraft carrier. Despite the limitations imposed by the Washington Navy Treaty in 1922, the *MN* was the fourth largest in the world, but growing tension with Italy after Benito Mussolini took power meant that a naval race developed between the two countries, with the Italian fleet growing rapidly to challenge the French. While Italy built light cruisers, the French response was to build super-destroyers, known as the *contre-torpilleur*, regarded by many as indeed being light cruisers. There were also new battlecruisers of the Dunkerque-class and the Richelieu-class battleships. A novelty was the *Surcouf*, a corsair submarine, which could use its gun in a surface engagement and also carried a small seaplane. No new aircraft carriers entered service between the wars, although two ships of advanced design, the *Joffre* and the *Painlevé*, were on order when war broke out. In the 1920s, some of the French Navy's fighter squadrons were transferred to the air force, the *Armée de l'Air*, but the service retained land-based maritime-reconnaissance.

The outbreak of war found the *MN* poorly prepared. New ships were being built, but not ready, while there was a desperate need for modern aircraft. Nevertheless, the service played its part in keeping the shipping lanes in the North Atlantic, the English Channel, the Bay of Biscay and the Mediterranean open. It shared the major naval base at Alexandria with the British Mediterranean Fleet, which moved the bulk of its ships from Malta in expectation of Italy entering the war, which it did not do until 10 June 1940. French naval units joined those of the Royal Navy in covering

Landing craft entering the stern dock of the French LHD *Mistrale*, one of two ships of this class, while a third has been sold to Russia. (*Marine Nationale*)

the despatch of an Anglo-French expeditionary force to Norway in April 1940 and were active in protecting Allied shipping during the campaign. Nevertheless, little progress was made ashore by the Allies and the forces were withdrawn as France herself came under pressure from the advancing German armies. The *MN* assisted the RN in covering the Dunkirk evacuation, but the French surrender and armistice meant that the *MN* withdrew from fighting, with its ships scattered in British ports and in North Africa as well as in its own home bases.

The dramatic change in the situation caused concern in the UK that the ships could be taken over by the German Navy (*Kriegsmarine*), causing the RN to seize those ships at Portsmouth and Devonport, while a stand-off at Alexandria was resolved by the French ships being disarmed and most of their crews being repatriated to France. Not all of the boardings were peaceful and a skirmish aboard the corsair submarine *Surcouf* led to four deaths. Many French sailors rejoined the Allies as part of the Free French Navy (*Forces Navales Françaises Libres*, FNFL). Despite French claims that no ships would be allowed to pass to the Germans, the British were worried that the new post-armistice Vichy regime might allow the substantial number of vessels at Mers-el-Kebir in Algeria or Dakar in West Africa to pass to Germany. When the demand to surrender the ships at Mers-el-Kebir was rejected, the RN opened fire, sinking a French battleship and severely damaging another two battleships and four destroyers.

Nevertheless, most of the French fleet remained intact and an attempt at destroying those ships at Dakar was also only partially successful.

The Germans did not take over the French warships in French ports, and when Vichy France was occupied after the Allied invasion of North Africa, as promised, the ships at Toulon, the main Mediterranean base, were either scuttled or left for either North Africa or neutral Spanish ports. After the invasion of North Africa, the remaining French warships outside France with their crews joined the Allies, and were present at the Allied landings in Normandy and later at those in the south of France. Once the invasion of Europe moved eastwards, the French Navy concentrated on the clearance of mines and rebuilding its bases, although the battleship *Richelieu*, after refitting in the USA, joined the British Pacific Fleet.

Post-war, the total tonnage of the *MN* was exactly half of that in 1939. The aircraft carrier *Bearn*, which had survived the war, led a task force of six ships to reoccupy French Indo-China in 1946. Nevertheless, this was the start of a war in which Communist forces sought to gain independence for the territory and the *MN* found itself supporting ground forces, including the use of air strikes from its aircraft carriers. The *MN* initially received the escort carrier HMS *Biter* from the Royal Navy, renaming her *Dixmude*, followed by the loan of the light fleet carrier *Colossus*, renamed *Arromanches* and eventually purchased. The USN loaned two of its Independence-class light carriers, *Langley* and *Belleau Wood*, respectively renamed *La Fayette* and *Bois Belleau*. These were returned to the USN in the early 1960s, but not before *La Fayette* had seen action off French Indo-China and in 1956 participated as a strike carrier during the Anglo-French invasion of the Suez Canal Zone.

The two Independence-class carriers were replaced by two French-built aircraft carriers, *Clemenceau* and *Foch*, which entered service during the early 1960s. From the outset, these incorporated angled flight decks and steam catapults, and operated jet strike aircraft as well as Alize ASW aircraft. They were complemented by a helicopter cruiser, *Jeane D'Arc*, which was designed to act as an ASW helicopter carrier, an assault ship and a cadet training ship.

Although France was one of the founder members of NATO, she withdrew from the command structure in the mid-1960s, not returning until the 1990s. Nevertheless, France has continued to maintain contact with most of the country's former colonies other than those in what was French Indo-China, especially in Africa and the Caribbean. A new naval base has been opened in Abu Dhabi to help protect shipping in the Gulf.

The withdrawal of the aircraft carriers *Clemenceau* and *Foch* and their replacement with a single nuclear-powered carrier, the *Charles de Gaulle*, has left the *MN* without two aircraft carriers despite the service's own policies requiring two. There are plans to buy a Queen Elizabeth-class conventionally-powered carrier, but these have been postponed several times due to budgetary constraints. The carrier-borne aircraft now include a naval version of the Rafaele fighter and the Hawkeye AEW aircraft, while the Super Etendard strike aircraft remain in service having been updated.

The *MN* is one of the few navies deploying ICBM nuclear-powered submarines, and relies entirely on French technology.

Today, the *MN* has 40,353 personnel, including 2,200 attached to the strategic nuclear forces, but excluding 12,800 marines who are counted under the army figures. There are four Le Triomphant-class nuclear-powered submarines, each with sixteen M-45 or M-51 SBLM and four single torpedo tubes, capable of firing submarine-launched Exocet AShM. There are also six Rubis-class nuclear-powered tactical or 'hunter-killer' submarines, each with four single torpedo tubes and also capable of firing submarine-launched Exocet AShM. The single aircraft carrier *Charles de Gaulle* is fitted with VLS Aster and Mistral SAM, and can accommodate up to forty Rafale or Super Etendard combat aircraft, or a lower number plus Hawkeye AEW aircraft and Dauphin helicopters. The *MN*'s air arm is usually known as *L'Aéronavale*.

Amphibious capability is provided by two Mistral-class LHDs, which can each carry up to sixteen medium helicopters as well as 450 troops and sixty armoured vehicles, and two Foudre-class LPDs, which can carry up to four helicopters, landing craft, twenty-two tanks and 470 troops, while there are also three Batral-class landing ships and nineteen landing craft.

Thirteen guided missile destroyers include two each of the Cassard and Forbin-classes, seven Georges Leygues-class and two Tourville-class, generally fitted with a 100mm gun, Exocet AShM, and either Crotale or Mistral SAM, as well as ASW torpedo tubes. The Georges Leygues-class vessels can accommodate two Lynx helicopters while the remainder carry a single Panther or NH90 helicopter. The more modern ships have Aster VLS SAM in addition to Crotale or Mistral. Eleven guided missile frigates include six Floréal and five La Fayette-class, all with 100mm gun, Exocet AShM and accommodation for a single Panther helicopter, while the former have Mistral SAM and the latter Crotale SAM, but with space for VLS SAM. Guided missile patrol craft include nine D'Estienne d'Orves-class with 100mm gun and space for a single medium helicopter. There are seven L'Audacieuse-class patrol craft, all based in either the Caribbean or the Pacific, and eight Leopard-class for training. There are eighteen MCMV, of which three are Antares-class and four Vulcan-class, also used as diving tenders, and eleven Eridan-class.

There are 107 auxiliaries and support ships, including four Durance-class replenishment ships with space for a medium-helicopter.

Main bases are at Toulon, home to the aircraft carrier and tactical nuclear submarines as well as much of the surface fleet; Brest, with the officers' training school and the MCMV vessels as well as survey ships, while the strategic missile submarines at nearby Ile Longue; Cherbourg with patrol craft; and L'Orient. Overseas bases are at Papeete in Tahiti; Dzaoudzi in Mayotte; Port-des-Galets on Reunion; Fort de France on Martinique and Noumea on New Caledonia, as well as Dakar, Djibouti, Cayenne and Abu Dhabi. The main naval air stations, BAN, are at Hyeres, Nimes-Garons, Landivisiau and Lanvéoc-Poulmic.

Mainstay of the *Aéronavale*'s maritime-reconnaissance force are twenty-two Atlantique aircraft, while there are thirty-eight Super Etendard, eighteen Rafale, and three Hawkeye, as well as twenty-six Lynx ASW, sixteen Panther SAR and eleven Dauphin helicopters, in addition to training and communications aircraft.

GABON

Population: 1.5 million
Land Area: 103,000 square miles (266,770 sq.km.)
GDP: $12.9bn (£8.4bn), per capita $8,574 (£5,567)
Defence Exp: $250m (£162.3m)
Service Personnel: 4,700 active, plus 2,000 paramilitary

GABON NAVY

Formerly part of French Equatorial Africa, Gabon became independent in 1960 and has since developed a small brown water navy for EEZ duties. It currently has about 500 personnel and has a French La Combattante-class patrol craft with Exocet AShM and two smaller French-built P-400 patrol craft with SS-12M SSMs, as well as an LST and twelve landing craft. It is based at Port Gentil.

GAMBIA

Population: 1.75 million
Land Area: 4,008 square miles (10,000 sq.km.)
GDP: $1.04bn (£675m), per capita $597 (£387)
Defence Exp: estimated at $7m (£4.5m)
Service Personnel: 800 active

GAMBIA NATIONAL ARMY MARINE UNIT

Gambia maintains a small army and has received assistance from the United States, Turkey and Communist China. There are about seventy personnel in the Marine Unit, which has four Hai Ou-class patrol boats and three smaller vessels, all based at Banjul.

GEORGIA

Population: 4.2 million
Land Area: 26,900 square miles (69,671 sq.km.)
GDP: $11.3bn (£7.34bn), per capita $2,690 (£1,746)
Defence Exp: $420m (£272.8m)
Service Personnel: 20,655 active

GEORGIA COAST GUARD

Georgia was briefly independent between 1918 and 1921, after the Russian Revolution, but the country was absorbed into the USSR in 1921. After the break-up of the Soviet Union, the country once again became independent in 1990, and immediately started to establish its own armed forces, including a navy. Equipment proved to be a problem as all Soviet naval vessels were withdrawn and although a division of the Black Sea Fleet was agreed between Russia and the Ukraine, Georgia was not a party to this. The Georgian Navy was established in 1993 using armed fishing vessels and eventually had nineteen vessels and 531 personnel, of whom no fewer than 181 were officers.

Relations with Russia remained difficult and hostilities flared up in 2008 over the status of the province of South Ossetia, during which most of the Georgian naval vessels were destroyed. Ukraine had contributed some ex-Soviet warships, but these were taken by the Russians later to settle part of Georgia's debts.

In 2009, the remains of the Georgian Navy were merged with the Georgian Coast Guard, itself part of the paramilitary Border Guard. Training was provided by the United States Coast Guard and once again Ukraine provided a number of small craft, as did Turkey, while Georgia became a member of the Black Sea Force, BLACKSEAFOR. The USCG also provided two Point-class cutters, the ex-USCG *Point Countess* became *Tsitne Dadiani* and the ex-*Point Baker* became *General Mazniashvili*.

Today, the GCG remains part of the Border Guard, which has total personnel strength of 5,400, but no figures are available for those involved with the GCG. There are seventeen patrol craft, of which one is an ex-Greek Kaan 33; seven Zhuk-class, of which three came from the Ukraine; two ex-US Point-class; two Dauntless-class; two ex-Greek Dilos-class and an Akhmeta-class. The main base is at Poti.

GERMANY

Population: 82.1 million
Land Area: 137,732 square miles (356,726 sq.km.)
GDP: $3.35tr (£2.18tr), per capita $40,781 (£26,481)
Defence Exp: $41.2bn (£26.8bn)
Service Personnel: 251,465 active, plus 40,396 reserves

For many years Germany was on what could have so easily have become Europe's frontline, but the country's own armed forces were not the strongest in Europe and had the Cold War have become a hot war, defence would have relied heavily on American and British forces based in the country, augmented by those of Canada and France. Some economists lauded the country for putting economic growth before defence, but without the means of defending the country, the opposing argument would be that no matter how successful, the economy and the country as a whole remained vulnerable. Deterrent is not simply nuclear and the value of strong conventional forces is so often underrated by politicians and the wider public.

No doubt as a result of having been the instigator of two world wars, the two largest conflicts in history, there was also strong German reluctance to do anything outside the strict North Atlantic Treaty Organisation area. This was matched by those in the other western democracies who opposed German reunification on the collapse of the Soviet Union and the Warsaw Pact, even though such objections were bound to fail and were impossible to justify on any rational grounds. The emotions that feared German resurgence were nothing compared to those of Germans wishing to be reunited.

Post-German reunification, the situation has changed considerably. Germany has Europe's strongest army, and while one might argue that her armed forces could be stronger, the same can be said about those of all the leading European powers. Germany is now participating in many UN operations, although there has been criticism of her troops in Afghanistan, who have been accused of sitting safely in Kabul and leaving American and British forces to face the full force of the Taliban.

The real danger is that while Germany is participating in all multi-national corps active in Europe, the spread of these in itself undermines NATO, the most successful and enduring alliance of all time, and the one that ties the United States and Canada into Europe. These two countries can cope without Europe, but Europe cannot cope in the long term against threats still to come without US involvement at the very least, and the Second World War showed Canada to be another worthwhile ally, not

The German air defence frigate *Mecklenburg* preparing to enter port. (German Navy)

least in her contribution to the safety of the North Atlantic convoys. The attitude of Russia to her neighbours is not one to engender confidence and complacency would be dangerous, for we should never forget that Russian expansion predated the Revolution. There is a danger that one day Germany may once again be on a potential frontline between East and West, and if not actually on the frontline, be no more than one step away from it behind Poland.

GERMAN NAVY

The German Navy (*Deutsche Marine*) was officially founded in 1956 when the country was once again allowed to have her own armed forces, although there was a second reformation when East and West Germany re-united to form the current state in 1990. Nevertheless, when Germany was united in 1872, it inherited the Prussian Navy, which evolved into the Northern Germany Federal Navy. On Germany's first unification, the country was a monarchy and the service was known as the Imperial Navy (*Kaiserliche Marine*), one of many changes of name as between 1919 and 1921 it became the Temporary Imperial Navy (*Vorlaufige Reichsmarine*) before simply becoming the State Navy (*Reichsmarine*) in 1921, and then after German re-armament was unveiled in 1935, it became the War Navy (*Kriegsmarine*). Further changes followed the Second World War.

The overriding ambition of the rulers of the new German State in the late nineteenth and early twentieth century was to create a blue water navy capable of rivalling the Royal Navy. Initially, the German Army had precedence over the German Navy but, in 1900, the Kaiser decreed that both services had equal standing. Because of Germany's relatively short North Sea coastline and the shallowness of the Kattegat and Skagerrak, access to the open sea was a problem and so between 1887 and 1895, the Kiel Canal was constructed so that shipping, and especially warships, could navigate between the Baltic and the North Sea in any weather and all states of the tide. In 1906, a programme of widening the Kiel Canal started and this was completed in time for the outbreak of hostilities in Europe in August 1914. Earlier, a Naval Act in 1898 had authorised the creation of a substantial German navy. Germany was also helped by the British government ceding the island of Heligoland to Germany in 1890, without consulting either Queen Victoria or Parliament. This not only removed a potential thorn in Germany's side in the event of war, but also provided a convenient forward base for raids on the British east coast.

In common with the other major maritime powers, the Germans constructed battleships that were seen as the defining standard of naval power at the time. When the Royal Navy's first all-big-gun battleship, HMS *Dreadnought*, went to sea for the first time in autumn 1906, every other battleship was obsolete. The paradox was that the advantage of having such an advanced ship also meant that the Royal Navy's advantage in size was gone, and the important factor became industrial capacity. In the years that led up to the First World War, the Germans built substantial numbers of Dreadnought-type battleships and battlecruisers in what became a great naval race between Germany and the UK.

Initially, the main emphasis of the First World War was the land battle, but the German Navy moved quickly to use its submarine fleet to good effect, especially in the North Sea and against the Royal Navy. Wider submarine warfare against merchantmen was restricted by the prize rules and the intensity varied as priorities wavered between inflicting maximum damage to the Allied war effort and not bringing the United States into the war. The most significant and best-known attack was the sinking of the Cunard liner *Lusitania* off the coast of Ireland.

There were attacks on British east coast towns by German warships, but the one set piece naval battle that both sides had anticipated so keenly was at Jutland on 31 May-1 June 1916. The Germans inflicted heavy losses on the Royal Navy and in this sense were the victors, but this was the only occasion when the two great fleets, the British Grand Fleet and the German High Seas Fleet, clashed, and in this sense, the British were able to claim a strategic victory.

The naval war was not confined to northern waters and in addition to German surface raiders in the South Atlantic, Indian Ocean and Pacific,

German naval forces also engaged the Royal Navy at Coronel, off the coast of Chile, where they were victorious, and at the Falklands, where they were defeated. There were also actions on the lakes of East Africa.

Although at one stage the German Navy almost inflicted starvation on Great Britain's population, far more successful in the end was the blockade of Germany in the closing months of the war. After the Armistice in November 1918, the German High Seas Fleet was ordered to steam to the anchorage of Scapa Flow in Orkney, to the north of the Scottish mainland, where the ships and their crews were interned, but most of the ships were subsequently scuttled.

The Treaty of Versailles limited Germany to six coastal battleships and a number of minor craft, including minesweepers, but no submarines. German submarine technology was kept alive by building outside Germany boats for other nations. The size of all navies was restricted soon after by the terms of the Washington Naval Treaty of 1922.

Despite tremendous economic problems within Germany, the 1920s saw the start of reconstruction of what had become the *Reichsmarine* (State Navy). A series of six light cruisers was built between 1925 and 1934, most of them before 1930. These ships were sent on goodwill visits across the world. The 1930s and Hitler's accession to power marked the start of a major programme of construction involving heavier warships. The London Naval Treaty of 1935 allowed Germany to increase the size of her fleet and strangely allowed her scope to match the Royal Navy in submarine tonnage. The elderly coastal battleships were replaced by three *Panzerschiffen* (armoured ships), although these were known to the media in the English-speaking world as 'pocket battleships', *Deutschland, Admiral Graf Spee* and *Admiral Scheer*. The first of these was renamed *Lutzow* in November 1939, shortly after the start of the Second World War, when the realisation dawned that it would be bad for national morale if a ship named *'Germany'* was sunk! Meanwhile, the name of the service had been changed to the more aggressive *Kriegsmarine* (War Navy).

Two old battleships, *Schlesien* and *Schleswig-Holstein*, were reclassified as training ships, although they were both pressed into active service on the outbreak of the Second World War.

Two large new battleships were built, with the first, *Bismarck*, commissioned in August 1940, and the second, *Tirpitz*, commissioned the following January. There were also two battlecruisers, *Scharnhorst* and *Gneisenau*, although to the Germans these ships were always classed as battleships. Three heavy cruisers also joined the fleet in 1939 and 1940.

Ambitious plans were prepared for the expansion of the fleet, with first 'Plan X', then 'Plan Y' and finally 'Plan Z' being prepared. These plans were drawn up on the expectation that war would not break out until 1942 or 1943, with a decisive naval battle with the Royal Navy in 1945. A large submarine fleet was envisaged in a modification of Plan Z, as well as additional battleships and cruisers, while aircraft carriers were also planned and at the outbreak of war, one, the *Graf Zeppelin*, had been launched and was nearing completion. Work on the aircraft carrier fleet was delayed due to arguments between the *Kriegsmarine* and the *Luftwaffe* over control of naval aviation, but carrier versions of the Junkers Ju87 'Stuka' dive-bomber and the Messerschmitt Bf109 fighter were developed, although they never entered series production.

The outbreak of the Spanish Civil War in July 1936 saw German armed forces involved on the side of the Nationalists, who were also supported by Italy, while the Soviet Union supported the Republicans. Unlike the *Luftwaffe* and the Germany Army, the Navy did not get so heavily involved in combat, but *Deutschland* was deployed and on 29 May 1937, she was bombed by Republican aircraft while in the Roads of Ibiza, with at least two bombs hitting the ship and killing more than thirty of her crew.

Plan Z had only been completed in late 1938 and approved by the Führer, Adolph Hitler, early in 1939, so when the Second World War broke out, the *Kriegsmarine* was far from its planned strength. It had the two old battleships, but the two new ships were far from ready. There were two battlecruisers, three armoured cruisers, three heavy cruisers and six light cruisers, twenty-two destroyers, twenty torpedo boats and small destroyers, fifty-nine submarines, of which fewer than twenty were capable of deep sea operation, and minesweepers. The aircraft carrier had been launched, but was not completed.

On the outbreak of war, the first shots in the war at sea were fired by the elderly battleship *Schleswig-Holstein* on 1 September 1939 against the Polish territory of the Westerplatte, a spit of land on the estuary of the river Vistula near Danzig, today's Gdansk. Two days later, on the expiry of the Anglo-French ultimatum, against orders, *U-30* torpedoed the passenger liner *Athenia* without warning, with the loss of many of her passengers, including children being evacuated to safety in Canada, and crew. From the outbreak of war until the following summer, attacks on passenger ships were forbidden.

The first few months of the war were successful for the *Kriegsmarine*, with the sinking of the British aircraft carrier *Courageous* on 17 September and the battleship *Royal Oak*, at Scapa Flow, on 14 October. A serious reversal came before the end of the year with the loss of the *Panzerschiff Graf Spee* in the Battle of the River Plate, with the ship being scuttled after a gunnery exchange with a British heavy cruiser and two light cruisers, a supposedly inferior force with lighter firepower.

Augmenting the main force was a substantial number of auxiliary cruisers, ships taken up from trade and converted to act as commerce raiders. There were thirteen ships in this role, varying between converted liners and more modest cargo ships, usually with their armament hidden until they surprised an Allied merchantman.

The war saw most of Germany's warships lost. The destroyer force was weak to begin with, and even weaker after the two Battles of Narvik in April 1940, when ten destroyers were lost. On 10 April, the light cruiser *Konigsberg* became the first operational warship to be sunk by aircraft when the Fleet Air Arm attacked from a shore station at Hatston in Orkney, but the battlecruisers *Scharnhorst* and *Gneisenau* sank the British aircraft carrier *Glorious* during the withdrawal from Norway. The battleship *Bismarck*'s first operational cruise was her last, although either she or her escort, the cruiser *Prinz Eugen*, sank the British battlecruiser *Hood* before the *Bismarck* succumbed to attack by the Royal Navy's Home Fleet and Force H, aided by the Fleet Air Arm.

U-boats played a leading role in the war in the Mediterranean as well as in the North Atlantic, but while there were many successes, especially during 1940 and 1941, the early adoption of a convoy system by the Royal Navy and the arrival of escort carriers and MAC-ships soon proved to be an effective counter. The German 'Enigma' codes were broken by the British early in the war and meant that signals between the German submarine headquarters and submarines could be decoded and often the position of the wolf packs of submarines detected.

At the end of the war, Germany had lost almost all her major warships apart from the *Panzerschiff Gneisenau*, the heavy cruiser *Prinz Eugen*, later used as a target for US atomic bomb tests, *Hipper*, which was laid up due to design deficiencies, and the light cruiser *Nurnberg*, which was taken by the USSR and put into service in the Soviet Navy. The *Graf Zeppelin* capsized and sank while being towed away by the Russians, possibly because she had been too heavily loaded with captured goods and equipment.

Post-war, Germany was divided between the four main wartime Allies, and this eventually resulted in a Federal Republic, or West Germany, and a Democratic Republic, or East Germany. As tension between East and West increased, West Germany became a member of NATO in 1956 and was once again allowed to have armed forces, with the *Deutsche Marine* (German Navy) being formed that year, while in East Germany, the *Volksmarine* (People's Navy), was also formed. The two navies differed in many ways as the German Navy developed to become a blue water navy, albeit without anything larger than a frigate for many years, while the *Volksmarine* became largely a coastal protection force.

The initial ships for the DM came from the country's new NATO allies and included former USN destroyers of the Charles F. Adams-class and Fletcher-class. These were followed in the 1960s by the first German-built destroyers and frigates of the Hamburg-class and the Koln-class, as well as the Type 205 submarines, the first post-war German-built submarines. Naval aircraft started to be introduced in 1957 on the formation of a naval air arm, the *Marineflieger*. Early equipment consisted mainly of British-built aircraft such as Gannet ASW aircraft, Sea Hawk jet fighters, Pembroke

Sometimes referred to as frigates, this is the German corvette *Braunschweig*, one of five ships of the class. (German Navy)

transports and Sycamore helicopters, all of which were shore-based. During the 1960s, licence-built F-104 Starfighters followed and eventually the Gannets were replaced by the Franco-German collaborative Atlantique maritime-reconnaissance aircraft.

Reunification of Germany saw most of the former *Volksmarine* ships sold or scrapped.

Today, the DM has 19,179 personnel. There are seven destroyers, all of which have VLS SAM and can accommodate two Naval Lynx helicopters. Of these, four are of the Brandenburg-class with Exocet AShM, four single torpedo tubes and a 76mm gun, while the remaining three are Sachsen-class with Harpoon AShM. There are thirteen guided missile frigates, all of which have a 76mm gun, while the eight Bremen-class ships have two twin torpedo tubes, Harpoon AShM and Sea Sparrow SAM and can accommodate two naval Lynx helicopters, while the five Braunschweig-class have RBS-15 AShM and a helicopter landing platform. There are ten Gepard-class offshore patrol vessels with Exocet AShM, a 76mm gun and RIM-116 SAM. A thirty-seven-strong MCMV force includes nine Frankenthal and five Kulmbach-class, as well as five Ensdorf and eighteen Seehund-class. The conventional submarine force now consists of six Type 212A boats, each with six single tubes.

There are three landing ships, while the 'Ark Project' with Denmark provides a further three RO-RO cargo and troop ships, each of 20,000 tonnes and available for use by the two navies or for other NATO forces. Support

Germany is probably the main builder of conventional submarines today, with examples in many navies, including the country's own. This is a Type 212, *U-34*. (German Navy)

Mine countermeasures remains an important role, and these are some of Germany's MCMV, with the one closest being the *Siegburg*. (German Navy)

comes from thirty-one tankers, supply vessels and support craft, and oceanographic survey ships.

Naval aviation accounts for 2,227 of the service's personnel and includes eight AP-3C Orions, which have replaced the Atlantiques on maritime-reconnaissance; two Do.228 pollution control aircraft; twenty-two Lynx, which can be used on ASW with torpedoes or AShM with Sea Skua missiles, and twenty-one Sea King ASW helicopters.

The main bases are at Wilhelmshaven, Glucksburg, which is also the operational HQ, Warnemunde, Olpenitz, Eckenforde and Kiel.

GHANA

Population: 24.3 million
Land Area: 92,100 square miles (238,539 sq.km.)
GDP: $18.2bn (£11.8bn), per capita $748 (£485)
Defence Exp: $126m (£81.8m)
Service Personnel: 15,500 active

GHANA NAVY

Although the Ghana Navy dates from 1959, it can trace its origins to the Gold Coast Naval Volunteer Force formed by the Royal Navy during the Second World War, when the country was still a British colony. The GCNVF was a seaward defence force and minesweeping organisation. After independence in 1957, the country began to organise its armed forces in 1959, with the naval force having its headquarters at Takoradi, although a second base was soon established at Accra. Initially, it was run by Royal Navy officers on secondment, but President Nkrumah ended this arrangement in 1961 and a senior army officer was transferred to head the navy.

By the late 1970s, the Ghana Navy had 1,300 personnel and the fleet included two British-built corvettes, unusual in having 4-inch guns, and four large patrol craft as well as four smaller patrol craft and a coastal minesweeper. Plans to add a frigate that doubled as a presidential yacht were abandoned and the ship served with the Royal Navy for a short time before being sold.

Today, the GN largely consists of ships bought second hand from other navies. It has 2,000 personnel. The fleet consists of two elderly Anzole-class patrol craft formerly operated by the United States Coast Guard for some fifty years; four German-built patrol craft and an ex-USCG patrol boat. There is a regional command structure with the naval HQ at Accra, while Western HQ is at Sekondi and Eastern HQ at Tema.

GREECE

Population: 11.2 million
Land Area: 50,534 square miles (132,561 sq.km.)
GDP: $306bn (£198.7bn), per capita $27,339 (£17,752)
Defence Exp: $9.66bn (£6.3bn)
Service Personnel: 138,936 active, plus 250,876 reserves

HELLENIC NAVY

Although Ancient Greece was one of the first maritime powers, the country at the time was a collection of city states. After the decline of the Roman Empire, Greece became first part of the Byzantine Empire and then, from 1453, part of the Ottoman Empire, but a war of independence began in 1821 and by 1828, the country was substantially free. During the war of independence, a naval force was established and, unable to meet the Turkish ships of the line on equal terms, much of the action involved the use of fireships. Only at the Battle of Navarino in 1827 did the major European powers become involved when a combined fleet of British, French and Russian ships defeated a combined Ottoman and Egyptian force.

Greece became a monarchy in 1833, and the service became the Royal Hellenic Navy, a title that persisted until the country became a republic in 1924. It was revived with the restoration of the monarchy in 1935, and dropped again when the country became a republic once again in 1970. The fleet in 1833 consisted of a corvette, three brigs, six gallettes, two gunboats, two steamboats and a few more small vessels. The first naval school was founded in 1846 on the corvette *Loudovikos*. The service was slow to modernise but, in 1855, four screw-driven steamers were ordered from the UK, and when rebellion broke out against Ottoman rule in Crete in 1866, the Royal Hellenic Navy was unable to assist. The closing years of the nineteenth century saw considerable modernisation and expansion, including the addition of three battleships to the fleet, so that when war broke out with Turkey in 1897, the RHN was the dominant naval force, but unfortunately the battles ashore went in Turkey's favour. In 1910, a British naval mission arrived and the service started to restructure on the lines of the Royal Navy.

By the outbreak of the Balkan Wars, the RHN had a battle fleet and a strong force of destroyers. Its war aim was to secure the Ottoman-occupied islands of the Aegean and control the seas. Two naval engagements with the Turkish fleet in 1912 and 1913 saw the RHN in control of the Aegean. A cruiser and additional battleships and destroyers were obtained, and two

Dreadnought-type battleships ordered, but these were not delivered due to the outbreak of the First World War in August 1914.

For some time after the outbreak of the First World War, Greece remained neutral, largely due to the government and the sovereign favouring different sides. To apply pressure, the French seized a number of Greek warships that then operated with French crews in the Aegean. It was not until June 1917 that Greece joined the Allies and the warships were returned. Greece supported the Allies in their bid to aid the White Russian forces during the Russian Civil War. This was followed by the Greco-Turkish War, 1919-1922, in which Greece was defeated.

Between the wars, Greece suffered from the poor state of the world economy and little was done to modernise the RHN, which became the HN in 1924 with the creation of a republic. In 1927, four destroyers were refitted and modernised and six submarines acquired from France, while four destroyers were obtained from Italy in 1929. In 1938, four Greyhound-class destroyers were ordered from British shipyards, but only two were delivered before the Second World War broke out the following year. This left what had become the RHN again with two battleships, an armoured cruiser, fourteen destroyers and six submarines.

The Second World War for Greece embraced the Greco-Italian War as Italy attempted to invade Yugoslavia and Greece. Convoy escorts were provided for the Ionian Sea, and the elderly Greek submarines managed to sink several Italian merchantmen. When Germany invaded Greece, the service lost no fewer than twenty-five ships to air attack. The surviving ships escaped to join the British Mediterranean Fleet at Alexandria. During the period of German occupation, a number of Royal Navy warships were transferred to the RHN, which not only operated in the Mediterranean but also had two destroyers present at the Normandy landings.

Post-war, the RHN received additional British warships and also ex-Italian warships as war reparations. On joining NATO in 1952, the country became eligible for US military aid. USN vessels transferred to Greece included five Gearing and six Fletcher-class destroyers as well as a Sumner-class destroyer. These were modernised, as were four Cannon-class frigates, and Guppy-class submarines. In the early 1970s, German-built Type 209 submarines were commissioned, while the service, by now once again the Hellenic Navy, became the first in the Mediterranean to operate fast missile-armed gunboats. In 1979, two Kortenaer-class guided missile frigates were bought from the Netherlands – the service's first new, as opposed to second-hand, major surface units in four decades.

Today, the HN has 20,000 personnel, of whom 3,100 are conscripts serving nine months' national service. Mainstays of the fleet are fourteen guided missile frigates, of which ten are Elli-class and modified Elli (Dutch Kortenaer), each fitted with a 76mm gun, Harpoon AShM, Sea Sparrow SAM, two twin torpedo tubes and accommodation for two AB-212 ASW helicopters. There are also four German-built Hydra-class (MEKO 200), each with a 127mm gun, Harpoon AShM and VLS Sea Sparrow SAM, two triple torpedo tubes, and accommodation for a Seahawk helicopter. There are up to seven Roussen-class corvettes, each with Exocet AShM, RIM-116 SAM and a 76mm gun. The later deliveries of some of the corvettes may see the withdrawal of the older units from the fleet of fifteen AShM-armed patrol craft, of which there are five Kavaloudis-class (French La Combattante-class), armed also with Penguin AShM, two torpedo tubes and two 76mm guns; four Lasko-class (French La Combattante-class), armed with two 76mm guns, two torpedo tubes and Exocet AShM; six Votsis-class (French La Combattante-class), of which two have Harpoon AShM and four Exocet AShM, as well as a 76mm gun. Smaller patrol craft include fourteen Armatolos, Kasos, Machitis and Andromeda-class vessels. There are nine conventional submarines, including eight Glavkos-class (German T-209), each with eight torpedo tubes, and a single German-built T-214, the *Papanikolis*, which can fire submarine-launched Harpoon AShM, as can four of the Glavkos. There are eleven MCMV, including two Evropi-class (ex-UK Hunt-class) and two Evniki-class (ex-US Osprey-class) and three Alkyon-class (ex-US MSC-294). There are five landing ships and seven landing craft. There are forty logistics and support ships, including the replenishment tanker *Etna*, smaller tankers, survey vessels and tugs.

The HN is responsible for maritime-reconnaissance and has two squadrons, with a total of six P-3B Orion aircraft, as well as a division operating eleven S-70 Seahawk and eight AB-212 helicopters on ASW, while there are also two Alouette III for communications duties.

The main bases are at Salamis, Patras and Soudha Bay.

GUATEMALA

Population: 14.4 million
Land Area: 42,042 square miles (108,889 sq.km.)
GDP: $40.9bn (£26.38bn), per capita $2,848 (£1,837)
Defence Exp: $169m (£214.3m)
Service Personnel: 15,212 active, plus 63,863 reserves and 19,000 paramilitary

GUATAMALAN NAVY

The Guatemalan Navy (*Marina Nacional*, MN), is a small force and although separate from the army, it depends on the larger service for logistics support and training. It has 897 personnel, while 650 marines are officially categorised as reservists. There are ten patrol boats, mainly US in origin, and there are two bases at Santo Tomas de Castilla and Puerto Quetzal.

The country maintains a claim to the neighbouring territory of Belize.

GUINEA

Population: 10.3 million
Land Area: 94,927 square miles (245,861 sq.km.)
GDP: $4.75bn (£3.1bn), per capita $443 (£287)
Defence Exp: $58m (£37.6m)
Service Personnel: 12,300 active, plus 7,000 paramilitary

REPUBLIC OF GUINEA NAVY

Guinea became independent from France in 1958 and started to establish its own armed forces. Since independence the country has been beset by internal unrest and changes of government by *coup d'état*, sometimes including mutinies amongst the armed forces due to poor conditions.

Today, the Guinea Navy has about 400 personnel and has two Swiftships patrol boats, although their operational status is uncertain. The main base is at Conakry.

GUINEA-BISSAU

Population: 1.64 million
Land Area: 13,948 square miles (36,125 sq.km.)
GDP: $845m (£548m), per capita $513 (£331)
Defence Exp: estimated at $14m (£9.9m)
Service Personnel: 4,458 active

GUINEA-BISSAU NAVY

Formerly Portuguese Guinea, the country became independent in 1974, but since then has been beset with economic problems and unrest, including an army mutiny in 1998, and again in 2010.

The small navy has about 350 personnel and two patrol boats, based at Bissau, but their operational status is uncertain.

GUYANA

Population: 761,442
Land Area: 83,000 square miles (214,970 sq.km.)
GDP: $2.2bn (£1.42bn), per capita $2,895 (£1,867)
Defence Exp: $128m (£82.6m)
Service Personnel: 1,100 active, plus 670 reserves and 1,500 paramilitary

GUYANA DEFENCE FORCE COAST GUARD

The Guyana Defence Force was established in late 1965, after independence from Great Britain, and includes the Coast Guard, which accounts for 100 of its total personnel. An ex-RN River-class minesweeper, originally used for training reservists, is the largest vessel, while there are also four Barracuda-class patrol craft. The main base is at Georgetown.

HAITI

Population: 10.2 million
Land Area: 10,700 square miles (27,713 sq.km.)
GDP: $6.65bn (£4.3bn), per capita $653 (£424)
Security Exp: 0 (£0m)
Service Personnel: None

HAITIAN COAST GUARD

Until 1920, Haiti had a small navy, but this was disbanded and it was not until the late 1930s that the Coast Guard was formed, initially with just two small picket boats. Although the country was neutral during the Second World War, six 83ft cutters were transferred from the United States Coast Guard in 1942, followed by three 121-ton submarine chasers in 1947, allowing the two picket boats to be withdrawn. Further vessels were provided by the USA at times. The crews of three ships mutinied in 1963 and shelled the presidential palace in Port-au-Prince, before being driven off by fighter aircraft and retreating to the US sovereign base at Guantanamo Bay in Cuba. The vessels were disarmed and transferred first to Puerto Rico and then returned to Haiti, where the dictator, Duvalier, celebrated by renaming the Coast Guard the Haitian Navy (*La Marine Haitienne*).

Plans to expand the 'new' navy remained unfulfilled although, later, five small patrol craft were obtained from the USA. In 1994, the dictatorship was ended and a civilian administration installed, which disbanded the armed forces, although the Haitian Navy was renamed the Coast Guard and became part of the National Police in 1996.

The National Police and Coast Guard were disbanded in 2004 to enable a new National Police Force to be formed, but these plans were thrown into disarray by a major earthquake in January 2010, and the country is now dependent on the United Nations for internal security.

HONDURAS

Population: 7.6 million
Land Area: 43,227 square miles (111,958 sq.km.)
GDP: $15.4bn (£10bn), per capita $2,021 (£1,312)
Defence Exp: $138m (£89.6m)
Service Personnel: 12,000 active, plus 60,000 reserves and 8,000 paramilitary

HONDURAN NAVY

Honduras became independent from Spain in 1821 and, although a member of the Central American Confederation until 1838, its armed forces date from 1825. The country has had an unstable past with many *coups d'état*, but has maintained a small navy with patrol and coastal vessels. Although it had just five patrol boats in the late 1970s, the following decade saw substantial US military assistance due to instability in neighbouring countries. Currently, it has 1,400 personnel and 830 marines, while it operates fifteen patrol boats and a landing craft, and it has bases at Puerto Cortes, Puerto Castilla and Amapala.

ICELAND

Population: 329,279
Land Area: 39,758 square miles (102,846 sq.km.)
GDP: $12.9bn (£8.4bn), per capita $39,265 (£25,496)
Security Exp: $32m (£20.8m)
Service Personnel: 130 active

ICELANDIC COAST GUARD

Known locally simply as 'The Guard', the Icelandic Coast Guard is a paramilitary organisation whose main role is fisheries protection. Although it dates its history from 1859, Iceland was still a part of Denmark at the time and, while this was still the case in 1920, it was in this year that the island assumed responsibility for protection of its coastline. However, it was not until 1924 that a trawler was armed, and the first purpose-built ship was not commissioned until 1926. Iceland became independent of Denmark when the latter was occupied by German forces in 1940, but Iceland was later occupied first by British forces and then by US forces to prevent any German occupation and formally became a republic in 1944.

Although a member of NATO, Iceland no longer has any armed forces of its own, largely due to the small population but also because NATO maintains a base on the island.

In 1955, the ICG formed an aeronautical division with a Consolidated PBY-6A Catalina amphibian, which came from the now defunct Icelandic Defence Force.

The ICG is best known for its role during the so-called Cod Wars with the UK and West Germany between 1972 and 1975, after unilaterally extending its territorial waters to 200 miles.

Today, the ICG has just 130 personnel. There are two Aegir-class coastal patrol craft and a support ship, the *Baldur*. Aerial surveillance is provided by a modified DHC-8-300, while there is a shipboard Dauphin helicopter and two Super Puma transport helicopters.

INDIA

Population: 1,214.5 million
Land Area: 1,262,272 square miles (3,268,580 sq.km.)
GDP: $1.55tr (£1.01tr), per capita $1,273 (£827)
Defence Exp: $38.4bn (£24.9bn)
Service Personnel: 1,325,000 active, plus 1,155,000 reserves

After many years of struggling with poverty, in the closing decade of the twentieth century India became one of the fastest growing economies in the world and, despite progress faltering early in the present century, it has since resumed. It would be an exaggeration to describe India as a prosperous country, but it has joined the list of donor nations and is in stronger shape financially and militarily than at any time since independence in 1947. The world's most populous democracy, relations with neighbouring Pakistan have improved over the past decade, but Communist China remains a strategic concern and India also takes piracy, especially in the Red Sea and western Indian Ocean, seriously as the country has a large and expending merchant fleet.

Contributing to the country's growing financial strength has been the capability of Indian industry, including aircraft production, shipbuilding, vehicle manufacturing and, of course, defence equipment.

As with its neighbours Pakistan and Communist China, India is now a nuclear power, but as yet has no nuclear-powered warships. Equipment, including warships, is purchased from a variety of sources, even including the United States, with Russia remaining a major supplier, with much built under licence or assembled in India. Nuclear weapons are handled by the Strategic Forces Command, with a Political Council, which is the only body that can authorise the use of nuclear weapons, advising an Executive Council. Just as the devastation that nuclear weapons can bring provided stability and peace during the Cold War, it can only be hoped that they will also have a similar impact in Asia.

INDIAN NAVY

The history of the Indian Navy predates the country's independence and partition into the states of India and Pakistan on 15 August 1947. Until 1935, the Royal Indian Navy was known as the Royal Indian Marine, but the history of the service actually dates from the formation of the Honourable East India Company's Marine in 1612. This was a strictly private enterprise venture designed to protect the 'Honourable Company's' ships in the Gulf of Cambay and in the Narmada and Tapti Rivers. It was not until 1830 that the force came under the control of the colonial administration as His Majesty's Indian Navy with British officers and Indian ratings. Early action included the First Opium War in 1840 and in the Second Anglo-Burmese war of 1852. A further change of name came before the First World War, when it became the Royal Indian Marine, providing minesweeping, convoy and harbour protection and facilities for visiting Allied warships.

The first Indian to be commissioned was Sub-Lieutenant D.N. Mukherji, an engineer, in 1928.

In 1935, the name was changed again to the Royal Indian Navy, following the practice in the dominions.

During the Second World War, the RIN was vastly expanded and its ships were deployed in operations far from India, the most significant being 'Operation Husky', the Allied invasion of Sicily in 1943, when two sloops joined the Allied naval force offshore. Closer to home, the RIN provided convoy escorts and minesweeping as well as supplying Allied warships in the India Ocean and in Indian coastal waters.

The end of the war in 1945 saw the number of vessels and personnel much reduced. The following year a large scale mutiny occurred, eventually affecting seventy-eight ships and twenty shore establishments and involving

20,000 Indian sailors throughout India in protest against perceived discrimination against Indian officers and ratings by the British.

On independence and partition in 1947, the remaining ships and personnel were divided equally between the Union of India and the Dominion of Pakistan. India became a republic on 26 January 1950, and the 'Royal' prefix was dropped while ships changed from 'His Majesty's Indian Ship' (HMIS), to 'Indian Naval Ship' (INS). Even after independence, many Royal Navy officers remained on secondment with the Indian Navy and it was not until April 1958 that the first Indian Chief of Staff, Vice-Admiral Ram Dass Katari, was appointed.

India has always been comprised of a large number of small states, almost all of which were colonised by the British, although some had originally been in French hands. The remaining exceptions on independence were Goa, Daman and Diu, which remained Portuguese colonies. In late 1961, Indian forces invaded Goa, followed by the two small statelets of Daman and Diu, seizing the territories and forcibly incorporating them into India. The cruiser INS *Delhi* sank a Portuguese patrol boat while the British-built Leopard-class frigates *Betwa* and *Beas* sank the Portuguese frigate *Afonso de Albuquerque*. The following year's war over territory in the Himalayas between India and China did not involve the IN.

The most usual foe for the Indian armed forces became neighbouring Pakistan, with the first major conflict between the two states in 1965, during which the IN provided coastal patrols, especially after the Pakistani Navy bombarded Dwarka. During the period that followed, the IN enjoyed considerable growth, largely with Russian equipment. One of the last major purchases from the UK was the aircraft carrier INS *Vikrant*, formerly HMS *Hercules*, which arrived in 1961 and enabled Indian Naval Aviation, which dated from the creation of a Fleet Requirements Unit in 1950 for target towing and communications duties, to put to sea using Sea Hawk fighter-bombers, Breguet Alize ASW aircraft and Alouette III helicopters.

The *Vikrant* played an important part in the Indo-Pakistani War of 1971, backing the naval blockade of both West and East Pakistan, which broke away from West Pakistan to become the new state of Bangladesh the following year. Sea Hawk and Alize aircraft from the carrier sank Pakistani gunboats and merchantmen and prevented relief supplies reaching Pakistani forces in East Pakistan. During the war, the destroyer *Raiput* sank Pakistan's only long-range submarine during the night of 3-4 December, while an attack on the main Pakistani naval base at Karachi, on 4 December 1971, sank a destroyer, a minesweeper and an ammunition ship, as well as damaging other ships and shore installations. Later that month, the Indian Navy lost the frigate *Khukri*, with another damaged.

In the mid-1980s, *Vikrant* was joined and then replaced by the former HMS *Hermes*, which was renamed INS *Viraat*. The ship was already fitted with a ski jump for STOVL operation of the Sea Harrier, of which the FRS1 fighter and T60/T4 conversion trainer variants were introduced at the same time.

An attempted *coup d'état* in the Maldives in 1988 was thwarted by Indian naval intervention, recovering a ship hijacked by the rebels and arresting those aboard. In 1999, during the Kargil War, the IN once again found itself

The Indian Navy still operates the former British aircraft carrier *Hermes*, in Indian service named *Viraat*. She will be replaced by a new ship built in India in due course. *Hermes* was converted with a ski jump to handle the Sea Harrier V/STOL jet fighter, but the outline of the angled deck can still be seen. (Indian Naval Service)

facing Pakistani forces as they attempted to blockade Indian ports. Tension between the two countries resurfaced during 2001-2002, with more than a dozen Indian warships deployed. At the same time, in 2001 the Indian Navy conducted operations in the Strait of Malacca to release US warships for Operation Enduring Freedom, the invasion of Iraq.

Following a sub-sea earthquake in the Indian Ocean in December 2004 and the ensuing tsunami, the Indian Navy was immediately mobilised to provide disaster relief not only in coastal communities in India itself and its offshore Nicobar and Andaman Islands, but also in neighbouring Sri Lanka, in Indonesia and the Maldives, with more than 5,000 personnel and almost thirty ships involved, many equipped with helicopters. Another humanitarian mission arose during the 2006 conflict between Israel and the Lebanon, when the Indian Navy mounted Operation Sukoon to evacuate some 2,300 Indian nationals as well as those of Sri Lanka and Nepal. In both 2007 and 2008, the IN provided relief for victims of tropical cyclones. One outcome of the post-tsunami relief operations was the decision to add LPDs, including the *Jalashwa*, to the fleet for amphibious manoeuvres.

Anti-piracy operations have also become an important aspect of Indian naval operations. In 1999, the IN and the Indian Coast Guard recovered a Japanese cargo ship captured by pirates while, since 2008, frigates and destroyers have been deployed off Somalia and off the Seychelles, at the request of the Seychelles government, to escort merchant shipping through waters in which piracy has become commonplace.

INS *Porbander* is a former Soviet mine countermeasures vessel. (Indian Naval Service)

The Indian frigate *Ganga* was amongst the first such vessels to be built in India as an enlarged version of the British Leander-class, some of whose lines can still be seen in the foredeck and the funnel. (Indian Naval Service)

Today, the Indian Navy has 58,350 personnel, including 7,000 involved in naval aviation, 1,200 marines and 1,000 personnel in the *Sagar Prahari Bal*, a special force created to protect naval bases from terrorist attacks. The newest of some 170 ships is the aircraft carrier *Vikramaditya*, bought from Russia and commissioned in 2012 with MiG-29K fighters, complementing the *Viraat*, but two 40,000-ton aircraft carriers are being built, one for V/STOL aircraft and the other for conventional aircraft. Amphibious warfare has been developed considerably and now includes the US-built LPD *Jalashwa*, formerly one of the USN's Austin-class ships, which can carry up to six medium helicopters, as well as landing craft and up to 930 marines. In addition, there are five Kumbhir-class LSM and five Magar and modified Magar-class LST. There are eleven destroyers, with guided missile and helicopter ships, including three of the Delhi-class with anti-ship missiles, 100mm gun and two medium ASW helicopters, and three of the new Shivalik-class with surface-to-air missiles, a 76mm gun and a single medium ASW helicopter. The five guided missile-armed Raiput-class have a 76mm gun, surface-to-air missiles and a single light helicopter, usually a Kamov Ka-25 or Ka-28. Twelve frigates include nine anti-ship and SAM guided missile and helicopter-equipped ships with three each of the Brahmaputra-class and Godavari-class, with 76mm guns, and the Talwar-class with 100mm guns. These can carry Chetak (Alouette III), ALH or Ka-31 or Ka-38 helicopters. Three Nilgri-class frigates have 114mm guns, torpedo tubes and either a Chetak or ASW Sea King helicopter. All frigates and destroyers

Ranjit is a former Soviet Navy Kashin-class destroyer, with the old USSR and now Russia being amongst the main armaments suppliers to India.

have ASTT. There are fourteen submarines, all of which are conventionally powered and which include four of the small German-built Shishumar-class with a single 533mm torpedo tube, while ten Russian-built Kilo-class boats are, in Indian service, known as ten Sindhughosh-class, with six torpedo tubes each and submarine-launched cruise missiles. A Russian Nerpa-class submarine is being evaluated while on loan, but is not fully operational.

There are twenty-four corvettes, all armed with 76mm guns, while twenty are also missile-armed, usually with ASM and SAM. These include four Khukri-class and four Kora-class, each capable of handling a light helicopter, usually a Chetak or a Dhruv. Helicopters cannot be carried aboard the ten Veer-class, and the two Prabal-class, modified from the Veer-class. The four Abhay-class corvettes have SAM and torpedo tubes, but no helicopter. There are twenty-eight patrol craft, of which the six Sukanya-class can carry a Chetak helicopter. MCMV include ten Pondicherry-class.

The fleet is supported by forty-eight oilers, ammunition ships and replenishment vessels, and survey ships.

The main bases are at Mumbai, Calcutta, Kochi, Vishakhapatnam and Port Blair (in the Andaman Islands), and the new base at Karwar, while naval aviation is based on Goa, where the Sea Harrier force of eleven aircraft is based alongside eight Mig-29K 'Fulcrum'. The IN includes land-based maritime-reconnaissance aircraft: Ilyushin Il-38 'May' and Tupolev Tu-142M 'Bear F', as well as twenty-four Indian-built Dornier Do-228 and seventeen Britten-Norman Islander, and will be amongst the world's most advanced maritime-reconnaissance forces by 2013, when the first of eight Boeing P-8A aircraft, based on the 737, are delivered. ASW helicopters include thirty-five S-61 Sea King and almost twenty Ka-25 'Hormone' and Ka-28 'Helix'. AEW is provided by nine Ka-31 'Helix B'. Transport helicopters comprise eleven Sea Kings of both Westland and Sikorsky manufacture. There are more than fifty light helicopters.

Weapons include anti-shipping missiles such as Sea Eagle and Sea Skua, and these British missiles can be fired from Russian-built aircraft, while there are also PJ-10 *Brahmos*. Air-to-air missiles (AAM) include versions of the French-built Magic as well as Russian AA-10 and AA-11. Medium and heavy UAV are also deployed.

Augmenting the Indian Navy is the 9,550-strong Indian Coast Guard, which is also controlled by the Ministry of Defence. It is divided into eleven districts and operates fifty-seven patrol and coastal protection craft as well as twenty-four Do-228 patrol aircraft and seventeen Chetak helicopters, which may be replaced by the Dhruv in due course.

INDONESIA

Population: 232.5 million
Land Area: 736,512 square miles (1,907,566 sq.km.)
GDP: $693bn (£450bn), per capita $2,981 (£1,935)
Defence Exp: $4.47bn (£2.9bn)
Service Personnel: 302,000 active, plus 400,000 reserves and 280,000 paramilitary

INDONESIAN NATIONAL DEFENCE – NAVY

The Indonesian Navy dates from 22 August 1945, before the country's independence from the Netherlands and during the lull between the Japanese surrender at the end of the Second World War and the Netherlands being able to re-occupy her colonies in the East. Initially it was known as the People's Security Sea Service and several changes of name followed before independence in 1949. Following independence, the Indonesian Navy (*Tentara Nasional Indonesia-Angkatan Laut*, TNI-AL) had an assortment of minor warships for coastal patrols and communications with the many islands in this straggling archipelago, as well as abandoned Japanese landing ships, but in the years that followed, warships were bought mainly from Italy until, in the early 1970s, ex-USN warships were transferred and modernised locally with Russian secondary armament.

Assistance was provided by a number of European countries, including the UK, and by India, but by 1962 an increasingly aggressive and expansionist foreign policy saw conflict with the Netherlands following an invasion of West Irian, formerly Dutch New Guinea, which was ceded to Indonesia the following year. At this time, Indonesia also started a confrontation with the UK and the Federation of Malaysia and Singapore, which lasted until 1966 and brought the country into conflict with UK, Australian and New Zealand forces. Western supplies were cut off and the country obtained its first supplies from the Eastern Bloc, including its first submarines, fourteen 'Whiskey'-class boats from the USSR. In 1975, the Portuguese territory of East Timor was seized.

By the late 1970s, the TNI-AL had four ex-USN Claude Jones-class frigates; two Italian-built Surapati-class frigates; two Italian-built Pattimura-class frigates; more than forty small patrol craft; three of the 'Whiskey'-class submarines, with nine in reserve and the remainder broken up for spares; and up to sixty landing ships and landing craft; and about twenty auxiliaries and support ships. Naval aviation included five HU-16 Albatross amphibians, a number of C-47 transports, six Australian-built Nomad maritime patrol aircraft and Bell 47 and Alouette II/III helicopters.

The return of a civilian government in recent years has led to a less aggressive foreign policy, while East Timor has become independent as the state of Timor Leste.

Today, the TNI-AL is involved in an annual series of bilateral maritime training exercises, Co-operation Afloat Readiness and Training (CARAT), between the US Navy and the armed forces of Singapore, Thailand, Malaysia, Indonesia, Brunei and the Philippines.

Currently, the TNI-AL has 45,000 personnel, of whom 1,000 are engaged in naval aviation and 20,000 are marines. It continues to have a large number of minor warships, but also has eleven frigates, of which six are Ahmad Yani-class, each with Harpoon AShM, Mistral SAM, two triple ASTT and a 76mm gun, as well as accommodation for a light helicopter, usually a Bo-105 or a Wasp; a single Hajar Dewantara-class is used for training, but has Exocet AShM, two single ASTT and accommodation for a light helicopter, usually a Bo-105 as, although a Wasp is usually quoted as an alternative, these are unlikely to be airworthy; four Sigma-class have Exocet AShM, Mistral SAM, two triple ASTT, a 76mm gun and have a helicopter landing platform. Ex-East German Parchim-class corvettes form the backbone of the fleet of nineteen corvettes, with sixteen of these ships as the Kapitan Patimura-class, and, although their serviceability is doubtful, each is supposed to have 'Grail' SAM, four single ASTT and rocket launchers, while there are also two Fatahillah-class and a Nala-class, with all three ships having Exocet AShM. There are about forty-five to fifty smaller patrol and fast attack craft. MCMV has eleven vessels. There are just two Cakra-class conventional submarines, each with eight torpedo tubes, but their serviceability is in doubt. A variety of four landing ships with floodable docks and twenty-six landing ships as well as fifty-four landing craft provides a strong amphibious force, while there are thirty-two auxiliaries and support ships.

Naval aviation includes twenty-two N-22B Searchmaster and two CN-235 MPA, as well as a variety of light aircraft and transports, elderly Wasp helicopters that are likely to be in store, Bo-105s, Super Pumas and Bell 412s, while the force of Mi-17s currently stands at four, with additional aircraft on order.

The service is organised into two fleets, East, based on Surabya, and West, based on Jakarta, but this is being replaced by three commands: Riau or West; Papua or East; and Makassar or Central. There are also bases at Kupang, in West Timor, and Tahuna, in North Sulawesi.

IRAN

Population: 75.1 million
Land Area: 627,000 square miles (1,626,520 sq.km.)
GDP: $356bn (£231bn), per capita $4,739 (£3,077)
Defence Exp: $9.02bn (£5.86bn)
Service Personnel: 523,000 active, plus 350,000 reserves and 40,000 para-
    military

In the case of Iran, writing on any branch of the armed forces presents a challenge as the Iranian Army, Air Force and Navy are duplicated by the Iranian Revolutionary Guard Corps and its Air Force, and the Iranian Revolutionary Guards Corps Naval Forces, with the latter actually stronger in manpower terms than the official Iranian Navy. The Revolutionary Guard Corps were originally formed after the revolution due to suspicions over the loyalties of the established armed forces, but more than three decades later, they remain. Nevertheless, as the history of the service predates the revolution, the Iranian Navy is given priority here, but any review has to include the IRGCNF, especially as this has, on occasion, been involved in activities that have sparked international incidents.

IRANIAN NAVY

Situated on the north-eastern shores of what was the Persian Gulf, Iran, or Persia in the past, for many centuries the navy was the lesser of the two services and neither well organised nor very strong, with the exception of the Achaemanid era, in about 500BC. It was not until the Pahlavi dynasty that sea power became important, with the Shah planning a service, the Imperial Iranian Navy, that could project power not only in the Gulf but into the Indian Ocean as well, starting in 1923.

Despite this, by 1939, the Imperial Iranian Navy consisted mainly of gunboats suitable only for operation in the Gulf. In August 1941, even this small force was destroyed by the Royal Navy in a combined British and Soviet invasion of Iran, intended to secure one of the three routes used to supply the Soviet Union with British and American arms, equipment and other supplies following the German invasion of the USSR earlier that summer.

Post-war, the British and Soviet forces withdrew and the work of re-building the Imperial Iranian Navy began. As Iran post-war moved firmly into the 'Western' camp, most of its equipment was obtained from the US and UK, and while gunboats were obtained, attention was also paid to larger ships such as destroyers and frigates, as well as hovercraft. By the late 1970s, the Imperial Iranian Navy had 28,000 personnel. Its ships included an ex-Royal Navy Battle-class destroyer modernised to carry Standard SSM and Seacat SAM; two ex-USN Allen M Sumner-class destroyers modernised with Standard SSM and accommodation for an ASW helicopter; four British-built Saam-class (Vosper Mk5) guided missile frigates with Seacat SAM and Sea Killer rocket launchers; four US-built PF103-class corvettes; three ex-USN Tang-class submarines, also modernised; twelve French-built Kaman-class fast attack craft armed with a 76mm gun and Harpoon AShM; three PGM71-class large patrol craft and four ex-USCG patrol craft. There were also minesweepers and four landing ships as well as more than a dozen auxiliaries, including tankers and supply ships. Naval aviation was provided by a maritime-reconnaissance squadron of Orions, an ASW Sea King helicopter squadron and a variety of smaller aircraft and helicopters for communications and liaison.

Although some reviews maintain that as many as six Italian Lupo-class frigates were on order, which were a popular design at the time, these do not seem to have joined the IIN, while four US-built destroyers were not delivered following the revolution of 1979 that saw the Shah over-thrown and an extreme Islamic regime take power. Instead, the ships were assigned to the USN as the Kidd-class frigates.

Post-revolution, the Iranian Navy was not heavily involved in the war between Iraq and Iran that started in 1979 and continued throughout the 1980s, but the seizure of staff at the US Embassy in Tehran and this conflict made relationships with the West even more difficult and Iraq received weapons to enable her to fend off Iranian attacks. The war was essentially an air and ground conflict.

While a number of ships were purchased from Russia and China, especially submarines, as well as some domestic production of minor war-ships, the main activity since the 1980s has been the modernisation of existing ships with Chinese and Russian missile systems. Naval exercises have been held with Pakistan.

Today, the Iranian Navy has 18,000 personnel, including 2,600 marines and 2,600 engaged in naval aviation. Its three destroyers are kept in reserve at Bushehr, but are unlikely to be returned to service as all date from the 1940s. The four UK-built frigates are now generally classified as corvettes, and are no longer the Saam-class but Alvand-class, with one modernised with 'Styx' AShM, SM-1 SAM, two triple ASTT and a 76mm gun, as well as a helicopter landing platform, with the other three also due to receive the same treatment, although they have already been fitted with 'Styx' and ASTT, but have a 114mm gun; only two out of the four US-built Bayandor-class (US PF103) corvettes have survived, with both having two 76mm guns and ASTT, but one has C-802 AShM. There are now thirteen Kaman-class fast attack craft, all fitted with 'Styx' AShM, while another four patrol craft have Kosar AShM. There are about seventy-five other small patrol craft. There are three Russian-built Kilo-class submarines, each with six torpedo tubes; twelve Qadir-class submarines and another eight submarines for minelaying and insertion of special forces. There are five MCMV, one of which is based in the Caspian Sea for training. There are four LSTs and three LSMs, as well as six LSL and ten landing craft. There are twenty-six auxiliaries, including three replenishment ships capable of taking a helicopter.

Naval aviation still has three P-3F Orion, ten Sea King and three Sea Stallion helicopters, and a number of light helicopters.

Main bases are at Bushehr, Bandar-e-Abbas, Bandare-e Khomeini, Bandar-e Anzelli, Kharg Island, Chah Bahar and Jask.

IRANIAN REVOLUTIONARY GUARDS CORPS NAVAL FORCES

Formed after the 1979 revolution, largely while the loyalty to the former regime of the established armed forces was assessed, today the Iranian Revolutionary Guards Corps Naval Forces have more than 20,000 personnel, of whom 5,000 are marines, and claim to have as many as 1,500 fast attack boats, although many of these are below 10 tonnes displacement and a more realistic assessment is that the IRGCNF have about forty fast attack craft, many with AShM. There are also four landing ships. Bases are believed to be at Abu Musa, Farsi Island, Larak Island and Sirri Island.

The IRGCNF are essentially a 'wild card', not adverse to provocation. On 21 June 2004, eight British naval personnel training Iraqi naval personnel in the Gulf were seized, and this was followed, on 23 March 2007, with the seizure of fifteen British naval personnel from the frigate *Cornwall* who had been intercepting shipping in the Gulf. In both cases the personnel concerned were eventually released. On 7 January 2008, the USA claimed that five Iranian speedboats harassed US naval vessels, making threatening moves and, on one occasion, threatening a suicide attack, forcing the crews to take up defensive positions and man their guns.

IRAQ

Population: 31.5 million
Land Area: 169,240 square miles (435,120 sq.km.)
GDP: $83.3bn (£54.1bn), per capita $2,679 (£1,739)
Defence Exp: $4.9bn (£3.2bn)
Service Personnel: 245,782 active, plus 413,613 paramilitary

IRAQI COASTAL DEFENCE FORCE

The Iraqi Navy was not formed until 1937, when it was equipped with four small patrol craft, essentially for riverine operations, and remained in this position until 1958, when the monarchy was overthrown. Over the next thirty years, it expanded and eventually reached a personnel strength of 5,000, but did not play any significant role in the war between Iraq and Iran (sometimes referred to as the 'First Gulf War') that started in 1979 and lasted throughout the 1980s.

At this time, the fleet consisted of three submarine chasers, and twelve Soviet-built Osa-class no larger than about 100 tonnes. There were also minesweepers and three landing craft. Many of these ships were destroyed in the war with Iran, but replaced by the West. Attempts to buy Lupo-class frigates and corvettes from Italy came to nothing due to international sanctions after the invasion of neighbouring Kuwait in 1990, and, in the Gulf War that followed, the Iraqi Navy was almost completely destroyed in 1991, with those left being annihilated during the Allied invasion of Iraq in 2003.

Post-war reconstruction led to the creation in 2004 of an Iraqi Coastal Defence Force using instructors provided by the Royal Navy, with an initial 214 personnel. The current title was adopted in 2005. An attempt to buy two Assad-class corvettes built in Italy during the 1980s was abandoned as the ships were found to have deteriorated badly over the intervening period. Instead, four smaller Diciotti-class vessels were selected.

Today, the Iraqi Navy has about 5,000 personnel, of whom more than 1,000 are in the marines. It has four Saettia-class (Italian Diciotti-class) patrol craft and eleven smaller patrol craft. The main base is at Umm Qasr, but it also protects the oil terminals at Basra and Khawr al-Amaya and the port of al-Zubair.

IRELAND

Population: 4.6 million
Land Area: 26,000 square miles (68,894 sq.km.)
GDP: $207bn (£134.4bn), per capita $45,030 (£29,240)
Defence Exp: $1.4bn (£0.91bn)
Service Personnel: 10,460 active, plus 14,875 reserves

NAVAL SERVICE (IRELAND)

Between 1800 and 1922, Ireland was part of the United Kingdom and maritime security was provided by the Royal Navy, which had two major bases in Ireland. Although the Anglo-Irish Treaty of 1921 allowed Ireland to have responsibility over customs and fishing other than in Northern Ireland, which remained in the UK, it left overall control of Irish waters with the UK. A Coastal and Marine Service (CMS) was established in 1923, but disbanded the following year. Meanwhile, civil war raged in what had become the Irish Free State, and a ferry from the British & Irish Steam Packet Company had to be chartered to take government troops to Tralee in Co. Kerry.

The UK had retained the right to use three ports, known as the Treaty Ports – Cork, Bere Haven and Lough Swilly – but these were handed over to the Irish in 1938. The Irish government had two ships at the time, one of which was an old steam yacht that had been used by the CMS, and the other was the *Fort Rannoch*. The following year, two MTBs were ordered from Vosper Thorneycroft and, when the Second World War started in Europe, a Marine and Coastwatching Service was established as it was clear that if Ireland was to demonstrate its neutrality, a naval service would be required. The order for MTBs was increased from two to six, while four other vessels were also operated and personnel strength grew to 300. The MCS spent the war years inspecting merchant shipping and protecting fisheries while also laying protective minefields off Cork and Waterford. In 1942 the MCS was renamed the Marine Service.

Post-war, the Marine Service was disbanded in September 1946 and a Naval Service created as part of the Irish Defence Forces. Three ex-wartime corvettes were bought from the UK and a tradition of naming ships after figures in Celtic mythology began. All ships' names were prefixed with LE

The Irish navy has been considerably modernised in recent years, with one of the more modern corvettes being *Eithne*, seen here alongside in Cork. (Irish Armed Forces)

(*Long Éireannach*), Gaelic for 'Irish Ship'. Irish officer cadets were trained at the Britannia Royal Naval College, Dartmouth, Devonshire. The corvettes remained in service until the late 1960s, when they were replaced by three minesweepers.

The first new ship to be ordered for the Naval Service followed in 1972, LE *Dierdre*, built at the Verlome yard in Cork, and later followed by a sister ship, *Emer*. When Ireland's EEZ was extended from 12 miles to 200 miles in 1976, funding was obtained from the then European Community to build and purchase seven ships. In 1999, the first of a new larger class of ship, the *Roisin*, joined the fleet and has since been joined by a sister ship, while two more vessels of this class will be built between 2012 and 2015. These have a single 76mm gun. The largest ship is the *Eithne*, which has a helicopter platform. The NS also acquired three ex-RN Peacock-class offshore patrol vessels, known in the NS as the Emer-class, which also have a 76mm gun. Personnel now stands at 1,110, and the main base is at Haulbowline, near Cork. Helicopters are operated by the Irish Air Corps, which also has two CN-235 aircraft for unarmed maritime-reconnaissance.

Essentially, the Naval Service remains a brown water navy, albeit often in difficult weather conditions off Ireland's west coast. Nevertheless, courtesy visits have taken ships as far as Argentina and India, while *Niamh* delivered supplies to Irish troops serving with the United Nations in Eritrea.

ISRAEL

Population: 7.3 million
Land Area: 7,993 square miles (20,850 sq.km.)
GDP: $219bn (£142bn), per capita $30,126 (£19,562)
Defence Exp: $15.6bn (£10.1bn)
Service Personnel: 176,500 active, plus 565,000 reserves and 8,050 para-
    military

ISRAELI NAVY

The Israeli Navy traces its origins to the formation of marine sports clubs in
the late 1920s, while a maritime training college was founded in Bosmat
in 1938. The Palmach movement founded the Palyam, a naval branch, in
1943, using the college for training, while a small number of cargo ships
were acquired as the foundation of a merchant service. During the Second
World War, 1,100 volunteers from the Zionist Haganah underground
movement joined the Royal Navy, mainly in technical roles, while a
number also joined the United States Navy.

Post-war, as the British mandate in Palestine drew to a close, the former
members of the Royal Navy worked on captured ships that had been
used to take illegal immigrants to Palestine and restored them to service.
On independence, the Israeli Defence Force was founded and used the
restored ships as the basis of its navy, which used the former Royal Navy
and United States Navy personnel, as well as members of the Palyam, who
often had no real seagoing experience. The first few years of the Israeli
Navy were largely dominated by political infighting and inexperienced
Palyam personnel were often promoted over the heads of the experienced former RN and USN officers. Order and organisation did not come
until the early 1950s, when Israeli naval officers were trained in the UK
and France, with a number also trained at the major British naval base at
Malta. Destroyers, frigates, torpedo boats and submarines were acquired.
In addition to its bases on the Mediterranean coast, in 1951 a base was
established at Eilat for operations in the Red Sea.

The subsequent history of Israel has proven to be one of constant tension
with the country's Arab neighbours, interrupted by a number of serious
conflicts, and while the Arab countries received constant Soviet support
during the period of the Cold War, support for Israel has wavered, even
from its main ally, the USA. The Israeli Navy did not play a prominent part
in the Suez Crisis of 1956, leaving this to the Royal Navy and the French
Marine Nationale, with most of the naval action being by carrier-borne
aircraft while the Royal Navy made the first heli-borne assault.

Israel maintains a navy mainly for coastal defence duties and to prevent arms smuggling to terrorist groups. This is a Eilat-class corvette at Eilat, with a Royal Navy Type 42 destroyer on the other side of the pontoon. (Israeli Defence Force)

The many wars between Israel and the country's Arab neighbours, mainly Egypt and Syria, did not always involve the Israeli Navy. The conflict that did was the Yom Kippur War, 6-25 October 1973, which was also known as the Fourth Arab-Israeli War. The conflict was notable for the first naval engagement between missile boats using SSM at the Battle of Latakia on 7 October between the Israeli Navy and the Syrian Navy. The battle established the IN as having a rightful place amongst the country's armed forces as previous wars had been fought mainly in the air and on the ground. After Latakia and a number of minor skirmishes, the Syrian Navy stayed in its ports and this allowed the Mediterranean sea lanes to Israel to remain open throughout the war, although for a while the Egyptians were able to enforce a blockade of Eilat, at the head of a gulf off the Red Sea. That same day, two Israeli boats patrolling the Gulf of Suez foiled an Egyptian attempt to land commandos. The Israeli Navy also inserted a team of commandos at the Egyptian port of Arkada during the night of 9-10 October, sinking an Egyptian fast attack missile boat. After the war, it was estimated that as many as fifty SSM were fired at Israeli warships, but none struck home and no Israeli ships were lost.

By the late 1970s, the Israeli Navy had 5,000 personnel, of whom 1,000 were conscripts, as well as 3,000 reservists. It was very much a coastal navy, with two corvettes planned, but not actually in service, but it did have three German-built Type 206 submarines. While the fleet included twelve missile-armed fast attack craft of the Saar-class built in France, Israel had already started to build its own small warships and the twelve Reshef-class missile-armed fast attack craft were amongst the first. There were also more than forty patrol craft and a dozen landing ships and landing craft. The main missile in use at the time was also Israeli-built, the Israeli Aircraft Industries' (IAI) Gabriel, with a range of up to 22km (13 miles).

In more recent times, the Palestinians have established their own state in the Gaza Strip and on the West Bank of the river Jordan, and Israel has suffered rocket attacks and terrorist incursions from these areas and from militant Hezbollah camps in the south of Lebanon. Hezbollah rocket attacks from Lebanon in 2006 led to a further war, known variously as the 2006 Lebanon War or the 2006 Israel-Hezbollah War. The conflict lasted for thirty-four days and saw the Israeli Navy maintain a blockade of Lebanese ports, which was not lifted until 6 September, after the fighting between ground forces had stopped. More recently, in 2010, Israeli naval forces stopped and boarded a Turkish-led relief convoy carrying supplies to the Gaza Strip.

The Israeli Navy has in recent years been planning to buy Littoral Combat Ships from the United States, which would bring about a significant improvement in capability, but these plans have now been shelved due to the rising costs of these ships. There are plans to build corvettes in Israeli yards with German assistance, possibly building a stretched version of the MEKO 100 corvette.

Today the Israeli Navy has 9,500 personnel, of whom 2,500 are con-scripts, but on mobilisation its strength rises to 19,500. It has three Eilat-class corvettes, each with Harpoon AShM, VLS Burak SAM, two triple ASTT, a 76mm gun and accommodation for a Panther ASW helicopter or a Dauphin SAR helicopter. There are eight Hetz-class fast guided missile craft, each with Gabriel AShM, VLS Burak SAM and a 76mm gun; two Reshef-class fast attack craft with Gabriel and Harpoon AShM and a 76mm gun; thirteen Super Dvora-class torpedo boats have two single torpedo tubes, fifteen Dabur-class, while another sixteen craft of various classes can be fitted with torpedo tubes or SSM as required. There are three German-built Dolphin-class (variants of the standard Type 212) submarines, each with six torpedo tubes and capable of firing Harpoon AShM.

Naval aviation includes seven Panther ASW helicopters and two Dauphin SAR helicopters, as well as seventeen Bell 212, mainly for commando use, while there are also two C-130 Hercules transports.

The main base is at Haifa, with commandos at Atlit, and other bases at Eilat and Ashdod.

ITALY

Population: 60.1 million
Land Area: 116,280 square miles (301,049 sq.km.)
GDP: $2.06tr (£1.34tr), per capita $34,304 (£22,275)
Defence Exp: $30.5bn (£19.8bn)
Service Personnel: 184,609 active, plus 42,153 reserves

ITALIAN NAVY

The present day Italian Navy traces its origins to its formation in 1946, after the Second World War, but Italian naval history predates the creation of a united Italy in 1861, as many of the constituent states, especially Venice and Genoa, and later Sardinia and Naples, had substantial navies and wielded influence across the Mediterranean. This history is reflected in the arms in the centre of the Italian naval ensign, which incorporates emblems from the republics of Venice, Genoa, Pisa and Amalfi.

Founded as the *Regia Marina* (Royal Navy), on 17 March 1861, the new service inherited an assortment of steam and sail ships from the constituent

The Italian fleet at sea, with a Durand de la Penne-class destroyer and a frigate in the foreground and the aircraft carrier *Garibaldi* in the left background. (Italian Navy)

navies. Inevitably, there was a lack of standardisation of equipment, training, standards and practices, not helped by there being separate officer training schools at both Genoa and Naples, which was not resolved until a new officer training school opened at Livorno in 1881. Naval technology was undergoing rapid change at the same time, which could have helped towards standardisation except that Italy lacked the necessary modern shipyards and had to purchase ships built in foreign yards.

It took just five years before the new navy saw its first engagement in the Battle of Lissa against the Austrian Empire and was fought off the island of Vis in the Adriatic. Despite having the larger fleet, although only one was modern, the Italians were defeated and lost two armoured ships and 640 men. Regardless of this setback, the 1880s and 1890s saw the fleet rebuilt and modernised. In 1911-1912, during the Italo-Turkish War, or Balkan Wars, the Italian Navy was more than able to hold its own.

By the outbreak of the First World War, in which Italy was one of the allies with France and the UK, the fleet included six dreadnought battleships. Inevitably, most of the *Regia Marina* was committed to the Adriatic where it held the Austro-Hungarian Navy, which bombarded towns and cities along Italy's Adriatic coast. While operations in the Adriatic were less severe than in other waters, the *RM* lost two battleships. Nevertheless, its new *Motoscafo Anti Sommergibile* (MAS) anti-submarine torpedo boats sank two Austro-Hungarian battleships, one of them in the harbour at Pula where it succumbed to an early form of human torpedo.

Between the wars, the Italian government decided to rebuild the *RM* to challenge the British Mediterranean Fleet while a naval arms race began with France. Italian designers sacrificed gun calibre for longer range and defensive armour plating for speed. In 1935, during the Italian invasion of Abyssinia, modern Ethiopia, which was landlocked, the *RM* assisted in maintaining supplies through ports in Somalia and Eritrea. The following year, the start of the Spanish Civil War saw warships deployed in support of the *Corpo Truppe Volontarie* (Corps of Volunteer Troops), which reinforced the Spanish Nationalists, while some fifty-six submarines were engaged against the Republican naval forces and merchant ships carrying supplies for Republican forces in Operation Ursula, sinking at least two cargo ships, while two light cruisers shelled Barcelona and Valencia.

In early 1939, Italy invaded Albania, with its troops and their equipment crossing the Adriatic under the protection of the *RM*.

Italy did not enter the Second World War until 10 June 1940. At this time the *RM* was the world's fourth largest navy, and Benito Mussolini, Italy's dictator since 1923, viewed the Mediterranean as *Mare Nostrum*, 'Our Sea'. While the air force and army struck across the border into France, the *RM*'s priority was to secure the sea routes across the Mediterranean to North Africa, mainly present day Libya but then known as Tripolitania and Cyrenaica, and to the colonies in East Africa. The *RM*'s headquarters,

Supermarina, wanted to occupy Malta, but the High Command did not approve, even though the islands were close to the sea and air routes between Italy and North Africa.

On paper, the *RM* was the strongest navy in the Mediterranean with six battleships, of which only the two oldest were fully operational and the four newest were being updated. There were nineteen cruisers, fifty-nine destroyers, sixty-seven torpedo boats and 116 submarines. The Achilles heel was the shortage of oil, while replacing ships lost was also to prove difficult. Strengths were the torpedo boats, which engaged in many valiant actions, and the human torpedoes, which crippled two British battleships at Alexandria. While range-finder and fire control systems were good, none of the Italian ships had radar.

An aircraft carrier, the *Aquila*, was being converted from a liner, and although Germany donated the catapults from the *Graf Zeppelin* once work on this ship stopped, the *Aquila* was never completed. As in Germany, amongst the problems were friction between naval and air commanders over operation of the ship's aircraft.

An early setback was the successful British attack on the main forward base at Taranto on the night of 11-12 November 1940. Three battleships were put out of action, and a cruiser and shore installations damaged. Three heavy cruisers and two destroyers were lost at the Battle of Cape Matapan. Increasingly, British submarines and aircraft based on Malta cut the supply lines between Italy and North Africa, while those to the Red Sea were already closed due to British control of the Suez Canal.

The *RM* contributed thirty-two submarines to the Battle of the Atlantic, using Bordeaux in France as a base and accounting for 109 Allied ships. A planned attack on the port of New York was never carried out. Another collaborative operation with the Germans was the deployment of four MAS anti-submarine motorboats, another five motor torpedo boats and six submarines as well as five explosive motorboats to the Black Sea, which they reached by first crossing overland to the Danube and then under their own power to the Black Sea, using Yalta and Feodisia as bases. When Italy surrendered, these craft were transferred to the Germans, but the surface vessels then passed to the Soviet forces as they advanced westwards, although the submarines were transferred to the Royal Romanian Navy.

Before war broke out, the *RM* already had a flotilla based in the Red Sea, using Massawa in Eritrea as a port. While the land campaign went well at first with the capture of British Somaliland, British and Empire forces launched a successful counter-attack in January 1941. The Red Sea flotilla suffered badly and lost its base at Massawa in April 1941. Before this, two auxiliary cruisers and another ship escaped and although one of the auxiliary cruisers was sunk by the New Zealand cruiser *Leander* off the Maldives, the other two ships reached Kobe in Japan. Four submarines rounded the Cape of Good Hope to reach Bordeaux and some merchant ships reached Madagascar.

In the Far East, the RM had a base at Tientsin in China, a concession port, with a minelayer and a gunboat based there. Auxiliary cruisers used the port during the war and also used Japanese ports. Seven of the larger submarines were converted to carry goods between Italy and Japan, and plans were laid for an additional twelve transport submarines, but only two were completed and these were destroyed by Allied bombing before they could enter service.

After Mussolini was deposed in 1943, an armistice was agreed with the Allies and this required the *RM* to send all of its ships to an Allied port, which for most meant Malta. The ships bound for Malta were attacked and the *Roma* was sunk by glider bombs. The armistice split Italy into two as the Germans moved quickly to take control of the northern part of the country, which they still occupied. Mussolini returned to power with German support after being rescued from imprisonment in a daring commando raid and established a new regime, the *Repubblica Sociale Italiana* (RSI, or Italian Social Republic). This had its own navy, the *Marina Nazionale Repubblicana* (National Republican Navy), as did the government of Italy, which formed the Italian Co-Belligerent Navy (ICBN) to fight alongside the Allies. The ICBN operated nothing larger than light cruisers and destroyers, with its battleships taken to Ismailia in Egypt, partly because little opportunity remained to use them and partly because of doubts over the reliability of their crews. Nevertheless, few *RM* crews volunteered for the *MNR* and it remained only a fraction of the size of the Co-Belligerent Navy. Meanwhile, the port of Tientsin was occupied by the Japanese. In the rest of the Far East, most of the ships' crews surrendered to the Allies, although ships in Japanese ports were scuttled, but the submarines that had carried vital goods between Italy and Japan were seized and handed over to the Germans, and spent the rest of the war operating with mixed Italian and German crews.

In June 1944, the three newer battleships were allowed to return to Sicily for training, although the older ships remained in Egypt. Post-war, one of the newer ships, the *Guilio Cesare*, was transferred to the Soviet Navy.

Post-war, Italy became a republic in June 1946, and the current Italian Navy (*Marina Militaire*) was formed. While Italy had been on the side of the Allies during the final years of the war, the earlier alliance with Germany and Japan was not forgotten in the negotiations for the peace treaty signed in Paris on 10 February 1947. Italy was devastated but the desire to rebuild its armed forces was restricted by the conditions of the treaty, which banned not only nuclear weapons but also any self-propelled weapons or their launchers, and extended to a ban on battleships, aircraft carriers, submarines and vessels for amphibious warfare. Reparations included placing major fleet units at the disposal of the victorious nations, the four wartime allies, plus Greece, Yugoslavia and Albania. The total displacement allowed was limited to 67,500 tons and personnel was capped at 25,000.

Nevertheless, the post-war world was different and the Cold War was already starting. Although one battleship was transferred to the Soviet Navy, the UK and the US decided against any further transfers to the USSR, but two cruisers did pass to France and one to Greece. Italy was also strategically important, occupying a central position in the Mediterranean. The country was admitted to NATO in 1949, the 1947 treaty restrictions were revoked in 1951, and the US included the country in its Mutual Defence Assistance Programme (MDAP), qualifying it for supplies of US-built equipment. The only outstanding restriction was the ban on aircraft carriers, which was withdrawn in 1989.

Within NATO, the *Marina Militaire* was assigned control of the Adriatic Sea and the Strait of Otranto as well as defence of the sea lanes in the Tyrrhenian Sea. While the Italian shipbuilding industry recovered from its wartime damage and the economy improved to be able to afford the necessary defence budget, equipment was supplied from the USN. Amongst the ships were Fletcher-class destroyers and Guppy-class submarines.

The *Fenice*, a Minerva-class corvette, sometimes referred to as a light frigate, powers away from the camera. Note the heavy armament, typical of Italian warships. (Italian Navy)

Italy also began to build ships to its own designs, including a number of notable designs that did well in export markets, such as the Lupo-class guided missile frigates, while the *MM* was noted for its helicopter cruisers, starting with the guided missile cruiser *Andrea Doria*, commissioned in 1963 and able to handle four ASW helicopters, joined by a sister ship the following year, and then by the *Vittorio Veneto*, another guided missile cruiser with accommodation for up to nine ASW helicopters.

The first Italian aircraft carrier to become operational, the *Garibaldi*, entered service in 1989, operating AV-8A Harriers and Sea King helicopters, capable of carrying up to eighteen AV-8B Harrier II or 17 SH-3D Sea King.

Today, the *MM* has 34,000 personnel, including the *San Marco Regiment*, which acts as a marine formation. There are now two aircraft carriers, with the *Garibaldi* having been joined by the larger *Cavour*, allowing the older and smaller ship to be converted to become a landing ship assault (LHA) in 2014. The *Cavour* can carry up to twenty Harrier II or twelve Merlin helicopters. Both ships have SAM, with the *Cavour* having VLS. There are two Andrea Doria-class and two Luigi Durand de Penne-class (ex-Animoso-

The Italian aircraft carrier *Garibaldi* as seen from the air with AV-8B Harrier II aircraft on her flight deck and escorted by a destroyer and a frigate, with a replenishment ship following. (Italian Navy)

class) destroyers. The former have three 76mm guns, Otomat AShM and Aster VLS SAM, two twin torpedo tubes, and can carry a Merlin helicopter, while the latter has a 127mm gun, Otomat AShM, Aspide SAM, two triple torpedo tubes and can carry an AB-212 helicopter. There are four Artigliere frigates, each with a 127mm gun, Otomat AShM and Aspide SAM, and able to carry an AB-212 helicopter, as well as eight Maestrale frigates, each with one 127mm gun, Otomat AShM and Aspide SAM, and able to carry two AB-212 helicopters. There are six Commandante Cigala Fuligiosa-class corvettes with a 76mm gun and an AB-212 or NH-90 helicopter. Offshore patrol craft include four Cassiopa-class with accommodation for an AB-212 or NH-90 helicopter, as well as four Esploratore patrol boats. Conventional submarines include four Pelosi-class (improve Sauro-class), each with a single torpedo tube, and two Salvatore Todaro-class, each with a single torpedo tube. There are three amphibious ships, of which two are San Giorgio-class with a 76mm gun and accommodation for up to six helicopters, including a single Chinook, as well as thirty to thirty-six armoured vehicles and 350 troops. The *San Giusto* has a similar armament and capacity to these ships. There are eight Gaeta-class and four Lerici-class MCMV. There are twenty-six landing craft. Ninety auxiliaries and support ships include oilers, survey vessels and tugs as well as training craft.

The MM is divided into six subordinate operational commands, with the COMFORAL frontline forces based at Taranto along with COMFORSUB, submarine forces; the COMFORPAT patrol forces based at Augusta;

Italian corvettes underway at sea. (Italian Navy)

The Italian patrol boat *Comandante Foscari* at sea – note the helicopter and hangar on such a small ship. (Italian Navy)

COMFORDRAG MCM forces are based at La Spezia; COMDFORSBARC amphibious forces are based at Brindisi, and the naval aviation force, COMFORAER, is based at Rome.

JAMAICA

Population: 2.7 million
Land Area: 4,411 square miles (11,424 sq.km.)
GDP: $13.7bn (£8.8bn), per capita $5,000 (£3,225)
Defence Exp: $91m (£58.7m)
Service Personnel: 2,830 active, plus 953 reserves

JAMAICAN COAST GUARD

Jamaica became independent and formed its own Jamaican Defence Force with the disbandment of the West Indies Federation in 1962. Within this service, which traces its origins to the formation of the West Indies Regiment, the small Coast Guard was established, although by the late 1970s it had just 133 personnel and six small patrol boats.

Today, the Jamaican Coast Guard has 190 personnel and eleven patrol craft of up to 31 metres, and a main base at Port Royal. It is supported by the JDF's Air Wing, which includes light aircraft for maritime surveillance, largely to counter smuggling.

JAPAN

Population: 127 million
Land Area: 142,727 square miles (370,370 sq.km.)
GDP: $5.39tr (£3.5tr), per capita $42,422 (£27,546)
Defence Exp: $52.8bn (£34.3bn)
Service Personnel: 247,746 active, plus 56,379 reserves and 12,636 para-
  military

JAPAN MARITIME SELF-DEFENSE FORCE

When Japan was again permitted to have armed forces in 1954 because of the pressures on the Allied military caused by the Korean War, it was considered prudent to describe the services as 'self-defense forces', and these were established with US help for air, ground and sea. They were preceded by the National Police Reserve, founded in 1950.

Although Japan has a long history of naval warfare, the country underwent two centuries of isolationism during the Edo period and it was not until United States intervention forced the country to trade internationally in 1854 that this ended. By that time, the country's maritime power had atrophied. Under the Meiji Restoration, the country underwent rapid industrialisation and modernisation. As part of this, an Imperial Japanese Navy was formed in 1869. Before this, the Shogunate acquired its first steam warship with assistance from the Netherlands in 1855, while in 1857, a naval school was founded at Nagasaki, although transferred to Tsukiji near Tokyo in 1859. Naval students were sent abroad to study. Meanwhile, a modern shipbuilding industry was established and in 1863 this supplied the first Japanese-built steamship, the *Chiyoda*. This ship, a wooden-hulled gunboat, had an eventful early history as having been built for the Shogun, and seized by the government in 1868, she was taken by rebels later that year, recaptured and withdrawn from service in 1869, before being later sold to a whaling company.

The country continued to receive foreign advice. French assistance saw the creation of two modern naval arsenals at Nagasaki and Yokosuka during 1867-1868, while the British sent a naval mission to assist in the development of the navy and of the naval school at Tsukiji. The Shogunate ended in 1867, although conflict between pro and anti-Imperial forces continued until 1869 with the naval Battle of Hakodate. Meanwhile, the country's first naval review had already been held in Osaka Bay the previous year with six ships from the private navies of six major port cities, although the total tonnage of these ships at 2,252 tons was less than that of the sole visiting foreign vessel, which was from France.

With the formation of the Imperial Japanese Navy, the private navies were abolished, providing a total of eleven ships to add to the seven ships that had belonged to the Shogunate. In 1870, the government prepared a plan calling for an Imperial Japanese Navy of 200 ships that would be organised in ten fleets, but this had to be abandoned the following year due to the shortage of resources. For the next two decades, the IJN developed as a brown water navy, essentially a coastal defence force. Nevertheless, new ships continued to be commissioned, British advisers assisted with such matters as gunnery training, while an Imperial decree ordered that the model for the future was to be the UK's Royal Navy rather than that of the Netherlands or France.

Foreign interventions by Japan followed, initially concentrating on the Korean peninsula and starting in 1875. This led to Korea in turn opening up to foreign trade. Further development was stifled by unrest in Japan itself, with the Saga Rebellion of 1874, followed by the Satsuma Rebellion of 1877, so that the military priority became a substantial army and coastal defences.

It was not until 1883 that larger warships began to be ordered, initially from British yards. An arms race developed with China at this time, with the Chinese buying even larger warships from German yards. In 1885, French influence began to be felt, with the emphasis on what became known as the *Jeune Ecole* (Young School), of naval warfare, which emphasised small, fast warships, such as cruisers (at the time, cruisers had the tonnage of a Second World War destroyer and about the same as many modern frigates) and torpedo boats rather than larger units such as battleships. One reason for this move towards France rather than the UK at the time was because the British were suspected of being close to the Chinese. Nevertheless, by 1887, British-built warships were once again being ordered.

War with China eventually started, although the Sino-Japanese War, 1894-1895 was relatively short as the two countries fought to dominate Korea. At the Battle of the Yalu River, 17 September 1894, the Chinese were defeated, losing eight of their twelve warships. The big lesson, however, was that larger and more powerful warships were needed as the two large German-built battleships of the Chinese Navy proved, although one was finally sunk by torpedoes and the other captured, albeit little damaged. The Treaty of Shimonoseki, April 1895, saw Taiwan and the Pescadores Islands transferred to Japan until the end of the Second World War.

Japan joined the Western powers in 1900, helping to suppress the Boxer Rebellion, and the IJN provided more warships than any other nation, with eighteen out of a total fifty. The real value of this was that the Japanese became familiar with Western military and naval doctrine.

Meanwhile, Russian support for China had created new tensions in the area, with Japan forced to return territory to China. This led to the Russo-Japanese War, 1904-1905, and after an early victory against the Russian fleet in the Pacific, the Russians sent their Baltic Fleet to Japan, culminating in the Battle of Tsushima, 1905, when out of thirty-eight Russian ships, twenty-one were sunk, seven captured and six disarmed. Almost 11,000 Russian naval personnel were killed or taken prisoner, while the Japanese lost three torpedo boats and 116 men.

After the war, expansion continued, with Japan having received its first submarines in 1904 in kit form for assembly and completion in Japan. The policy implemented considered the most likely future conflict to be with the United States and called for the IJN to be 70 per cent of the size of the USN. As early as 1907, the intention was to create what became known as the Eight-Eight Fleet of eight modern battleships and eight modern battlecruisers. This never became a reality due to financial difficulties.

During the First World War, Japan fought on the side of the Allies, taking the German port of Tsingtao in the naval action of that name, but otherwise saw little action, although a force of destroyers was sent to reinforce the British Mediterranean Fleet, but these were instead of the four modern battleships requested to reinforce the Grand Fleet. The IJN also had a seaplane carrier, the *Wakamiya*, by this time and her aircraft flew reconnaissance missions before the Battle of Tsingtao.

In 1920, the IJN was the world's third largest navy. Once again, British assistance was provided to establish naval aviation, but after its departure, Japan ceased to seek assistance from abroad. Nevertheless, many contemporary British naval aircraft designs were built under licence in Japan. The Washington Naval Treaty of 1922 placed limits on the total warship tonnages of the world's leading navies, as well as on each type of warship, leaving Japan limited to a total of 315,000 tons, ahead of France and Italy with 175,000 tons each, but behind the UK and USA at 525,000 tons each.

Differences between Japan and the other Western powers were high-lighted during the Allied intervention in the Russian Civil War, which followed the Bolshevik Revolution and the end of the First World War. Japan intended to demonstrate that she was the leading power in the Pacific, but also intended to extend her grip on Korea into China and needed supplies of food, fuel and raw materials, such as rubber, which came from the British and Dutch colonies to the west. The start of the Second Sino-Japanese War in 1937 increased tensions, although the balance of power, especially at sea, was heavily in Japan's favour.

While Japanese admirals were as strongly in favour of the battleship as their American and British counterparts, Japan also started to create a substantial aircraft carrier force. Japan built the world's largest battle-ships, the Yamato-class, with 18-inch guns, the heaviest main armament of any warship. There were also technological advances, and the Japanese produced some of the world's best torpedoes. Secretly, Japan began to build ships that enabled her to exceed the Washington Naval Treaty limitations.

By 1939, the Imperial Japanese Navy had ten battleships with four under construction; six aircraft carriers and two aircraft tenders; thirty-seven cruisers; five coast defence ships, with guns up to 8-inch calibre; 114 destroyers; thirteen torpedo boats; six submarine chasers; ten minelayers; twelve minesweepers; forty-two ocean-going submarines and thirty smaller submarines; four submarine depot ships and nine river gunboats. This fleet was set to grow further in the two years that remained before the outbreak of war in the Pacific.

After a period of rising tension, Japan attacked the United States Pacific Fleet in its main base at Pearl Harbor on Hawaii on 7 December 1941, without first making a declaration of war. The attack was intended to give Japan enough time to advance across the Pacific and also westward to the Netherlands East Indies, Malaya, Siam and Burma, and possibly India. Senior naval officers realised that Japan could not face the entire United States Navy so it was important to defeat the Pacific Fleet first, although

In the Pacific Ocean off Hawaii, a joint exercise between the USN and the JMSDF, with, from left, the Military Sealift Command cargo and ammunition ship USNS *Washington Chambers*, the guided missile frigate USS *Crommelin* and the JMSDF destroyer *Kurama*. (USN)

the more thoughtful of the high command also realised that Japan could not hope to match America's industrial capacity or manpower.

The attack on Pearl Harbor was limited in its success as the Japanese Naval Air Force failed to put the base out of action, partly because plans to follow up the first two waves of aircraft with a third and even a fourth wave were abandoned. The Pacific Fleet's aircraft carriers were not in port and so remained at large and unscathed. While the IJN ranged as far west as Ceylon, sinking the small British carrier HMS *Hermes*, and as far south as Darwin in Australia, within six months it had suffered a setback in the inconclusive Battle of the Coral Sea, 3-5 May 1942, and a disastrous defeat at the Battle of Midway, 3-7 June 1942, when it lost four aircraft carriers in one day. Miniature submarines were used for attacks on the British at Diego Garcia and at Sydney, but these had no impact on the outcome of the war. A series of actions followed while the Americans were 'island hopping' towards Japan, but in each case the IJN attacked too late to affect the outcome and did not concentrate on sinking the troop transports before they had landed their men. The lack of an effective convoy system also meant that the long supply lines carrying fuel and rubber as well as food from Japan's new empire, or 'Greater Asian Prosperity Sphere', were vulnerable to increasingly daring USN submarine attack.

As Japanese forces fell back towards the Japanese Home Islands, an attempt to save the Philippines and bring the under-used surface fleet into the war resulted in the biggest naval battle in history at Leyte Gulf, 23-26 October 1944. This was yet another defeat despite the first significant use of *Kamikaze* suicide bombers, largely because of the poor training and inexperience of the pilots. By this time, while the US and Royal Navies were gaining in experience and had improved techniques and equipment, the reverse was true of the Japanese, who had lost their most experienced pilots and commanders. During the final months of the war, the IJN could not even protect the Japanese Inland Sea.

Despite elaborate plans for a last-ditch defence of the homeland, the use of two atomic bombs on first Hiroshima and then Nagasaki on 6 and 9 August 1945 eventually forced Japan to surrender. The IJN had few major ships left by this time. It was not formally disbanded until 1947.

The new constitution for the country claimed that the country denounced war, but left open the prospect of self-defence. The first step was the formation of the National Police Reserve in 1950, to help maintain internal order. This was followed by the creation of the Coastal Safety Force within the Maritime Safety Agency in 1952, which was given the surviving vessels from the old IJN's minesweeping fleet, while the US also donated surplus ships. In 1954, the Self-Defense Forces Law was passed, and the Coastal Safety Force was separated from the larger ships and became the foundation of today's paramilitary but non-combatant Japanese Coast Guard.

First ships of the new Japanese Maritime Self-Defense Force (JMSDF) were ex-USN destroyers, but these were joined in 1956 by the first post-war Japanese-built destroyer. Manpower inevitably included many former members of the IJN. Due to the Cold War and the threat of the Soviet Union's vast fleet of submarines, the initial tasks entrusted to the JMSDF included anti-submarine warfare and mine countermeasures.

By the late 1970s, the JMSDF had 41,000 personnel, of whom some 6,000 were involved in naval aviation, while there were 600 reservists. The service had its first guided missile destroyers, the Tachikaze-class, with two in service and two more being built, as well as another thirty-two destroyers, of which the four Haruna-class ships could accommodate three ASW helicopters as well as being fitted with ASROC launchers. By this time, the ex-USN ships had been withdrawn. There were fifteen frigates, with the eleven Chikugo-class ships having ASROC but no helicopters, while these were augmented by twelve corvettes and five fast torpedo boats. The sixteen-strong submarine force included eight boats of the Uzushio and Improved Uzushio-class, with six torpedo tubes, five of the smaller Ooshio-class, also with six torpedo tubes, and the three Hayashio and Natsushio-class boats with three torpedo tubes. There were also ten coastal patrol craft, six landing ships, about forty minesweepers and three depot ships, and twenty-seven auxiliaries, including two training ships and an icebreaker.

Naval aviation included eleven maritime-reconnaissance squadrons with P-2 Neptune and S-2F Tracker aircraft, all shore-based, and the Japanese-

The Japanese helicopter destroyer *Kurama*. (JMSDF)

125

designed PS-1, and seven helicopter squadrons with licence-built KV-107 (CH-46 Sea Knight) and 61 HSS-2 (S-61).

As with most of the world's major navies, the end of the Cold War meant significant changes. In 1991, after considerable pressure from her allies, the JMSDF sent MCMV vessels to the Gulf to clear mines sown by the Iraqi forces during the war to liberate Kuwait. A mission to Cambodia in 1993 saw Japanese ground forces supported by a JMSDF auxiliary. Nevertheless, Japan also came to face its own regional 'Cold War' with North Korea testing ballistic missiles over northern Japan in 1993 and 1998. A North Korean spy ship was sunk in 2001 by the JMSDF. One of the measures forced upon the service by these actions has been the deployment of a ship-based anti-ballistic missile system, first test-fired in late 2007.

Today the JMSDF has 45,518 personnel, of whom 9,800 are involved in naval aviation, while reserve personnel number 1,100. There are two small aircraft carriers of the Hyuga-class with Sea Sparrow-SAM, ASROC, two triple ASTT and two 20mm CIWS guns, and with space for three SH-60 Sea Hawk helicopters, although an extra seven can be carried on deck. There are two Atago-class guided missile cruisers using the Aegis command and control or 'command and decision' system, which co-ordinates sensors and firepower, with SS-1B AShM, Mk.41 VLS SM-2R SAM/ASROC, two triple ASTT, a 127mm gun and accommodation for a single SH-60 Seahawk ASW helicopter. Guided missile destroyers include six Asagiri-class, each with Harpoon AShM, Sea Sparrow SAM, two triple ASTT, ASROC, one 76mm gun and accommodation for a single SH-60 Seahawk ASW helicopter; nine Murasame-class, each with Harpoon AShM, Sea Sparrow SAM, two triple ASTT, ASROC, two 76mm guns and accommodation for a single SH-60 Seahawk ASW helicopter, plus five Takanami-class (or improved Murasame-class), each with SSM-1B AShM, SM-1 MR SAM, two triple ASTT, two 127mm guns and accommodation for a single SH-60 Seahawk ASW helicopter. Other destroyers include two Hatakaze-class, each with Harpoon AShM, Sea Sparrow SAM, two triple ASTT, ASROC, one 76mm gun and helicopter landing platform; four Kongou-class, each with Harpoon AShM, SM-2MR SAM, two triple ASTT, ASROC, and a 127mm gun; one Tachikaze-class, with Harpoon AShM, SM-1 MR SAM, two triple ASTT, ASROC, and a 127mm gun; one Haruna-class with Sea Sparrow SAM, two triple ASTT, ASROC, two 127mm guns and accommodation for three SH-60 Seahawk helicopters; two Shinane-class with Sea Sparrow SAM, two triple ASTT, ASROC, two 127mm guns and accommodation for three SH-60 Seahawk helicopters. Frigates include six Abukuma-class, each with Harpoon AShM, two triple ASTT, ASROC, and a 76mm gun; ten Hatsuyuki-class, each with Harpoon AShM, Sea Sparrow SAM, two triple ASTT, ASROC, and a 76mm gun as well as accommodation for a single SH-60 ASW helicopter. There are also six guided missile patrol boats of the Hayabusa-class, each with SSM-1B AShM and a 76mm gun. There are

The Japanese Oyashio-class submarine *Mochishio*, one of eleven boats of this class, each with six torpedo tubes and capable of launching Harpoon AShM. (JMSDF)

thirty-seven MCMV. Submarines are all conventional and include five Harushio-class, of which two are used for training, with six single torpedo tubes and able to use Harpoon AShM; eleven Oyashio-class with six single torpedo tubes and able to use Harpoon AShM; and the first two of a number of Soryu-class with air independent propulsion and with six single torpedo tubes and able to use Harpoon AShM. There are five landing ships and twenty landing craft. A formidable logistics and support force consists of seventy-seven ships, including replenishment vessels and a force of six training ships.

Naval aviation now includes six squadrons with the P-3C Orion; seven shipboard squadrons with SH-60 ASW helicopters; an EW squadron also with P-3 Orions; an MCM squadron with MH-53E Sea Dragon helicopters; SAR is provided by a squadron of US-1A flying boats and two with UH-60J Black Hawk helicopters; transport includes AW-101 Merlin helicopters, Beech King Air and YS-11M transports; while training uses OH-6D/DA helicopters and T-5, King Air and YS-11T trainers.

Bases are at Kure, Sasebo, Yokosuka, Maizuru and Ominato.

The Coast Guard is non-combatant, although paramilitary, and has 12,636 personnel, with about 350-360 patrol craft of different sizes, as well as Falcon 900 and Beech 200T aircraft and Bell 412 helicopters and a number of light helicopters.

JORDAN

Population: 6.5 million
Land Area: 36,715 square miles (101,140 sq.km.)
GDP: $27.5bn (£17.9bn), per capita $4,249 (£2,759)
Defence Exp: $2.53bn (£1.64bn)
Service Personnel: 100,500 active plus 65,000 reserves and 10,000 para-
military

JORDANIAN ROYAL NAVAL FORCE

Almost completely landlocked except for its southern extremity at the end
of the Gulf of Aqaba, Jordan was part of the Ottoman Empire and became
independent in 1923 as Transjordan, a British League of Nations mandated
territory. The mandate was terminated in 1946.

The Royal Jordanian Naval Force originated in 1951 as the Royal Coast
Guard, initially with its headquarters at Aqaba but this moved to the Dead
Sea coast from 1952 until 1967, the year in which the country suffered a
complete military defeat in an Arab-Israeli War. It acquired its current title
in 1991.

Because of the short length of coastline, just 16 miles (26 kilometres),
throughout its history it has been a coastal patrol force. Today it has about
500 personnel and has seven patrol boats, of which three are British-built
Al Hussein-class and four US-built Abdullah-class (USCG Dauntless). The
sole base and headquarters is at Aqaba.

KAZAKHSTAN

Population: 15.8 million
Land Area: 1,048,070 square miles (2,778,544 sq.km.)
GDP: $127bn (£82.5bn), per capita $8,081 (£5,247)
Defence Exp: $1.12bn (£727m)
Service Personnel: 49,000 active, plus 31,500 paramilitary.

KAZAKH NAVY

Landlocked Kazakhstan needs warships to patrol the Caspian and Aral
Seas. Formerly a part of the Soviet Union, the country became independent
in 1991 and its armed forces were created by taking over what had been
Soviet equipment and bases. Strictly speaking, the Kazakh Navy is the

'Naval Component of the Armed Forces of Kazakhstan', and it is by far the smallest of the three armed forces.

Today, the KN has 3,000 personnel operating seventeen patrol craft, all of which are ex-Soviet Navy.

KENYA

Population: 40.8 million
Land Area: 224,960 square miles (582,646 sq.km.)
GDP: $31.9bn (£20.7bn), per capita $782 (£507)
Defence Exp: $720m (£467m)
Service Personnel: 24,120 active, plus 5,000 paramilitary

KENYA NAVY

Kenya gained independence from the United Kingdom in 1963, and the following year the Kenya Navy was established, replacing the former Royal East African Navy that had been disbanded in 1962. Army officers were placed in command and to this day the Kenya Navy remains one of the few that uses army ranks rather than traditional navy ranks.

Kenya maintains a small coastal navy with patrol craft, such as the Nyayo-class, shown here. (Kenyan Ministry of Defence)

The new service received assistance from the Royal Navy at first. By the late 1970s, it had 400 personnel and the bulk of its fleet were seven British-built large patrol craft.

Today, the KN has 1,620 personnel, of whom 120 are marines. It has two Nyayo-class large patrol craft, both with Otomat AShM and a 76mm gun; two Shujaa-class patrol craft, both with a 76mm gun and a smaller patrol craft. There are two landing craft. The base is at Mombasa.

KOREA, DEMOCRATIC PEOPLE'S REPUBLIC OF (NORTH)

Population: 24 million
Land Area: 46,814 square miles (121,248 sq.km.)
GDP: Not known
Defence Exp: estimated at $4.38bn (£2.84m)
Service Personnel: 1,190,000 active, plus 600,000 reserves, and 189,000 para-
    military with 5,700,000 reserves

KOREAN PEOPLE'S ARMY NAVAL FORCE

Although Korea has a long maritime history, the country was occupied by Japan from early in the twentieth century until the end of the Second World War, when the north was occupied by Soviet troops and the south by US troops. More usually referred to as the Korean People's Navy, KPN, it was formed in June 1946 as the Marine Patrols with Soviet assistance and its early equipment also included abandoned Japanese warships in Korean ports. Initially based in Wonsan, it was moved to Pyongyang, the capital, shortly afterwards, but Wonsan remained the location of the officers' training school.

On 25 June 1950, North Korean troops invaded South Korea. At the time, the KPN had five submarine chasers, three minesweepers and a number of small patrol boats. Most of the invading forces simply crossed the border between the two countries, and when an armed steamer tried to land 600 troops near Pusan, it was sighted and sunk by a South Korean patrol boat. As this was happening, a North Korean convoy of two submarine chasers, a minesweeper and twenty schooners started to land four battalions of troops near Kangnung and another convoy landed a small force of guerrilla fighters near Samcheok. A short battle ensued at Samcheok between a South Korean minesweeper and a similar North Korean vessel, with the South Korean ship forced to withdraw, although not before it sank two North Korean schooners.

While most of the fighting was on the land, British, American and Australian aircraft carriers provided air cover in the early days of the war because of the shortage of secure land bases. There was one naval engagement, however, at Chumunjin on 2 July 1950. The cruisers USS *Juneau* and HMS *Jamaica*, accompanied by the frigate HMS *Black Swan*, sighted a North Korean convoy of ten trawlers carrying ammunition, escorted by four torpedo boats and two motor gunboats. The cruisers moved to intercept and the torpedo boats turned to attack, but within minutes one torpedo boat was sunk, one was dead in the water, another was heading for the coast to be beached and the last one was escaping seaward. This was the only naval engagement of the war and afterwards the cruisers moved to bombard the fortifications at Kangnung.

The Korean War ended in 1953, but what followed on the border amounted to an armed stand-off between the two countries, a dangerous potential flashpoint during the Cold War but set to last even longer, with both sides providing support for the armed forces of the former belligerents. While South Korea industrialised and the country became prosperous, the only development in the North was for the country to become the most militarised state in the world, down to substantial village paramilitary militias.

Given the country's geographical position, the KPN developed both an Eastern and a Western Fleet, with no exchange of ships or joint exercises. Some maintain that this is because the ships have very limited range, but it could also be because the long South Korean coastline could have made such a passage from one side of North Korea to another hazardous or that personnel might have taken the chance to seek asylum. By the late 1970s, the KPN had 27,000 personnel and three locally-built Najin-class frigates and fifteen mainly ex-Chinese submarines of the 'Romeo' and 'Whiskey'-classes, but most of the fleet could be described as a brown water navy intended for coastal operations with about 300 small patrol craft and about 100 landing craft. Surprisingly for the time, few were missile-armed, with a greater emphasis on gun armament, including 100mm and 76mm guns.

There were no naval engagements between 1950 and 1996, but in recent years there have been a number of clashes between the North and South Korean navies, with at least six engagements reported between 1998 and 2010. Attempts by South Korea to improve relations and provide food aid for the North and allowing families divided by the border to be reunited have not eased the situation. None of these could be described as a full-scale naval battle, but they are symptomatic of continued rivalry and tension.

Today, the KPN has grown to about 60,000 personnel. The three Nanjin-class frigates remain with a planned fourth ship never actually completed.

These ships have P-15 Termit (SS-N-2) AShM, RBU-1200 rocket launchers and two 100mm guns. There is a single Soho-class frigate, with a similar armament except for just one 100mm gun and a helicopter landing platform. The armament of the patrol craft has improved, with the eighteen vessels of the Osa II and Soju-classes, having P-15 Termit (SS-N-2) AShM, as do the sixteen vessels of the fast Huangfen, Komar and Sohung-classes, while the eighteen Hainan and Taechong-class boats and six small Chong-Ju-class boats have RBU 1200 rockets. There are another 320 or so small craft that are armed, usually with machine guns or cannon, but five have 85mm guns. Mine warfare accounts for another twenty-five vessels. There are no fewer than seventy conventional submarines, with twenty-two Chinese-built Romeo-class, each having eight torpedo tubes, but the remaining forty-eight boats of the Sang-O and Yugo/Yeono-classes have just two torpedo tubes each. There are ten landing ships and 257 landing craft, but the logistics and support fleet is small at just twenty-three ships, mainly converted cargo ships or former fishing vessels. There are few aircraft and no marines, but a substantial coastal artillery and AShM force.

As mentioned above, the KPN is organised into two fleets. The East Coast Fleet has its HQ at Toejo Dong and has eight operational commands with important bases at Majin and Wonsan. The West Coast Fleet has five operational commands and has its HQ at Nampo, with major bases at Pipagot and Sagon Ni.

KOREA, REPUBLIC OF (SOUTH)

Population: 48.5 million
Land Area: 38,452 square miles (99,591 sq.km.)
GDP: $992bn (£644bn), per capita $20,457 (£13,283)
Defence Exp: $25.4bn (£16.5bn)
Service Personnel: 655,000 active, plus 4,500,000 reserves and 4,500 para-
  military with 3,000,000 reserves

REPUBLIC OF KOREA NAVY

Although Korea has a long maritime history, dating back to the four-teenth century, the country was occupied by Japan from early in the twentieth century until the end of the Second World War, when the north was occupied by Soviet troops and the south by US troops. After liberation, a Marine Defences Group was formed in November 1945, and this soon transformed into the Korean Coast Guard. After the Republic of Korea was formed in August 1948, the Korean Coast Guard was formally named the Republic of Korea Navy, more often referred to as the ROK Navy or the ROKN. In April 1949, the Republic of Korea Marine Corps, ROKMC, was formed, initially as an autonomous force. The first warship of any significance was a submarine chaser purchased from the United States Navy.

On 25 June 1950, North Korean troops invaded South Korea. At the time, the ROKN had just 6,956 personnel and thirty-three naval vessels, mainly small. When an armed steamer tried to land 600 troops near Pusan, it was sighted and sunk by a South Korean patrol boat, but as this was happening, a North Korean convoy of two submarine chasers, a mine-sweeper and twenty schooners started to land four battalions of troops near Kangnung and another convoy landed a small force of guerrilla fighters near Samcheok. A short battle ensued at Samcheok between a South Korean minesweeper and a similar North Korean vessel, with the South Korean ship forced to withdraw, although not before it sank two North Korean schooners.

United Nations forces included warships provided mainly by the United States, United Kingdom and Australia, while another seven countries also made a contribution, allowing South Korea to have control of the seas around its coasts throughout the conflict, which ended in 1953.

The uneasy peace that followed saw a determined effort to create a more substantial ROKN, with many warships transferred from the USN. During the 1960s, ten destroyers were transferred. During the Vietnam War, the ROKN was able to assist its ally by sending five landing ships while the ROKMC sent a brigade of combat troops. In the meantime, on 19 January 1967, one of the ROKN's submarine chasers was sunk by North Korean coastal artillery north of the border on the east coast. In June 1970, a ROKN-manned radio broadcasting ship was captured by a North Korean patrol craft while in the Yellow Sea.

In 1973, the ROKMC became part of the ROKN. By the late 1970s, the ROKN had 32,000 personnel with another 25,000 reservists. The fleet included four ex-USN Gearing-class destroyers, modernised and fitted with a helicopter landing platform and hangar; two Allen M Sumner-class destroyers, also modernised, and three Fletcher-class destroyers, also ex-USN. There was a single ex-USN frigate and three Auk-class corvettes, converted from USN minesweepers, as well as a number of US-built fast attack craft armed with SAM missiles. A large force of about 300 mine-sweepers was also available and more than thirty small patrol craft. There were no submarines, but S-2 Tracker ASW aircraft were also acquired.

During the 1970s, an eight-year national defence plan was initiated to create an independent defence capability and, in the case of the ROKN, this meant introducing ships built in South Korean shipyards. The first locally-built ship was a small frigate, the *Ulsan*, 2,000 tons, launched in 1980, and followed in 1982 by a corvette.

The ROKN had developed into a brown water navy with a strong coastal defence force, but during the 1990s, the decision was taken to create a true blue water navy. In 1992, the ROKN obtained its first submarine from a German shipbuilder and in 1996, the first Korean-built destroyer was launched and the ROKN started to replace the elderly ex-USN destroyers in its fleet. In 1996, P-3C Orion maritime-reconnaissance aircraft were obtained to replace the elderly Trackers.

The period from 1998 onwards saw a number of incidents at sea with the North Korean Navy. Nevertheless, the ROKN continued its progress towards becoming a blue water navy and, in 2005, the first of a class of amphibious landing ships was launched, while Korean shipyards also started to supply submarines.

Today, the ROKN has 68,000 personnel, including 27,000 marines. It has three Sejong-class cruisers, each with the Aegis command and control or 'command and decision' system that co-ordinates sensors and fire-power, Harpoon AShM, VLS SM-2MR SAM, RIM-116 missiles, two triple ASTT, ASROC and a 127mm gun, as well as accommodation for two Lynx ASW helicopters. There are six Chungmuong Yi Sun-Jhin-class destroyers, each with Harpoon AShM, VLS SM-2MR SAM, two triple ASTT, a 127mm gun and accommodation for a Lynx helicopter. Frigates include three Gwanggaeto Daewang, each with Harpoon AShM, VLS Sea Sparrow SAM, two triple ASTT, a 127mm gun and accommodation for a Lynx helicopter; and nine Ulsan-class, each with Harpoon AShM, two triple ASTT and two 76mm guns. There are thirty-one corvettes of the Gumdoksuri, Po Hang and Dong Hae-classes, with the Gumdoksuri and some of the Po Hang vessels having Harpoon AShM, and all having two triple ASTT and one or two 76mm guns. There are more than eighty Sea Dolphin-class patrol craft and ten MCMV. There are twenty-three conventional submarines, with the nine Chang Bogo-class and three Son Won-ill-classes having eight torpedo tubes each, while the eleven Cosmos and Dolgorae-classes have just two torpedo tubes each. Amphibious forces include an LPD, the *Dokdo*, capable of carrying ten tanks, 700 troops and ten UH-60 helicopters; five landing ships and forty-one landing craft. The logistics and support fleet includes three replenishment vessels capable of accommodating a helicopter, while seventeen of the smaller vessels are Merchant Navy-manned and funded by the Ministry of Transport.

Naval aviation includes eight shore-based P-3C Orion for maritime-reconnaissance, twenty-four Lynx Mk99/99A and five Alouette III.

The main bases are at Pusan, with the Fleet HQ at Jinhae, which is also HQ for the 3rd Fleet; Donghae, HQ for the 1st Fleet; Pyongtaek, HQ for the 2nd Fleet; Mukho, Cheju and Mokpo.

KUWAIT

Population: 3.1 million
Land Area: 9,375 square miles (24,235 sq.km.)
GDP: $117bn (£76bn), per capita $38,359 (£25,103)
Defence Exp: $3.91bn (£2.54bn)
Service Personnel: 15,500 active, with 23,700 reserves, plus 7,100 paramilitary

KUWAIT NAVAL FORCE

Kuwait established the Kuwait Naval Force in 1961, shortly before the end of the country's status as a British protectorate and independence.

Manpower limitations and the country's position at the head of the Gulf meant that it developed essentially as a coastal force with small craft armed with Exocet AShM. When Iraq invaded Kuwait in August 1990, the KNF was almost completely destroyed, with Iraq capturing six missile-armed fast attack craft and another seventeen small craft destroyed. Post-liberation, the KNF has been rebuilt, mainly using French and German equipment, while after the invasion of Iraq and the rebuilding of the Iraqi Navy, there is now co-operation between the two services.

Today, the KNF has about 2,000 personnel, of whom 500 are in the Coast Guard. It has two German-built patrol craft, both with Exocet AShM and a 76mm gun, while eight French-built Um Almaradim-class patrol boats have Sea Skua AShM. The base is at Ras al Qalaya.

LAOS

Population: 6.4 million
Land Area: 88,780 square miles (231,399 sq.km.)
GDP: $6.42bn (£4.17bn), per capita $997 (£647)
Defence Exp: estimated at $14m (£9.1m)
Service Personnel: 29,100 active, plus 100,000 paramilitary

LAOS PEOPLE'S LIBERATION ARMY MARINE SECTION

Independent from France since 1949, landlocked Laos has suffered political upheavals and civil war, including occupation by Vietnamese troops. There is no navy but the People's Liberation Army has a Marine Section with fifty-two small patrol craft, mainly used on the Mekong River and its tributaries, while there are also a number of landing craft.

LATVIA

Population: 2.24 million
Land Area: 25,590 square miles (66,278 sq.km.)
GDP: $23.5bn (£15.3bn), per capita $10,508 (£6,823)
Defence Exp: $250m (£162.3m)
Service Personnel: 5,745 active, plus 10,866 reserves

LATVIAN NAVAL FORCES

Latvia was annexed by Russia in 1721, following the Great Northern War, and only regained its independence in 1918, after the Russian Revolution and the civil war that followed it. The country was occupied by the Soviet Union in 1940, and only regained its independence in 1991.

The Latvian Naval Forces were re-established in April 1991, with a single ship, *Sams*, and was formed into a Southern Region, Central Region, Coastal Defence Battalion and Training Centre. The Latvian Coast Guard is incorporated into the LNF. The LNF joined the Baltic Naval Squadron, BALTRON, when it was formed in 1999 to foster naval co-operation between the Baltic States. That year, the LNF was reorganised, albeit on the same structure as previously, but was reorganised yet again in 2004, with an LNF HQ, a Naval Forces Flotilla HQ and the Coast Guard.

Currently, the LNF has 587 personnel, including those of the Coast Guard. It has a patrol boat squadron and a mine countermeasures squadron. There are four Norwegian-built Storm-class patrol craft, each with a 76mm gun, and five MCMV, of which four are Dutch-built Imanta-class and the remaining ship is a Norwegian-built Vidar-class. There are two auxiliaries. The Coast Guard has six small patrol craft and is based at Riga, while the naval units are based on Liepaja and Daugavgriva.

LEBANON

Population: 4.3 million
Land Area: 3,400 square miles (8,806 sq.km.)
GDP: $39.4bn (£25.6bn), per capita $9,253 (£6,008)
Defence Exp: $1.16bn (£753m)
Service Personnel: 59,100 active, plus about 230,000 conscripts available for
    recall, and 20,000 paramilitary

LEBANESE NAVY

Part of the Ottoman Empire until the end of the First World War and then administered by the League of Nations until 1943, Lebanon did not form a navy until 1950, basing it at Beirut, the capital. The service functioned mainly as a coastal force.

The country has become the focus of military intervention by neighbouring Syria and Israel, as well as being used as a base by militant Palestinian organisations. This unstable mix led to civil war in the mid-1970s, which lasted for some twenty years, and more recently, there has been further action known as the 2006 Israel-Hezbollah War, which saw the Israeli Navy blockade the country's ports throughout the summer.

Today, the LN is being rebuilt with assistance from the United Arab Emirates, and has 1,100 personnel. It has eleven light patrol craft, of which the most numerous are five 'Attacker' and two 'Tracker' built in the UK, while the remainder are German and French in origin. There are two ex-French LCT. The base remains at Jounieh, Beirut, but a new naval base is being built at the Nahr el-Bared refugee camp.

LIBERIA

Population: 4.2 million
Land Area: 43,000 square miles (99,068 sq.km.)
GDP: $977m (£634m), per capita $238 (£154)
Defence Exp: $1.59m (£1.03m)
Service Personnel: 2,050 active

LIBERIAN COAST GUARD

Liberia came into existence in 1822 as a homeland for former American slaves and, over the next 150 years, considerable support was provided by the United States. It was not until 1959 that the Coast Guard was formed, and by the late 1970s, this had 300 men, four patrol craft and a landing craft.

The intervening years have seen the country ravaged by two civil wars requiring massive intervention by the United Nations. Today, the service has fifty men and eight Zodiac semi-inflatable craft.

LIBYA

Population: 6.5 million
Land Area: 679,358 square miles (1,750,537 sq.km.)
GDP: $76.4bn (£49.6bn), per capita $11,674 (£7,580)
Defence Exp: estimated at $1.71bn (£1.11)
Service Personnel: 76,000 active, plus 40,000 People's Militia reserve

LIBYAN ARAB REPUBLIC NAVY

The Libyan Navy was founded in 1962, and initially developed as a brown water navy able to patrol the coastal waters and police the EEZ. It acquired fast missile-armed patrol craft and by the late 1970s, its largest ship was a British-built light frigate, *Dat Assawari*, with a 4.5-inch main armament, Sea Cat SAM and anti-submarine mortars. It also had ten French-built and three British-built missile-armed fast attack craft, with the former having Exocet and the latter retrofitted with SS12 AShM missiles.

After the overthrow of the monarchy in 1970 by Colonel Gaddafi and the creation of an Arab republic, the title was changed and the extent of the navy's ambitions broadened. The harbour police were amalgamated with the navy. Submarines were provided by the Soviet Union, which also provided frigates and corvettes, minesweepers and landing ships and landing craft. Libya became strongly anti-Western and the fleet provided a measure of threat to NATO in the Mediterranean, although the operational status of the six ex-Soviet 'Foxtrot'-class submarines was uncertain throughout.

Egypt blamed Libya for sending a ro-ro ferry to the Red Sea in 1984 to sow mines south of the Suez Canal, although the Islamic Jihad Organisation claimed credit for the operation, which is believed to have damaged as many as nineteen merchantmen. Egypt had to request minesweeping support from NATO navies. A naval engagement with the US Sixth Fleet in the Gulf of Sidra followed in 1986, when Libyan warships used anti-tank weapons against American warships. In the action, Libya lost a corvette and a missile boat to attacks by A-4 Skyhawks.

The Libyan civil war that broke out in spring 2011 saw NATO air forces and the USN mount aerial attacks in support of the rebels, in which as many as nine warships are believed to have been sunk, while another two were captured by rebels before the end of the conflict in October 2011. During the conflict, Libyan naval vessels were claimed to have attacked rebel positions during the Battle of Ra's Lanuf, and then landed troops to outflank the rebels.

The operational status of the Libyan Arab Republic Navy is uncertain at present. Before the civil war, it had 8,000 personnel, including the Coast Guard. There may be two Al Hani-class (former Soviet Koni-class) guided missile frigates, each with SS-N-2C AShM, 'Gecko' SAM, two twin ASTT, RBU 6000 rocket launchers and two twin 76mm guns; a corvette, the *Tariq Ibin Ziyad*, with SS-N-2C AShM and 'Gecko' SAM; up to eleven fast missile-attack craft, and smaller patrol boats.

Aviation is provided by Libyan Arab Air Force Super Frelon helicopters.

The main bases are at Tripoli, Benghazi, Tobruk and Khums, but there are a number of minor bases as well.

It remains to be seen just what the future holds for the country and its armed forces, and what any future alliances may be. Nevertheless, pro-Islamic sentiment is strong, while some suspect that the country may divide into its two constituent regions, Tripolitania and Cyrenaica, unified by Italy to create the present state in the late 1930s.

LITHUANIA

Population: 3.3 million
Land Area: 25,170 square miles (65,201 sq.km.)
GDP: $35.9bn (£23.3bn), per capita $11,022 (£7,157)
Defence Exp: $323m (£209.7m)
Service Personnel: 10,640 active, plus 6,700 reserves

LITHUANIAN NAVY

At one time, Lithuania was a grand duchy and controlled territory stretching from the Baltic to the Black Sea, but united to Poland in 1385 before control passed to Russia in 1795. In common with the other Baltic States, it took the chance to seize independence in 1918, after the Russian Revolution and the ensuing Civil War, but the Lithuanian Navy was not established until 1935, although the first warship, a minesweeper, was commissioned in 1927 and was used for training.

Even before the outbreak of the Second World War, part of Lithuania was occupied by Germany on 22 March 1939. Once war broke out, Lithuanian warships were evacuated to Latvia, and once the Baltic States were occupied by the Soviet Union, the Lithuanian Navy became part of the Soviet Union's naval forces in the Baltic. Its first ship, the *Prezidentas Smetona*, was renamed *Korall* and saw combat against the German *Kriegsmarine* before sinking in the Gulf of Finland on 11 January 1945, after striking a mine. After this, Lithuanians served in the Soviet Navy.

Lithuania once again declared independence on the break-up of the Soviet Union and on 4 July 1992, the Lithuanian Navy was re-established. Later that year, two Grisha-class frigates were obtained. The service joined the Baltic Naval Squadron, BALTRON, on its formation in 1999 to enhance collaboration between the navies of the Baltic States, and became a member of NATO in April 2004.

Today, the Lithuanian Navy has 530 personnel, of whom 120 are conscripts. It has four patrol craft, of which three are Danish-built Standard Flex 300 and have a 76mm gun, while the other is an ex-Norwegian Storm-class. The four MCMW include two ex-German Suduvis-class (German

Lindau-class) and two ex-RN Hunt-class vessels that were added in 2011. The largest ship is the former Norwegian Vidar-class minelayer, *Jotvingis*. There are two auxiliaries and two tugs. The main base is at Klaipeda.

MACEDONIA, FORMER YUGOSLAV REPUBLIC

Population: 2.04 million
Land Area: 10,229 square miles (27,436 sq.km.)
GDP: $9.27bn (£6.02bn), per capita $4,538 (£2,946)
Defence Exp: $140m (£90.9m)
Service Personnel: 8,000 active, plus 4,850 reserves

MACEDONIAN ARMY

Created on the break-up of the former Republic of Yugoslavia in 1992, the Macedonian Army includes a small 'Marine Wing' with two patrol boats for river patrols.

MADAGASCAR

Population: 20.1 million
Land Area: 228,600 square miles (590,002 sq.km.)
GDP: $8.52bn (£5.53bn), per capita $423 (£274)
Defence Exp: $56m (£36.4m)
Service Personnel: 13,500 active, plus 8,100 paramilitary

MALAGASY PEOPLE'S ARMED FORCES NAVY

The former French colony of Madagascar became independent in 1960, and assumed control over its armed forces, although many Madagascans had previously served with the French armed forces. A small navy was created and, by the late 1970s, this had 600 personnel and four patrol craft as well as a landing ship and two auxiliaries.

Today, as part of the Malagasy People's Armed Forces, the Navy has 500 personnel, of whom 100 are marines. It has a large patrol craft, the *Chamois*, and six ex-US Coast Guard cutters as well an ex-French landing craft. The main base is at Diego Suarez, but there are another four minor bases, despite the small size of the fleet.

MALAWI

Population: 15.7 million
Land Area: 36,686 square miles (93,182 sq.km.)
GDP: $5.1bn (£3.29bn), per capita $325 (£209)
Defence Exp: estimated at $51m (£32.9m)
Service Personnel: 5,300 active, plus 1,500 paramilitary

MALAWI ARMY MARITIME WING

Landlocked Malawi has a small Maritime Wing within its Army, with a base at Monkey Bay on Lake Nyasa. There are 220 men assigned to the wing, which has a single patrol boat of uncertain operational status.

MALAYSIA

Population: 27.9 million
Land Area: 128,693 square miles (326,880 sq.km.)
GDP: $230bn (£149.4bn), per capita $8,237 (£5,348)
Defence Exp: $2.81bn (£1.82bn)
Service Personnel: 109,000 active, plus 51,600 reserves, and 24,600 paramilitary with 244,700 reserves

The Royal Malaysian Navy corvette *Laksamana*, seen at speed. (Royal Malaysian Navy)

ROYAL MALAYSIAN NAVY

As with the Republic of Singapore Navy, the Royal Malaysian Navy's origins can be traced back to the period of British colonial rule when the Straits Settlement Naval Volunteer Reserve (SSNVR) was formed in Singapore in April 1934. The SSNVR was formed to assist the Royal Navy in the defence of Singapore, where a major naval base was being constructed, as Singapore was vital to the defence of the Malay Peninsula as a whole. The following year, an Acacia-class sloop was transferred from the Royal Navy to serve as a headquarters and drill ship. In 1938, a branch was established actually in Malaya at Penang.

Japan's aggressive intentions were already clear, so when the Second World War broke out in Europe, members of the SSNVR were mobilised and recruitment of local personnel intensified in order to support the hard-pressed Royal Navy. By the time Japan entered the war on 7 December 1941, the SSNVR had 1,450 men, including 400 men of the Royal Navy Malay Section, and the combined force became known officially as the Malay Navy. The sloop was sunk early in 1942 as Japanese forces swept south through Malaya to take Singapore, but personnel from the Malay Navy served with the Allies in the Indian and Pacific Oceans. By the time of Japanese surrender in August 1945, just 600 personnel had survived.

The Malay Navy was disbanded in 1947 due to financial constraints, but reactivated in December 1948 at the start of the Malayan Emergency as Communist-backed guerrillas attempted to overthrow the colonial government. Its main role was coastal patrols to prevent supplies for the guerrillas being smuggled into Malaya by sea and also guarding the approaches to Singapore. In 1952, the Malay Navy became the Malayan Royal Naval Volunteer Reserve and was organised with a Singapore Division and a Federation (that is, Malayan) Division. A River-class frigate was transferred from the Royal Navy for training and, by 1950, the fleet also included an abandoned Japanese minelayer, an LST, a motor fishing vessel and a torpedo recovery vessel as well as seaward defence launches. A further change of title came in 1952, with the creation of the Royal Malayan Navy.

On independence in August 1957, the service was transferred to the new Federation of Malaya, but retained the title of 'Royal Malayan Navy' in deference to the Yang di-Pertuan Agong, the head of state. By this time, the fleet included an LCT, two Ham-class minesweepers, a coastal minelayer and seven patrol craft. With the formation of the Federation of Malaysia and Singapore in September 1963, the service had yet another name change and became the Royal Malaysian Navy. As coastal patrols remained important, eighteen Keris-class patrol boats were ordered from the UK, but these were small at just 103ft in length and so the force was augmented by four Perkasa-class fast patrol boats, similar to the RN's Brave-class, with gas turbine propulsion. The largest ship at this time was a Loch-class frigate transferred from the RN in 1964.

Indonesia opposed the newly-independent state until 1966, during which time the RMN joined the Royal Navy and Royal Australian Navy in securing its coastlines from infiltration. Afterwards, Malaysia and Singapore separated amicably and the RMN became the former's navy. It was decided that the RMN should move from being a brown water navy to a blue water navy. As a first step, the light frigate HMS *Mermaid* was acquired from the Royal Navy and renamed *Hang Tuah*, later becoming a training ship. Another light frigate was later acquired from a UK ship-builder, bringing with it the service's first guided missiles, Sea Cat SAM. Further missile systems followed with the purchase of fast attack craft equipped with Exocet AShM from France and Sweden during the 1970s and 1980s, while surplus USN LSTs were also bought.

By the late 1970s, the RMN had 6,000 personnel and was operating both of the light frigates mentioned, fourteen fast attack craft and twenty-two patrol boats, as well as five minesweepers and three LSTs. In 1977, an air arm was established with twelve ex-RN Wasp ASW helicopters.

In more recent years, the RMN has joined international efforts against piracy in the Gulf of Aden, rescuing a Malaysian chemical tanker in January 2011. In addition, the RMN is involved in an annual series of bilateral maritime training exercises, Co-operation Afloat Readiness and Training (CARAT), between the US Navy and the armed forces of Singapore, Thailand, Malaysia, Indonesia, Brunei and the Philippines.

Today, the RMN has 14,000 personnel, of whom 160 are involved in naval aviation. There are two British-designed Lekiu-class frigates, each with Exocet AShM, VLS Sea Wolf SAM, three triple ASTT and accommodation for a Super Lynx ASW helicopter; two German-built Kasturi-class frigates also have Exocet AShM, anti-submarine mortars, a 100mm gun and a helicopter landing platform; six Kedah-class (German MEKO) frigates have Exocet AShM, CIWS and a 76mm gun as well as a helicopter landing platform. A force of thirty-seven patrol and coastal combatants includes four Laksamana-class corvettes, each with Otomat AShM, Aspide SAM, two triple ASTT and a 76mm gun; four Perdana-class (French Combattante II) patrol boats with Exocet AShM; and four Handalan-class patrol boats with Exocet AShM. There are two Franco-Spanish-built Scorpene-class conventional submarines with six torpedo tubes each. There are four MCMV. An LST is on loan from the Republic of Korea Navy, but there are also 115 landing craft. Logistics and support is provided by fifteen ships, including oilers and supply vessels. Naval aviation consists of six Super Lynx ASW helicopters and six As-555 Fennec light helicopters, but plans exist for maritime-reconnaissance aircraft.

A marine commando unit also exists, but no details of its manpower are available.

The Malaysian guided missile frigate *Lekiu* dressed overall, possibly for a commissioning ceremony. (Royal Malaysian Navy)

The main bases are at Tanjung Pengelih, Kuantan, Labuan, Lumut and Semporna, with two new bases being completed at Langkawi and Sepanngar Bay.

MALI

Population: 13.3 million
Land Area: 464,875 square miles (1,204,350 sq.km.)
GDP: $9.3bn (£6.0bn), per capita $698 (£453)
Defence Exp: $208m (£135m)
Service Personnel: 7,350 active, plus 4,800 paramilitary and 3,000 militia

MALI NAVY

Mali became independent from France in 1960 and, although landlocked, has a small navy, which is probably no more than a unit within the army. There are fifty personnel and three patrol boats, all for riverine use, but of doubtful serviceability. There are four bases, including Barnako and Timbuktu.

MALTA

Population: 410,000
Land Area: 122 square miles (316 sq.km.)
GDP: $7.9bn (£5.13bn), per capita $19,259 (£12,505)
Defence Exp: $57m (£37m)
Service Personnel: 1,954 active, plus 167 reserves

ARMED FORCES OF MALTA MARITIME SQUADRON

While Maltese personnel served with the Royal Navy from the Battle of Trafalgar, 1805, onwards, it did not form its own armed forces until after the country became independent in 1964. While ground forces were a continuation of Maltese units within the British Army, the air and maritime elements had to be formed from scratch.

A number of small patrol craft were donated by the United States Coast Guard and also by Italy, and some former East German vessels were provided after German reunification. These were augmented by rigid-hulled inflatable boats for fast interceptor duties. The European Commission has provided 110 million Euros for the Armed Forces of Malta, and part of this money is being spent upgrading and modernising the capabilities of the Maritime Squadron as well as paying for a new maritime patrol craft.

The main functions of the squadron are EEZ as well as curbing smuggling and illegal immigration.

Today, the Maritime Squadron has a Diciotti patrol craft, four Austral 21m patrol craft purchased from Australia in 2010-2011, two Marine Protector-type patrol craft and an ex-East German Brense-class patrol craft, as well as two support vessels. The main base is at Pieta. Air support is provided by two Islanders of the Air Wing, while a joint AFM and Italian SAR unit has two AB-212 and is based at the island's airport at Luqa.

MAURITANIA

Population: 3.4 million
Land Area: 398,000 square miles (1,085,210 sq.km.)
GDP: $3.66bn (£2.37bn), per capita $1,088 (£706)
Defence Exp: $115m (£74.7m)
Service Personnel: 15,870 active, plus 5,000 paramilitary

MARINE MAURITANIENNE

A former French protectorate and colony, Mauritania has been independent since 1961.

The small armed forces include a navy, the Marine Mauritanienne, which has about 620 personnel and twelve small patrol boats, with its main base at Nouakchott and another at Nouadhibou.

MAURITIUS

Population: 1.3 million
Land Area: 720 square miles (2,038 sq.km.)
GDP: $9.44bn (£6.1bn), per capita $7,284 (£5,348)
Security Exp: $41m (£26.45m)
Service Personnel: Nil, but 2,000 paramilitary

MAURITIUS COAST GUARD

Mauritius does not have armed forces but maintains a paramilitary 'Special Mobile Force' and its Coast Guard, which also has some aircraft in addition to those of the Police Air Wing.

The Coast Guard has 500 personnel and its largest ship is the Canadian-built *Vigilant*, a large patrol craft with a helicopter landing platform, while there are four smaller patrol boats. Aircraft include a Defender and 2 Do-228-101.

MEXICO

Population: 110.6 million
Land Area: 760,373 square miles (1,972,360 sq.km.)
GDP: $1.01tr (£655.8bn), per capita $9,168 (£5,953)
Defence Exp: $4.6bn (£2.98bn)
Service Personnel: 280,250 active, plus 87,344 reserves and 51,500 paramilitary

MEXICAN NAVY

Mexico gained independence from Spain in 1821 and, almost immediately, a Ministry of War was established and this controlled both the army and the Mexican Navy (*Armada de México*, SEMAR) until 1939, when an independent ministry was set up. The first ships were bought from the United States, but at the time Mexican territory included a number of areas, including Texas, which are now part of the USA, and in 1836 Texas rebelled, declared independence and later joined the USA in 1845. In the ensuing Mexican War, 1846-1848, Mexico lost all territory north of the Rio Grande. Throughout this period, from 1810 and the first Mexican uprising until the middle years of the nineteenth century, there were also intermittent battles with Spain, which refused to recognise Mexican independence.

There was also a French intervention between November 1838 and March 1839, and a further intervention lasting from 1862 until 1867. The first French intervention was called the 'Pastry War' as it started with a claim by a French baker in Mexico City that his shop had been looted by Mexican officers. But Mexico at the time had also defaulted on the considerable sums it owed France. For the duration of the war, the French fleet blockaded Mexican ports.

The second French intervention was also caused by Mexico defaulting on payments to France, and to Spain and the United Kingdom as well. A Spanish fleet was sent, but withdrew when the French invaded with more than 38,000 men, a sixth of the French Army at the time, and in 1863, Mexico City fell to the invaders. Although the USA opposed the invasion, its ability to act was rendered impossible by the American Civil War. By the time the French withdrew, more than 6,600 of its men had died, with about 5,000 of them succumbing to disease. Despite the obvious naval intervention by the French to transport so many troops to and from Mexico, there was little in the way of naval engagement in the conflict, which was finally resolved by an uprising in Mexico against a French puppet dictator, which was aided by a US blockade of Mexico starting in 1866. Internally, there was political disorder until 1876.

The Vera Cruz incident with the United States in 1914 was prompted by the arrest of American ratings that had strayed into a prohibited area of Tampico. This came at a time of deteriorating relations between the two countries. The landing of US Marines and sailors from two battleships on 21 April 1914 brought the incident to an end with Mexican forces retreating.

Mexico remained neutral during the First World War. By 1939, the SEMAR consisted of a coast defence ship, effectively destroyer-sized but only capable of 15 knots, three sloops and about eleven gunboats. Although initially neutral on the outbreak of the Second World War, Mexico joined the Allies in 1942, placing bases at the disposal of the US forces, and in return received the first US military aid. Further US military aid followed Mexico joining the Organisation of American States in 1948.

By the late 1970s, SEMAR had 19,000 men, including 2,000 marines. The fleet included two ex-USN Fletcher-class destroyers and five ex-USN frigates as well as a frigate built in Spain. There were thirty-four corvettes and thirty-six patrol craft, including eight river patrol craft and twenty

British-built Azteca-class large patrol craft. Just 250 personnel were involved in naval aviation.

By this time, the nature of the service was that its main role was protection of the country's long coastline, anti-smuggling with increasing emphasis on anti-drug work, and protection of offshore oil and gas rigs. These priorities have increased in importance, so that the need has been for many fast but lightly-armed smaller warships capable of handling a light helicopter.

Today, the SEMAR has grown to 56,500 personnel, including 1,250 involved with aviation and 19,500 marines, with the latter force planned to grow to 30,000 personnel. There are seven frigates, of which six are ex-USN. These include four Allende-class (US Knox), each with Harpoon AShM, Sea Sparrow SAM, two twin ASTT, a 127mm gun and accommodation for a MD-902 helicopter, and two Bravo-class (ex-US Bronstein) with an ASROC launcher, two triple ASTT, a twin 76mm gun and a helicopter landing platform, as well as another frigate, *Quetzalcvoatl*, with a twin 127mm gun and a helicopter landing platform. There are no fewer than 119 patrol and coastal combatants, of which the most modern are the first four of a possible eight Oaxaca-class, with a 76mm gun and capacity for a single Panther helicopter, with this class replacing the ex-USN Leandro Valle-class. The other fast-growing class is the Polaris II-class, with nine vessels in service and more under construction. There is a small amphibious fleet with three ex-USN LSTs. There are seventeen logistics and support ships, including four devoted to training.

Naval aviation includes shore-based maritime-reconnaissance aircraft with a squadron combining CASA 212PM Aviocar and CN-235 MPA Persuader aircraft; five squadrons with Beech and Cessna twin-engined light aircraft; a transport squadron has An-32B 'Cline' aircraft, and also a VIP squadron of Beech, DHC and Learjet aircraft; while there are five squadrons of Mi-8 and Mi-17 transport helicopters; two with Fennec and Panther helicopters and two squadrons with Bo-105.

Although the ministry is based in Mexico City, the operational HQ is at Acapulco, below which there is an exercise HQ at Vera Cruz and two fleet commands, Gulf, with six zones, and Pacific, with eleven zones, giving eighteen bases in all.

MONTENEGRO

Population: 625,516
Land Area: 5,019 square miles (13,812 sq.km.)
GDP: $3.93bn (£2.55bn), per capita $6,280 (£4,078)
Defence Exp: $35m (£22.73m)
Service Personnel: 3,127 active, plus 10,100 paramilitary

MONTENEGRIN NAVY

Montenegro was created as an independent state in 2006, after the division of the Former Yugoslav Republic of Serbia and Montenegro. After independence, the government moved quickly to established armed forces and, as part of this, a separate navy is being developed. Currently, the Montenegrin Navy has about 400 personnel. It has five patrol ships, including two Rade Koncar-class capable of launching 'Styx' AShM, the *Kotar*, with a twin 76mm gun, and two small Mirna-class or Type 140 patrol boats operated on behalf of the police. It has two small swimmer delivery vehicles. There are five small landing craft and three support vessels. The main base is at Bar.

MOROCCO

Population: 32.4 million
Land Area: 171,388 square miles (466,200 sq.km.)
GDP: $92.2bn (£59.9bn), per capita $2,849 (£1,850)
Defence Exp: $3.19bn (£2.07bn)
Service Personnel: 195,800 active, plus 150,000 reserves and 50,000 para-
    military

ROYAL MOROCCAN NAVY

At one time a protectorate of both France and Spain, Morocco became an independent kingdom in 1956. Although the country had a long seafaring tradition dating back to the middle ages, the modern Royal Moroccan Navy dates from 1960.

Initially, the service was structured almost as a coastguard service and by the late 1970s, it had 2,000 personnel, including 600 marines, and was based on about twenty patrol craft, of which the largest was just over 300 tons displacement. Since then, it has expanded considerably to include frigates and corvettes, largely depending on French and Spanish equipment.

Today, the RMN has 7,800 personnel, of which 1,500 are marines. There are two guided missile frigates of the Mohammed V-class (French Floreal-class), both with Exocet AShM, a 76mm gun and accommodation for a Panther helicopter; a Spanish-built corvette, the *Lt Col Errhamani*, with Exocet AShM, Aspide SAM, two triple ASTT, and a 76mm gun; and about twenty patrol craft, of which the largest, the four Spanish-built Commandant El Khattabi-class, have Exocet AShM and a 76mm gun. The fisheries administration controls the five Rais Bargach-class patrol craft, and two of the four Danish-built El Hahiq-class are used by the customs. There are another seventeen patrol boats of various types. There are three LSM and an LST, a

149

landing craft and three auxiliaries as well as a tug. Naval aviation consists of three Panther helicopters.

The main bases are at Casablanca, Tangier, Agadir, Al Hoceima and Dakhla.

MOZAMBIQUE

Population: 23.4 million
Land Area: 302,250 square miles (771,820 sq.km.)
GDP: $9.08bn (£5.9bn), per capita $388 (£251)
Defence Exp: $73m (£47.4m)
Service Personnel: 11,200 active

MOZAMBIQUE NAVY

Mozambique became independent from Portugal in 1975, but the civil war that followed lasted for the next twenty years. The armed forces were reconstructed at the end of the fighting and the opposing armies were amalgamated as far as possible. The Mozambique Navy, which originally had 700 personnel and seven small patrol craft, was run-down by this time and manpower had dwindled to 200, about the present level. Details on equipment are scarce but, in 2004, South Africa donated two Namacurra-class harbour patrol boats. The main base is at Beira but there are two other Indian Ocean bases and one on Lake Malawi.

MYRANMAR

Population: 50.5 million
Land Area: 261,789 square miles (676,580 sq.km.)
GDP: $145bn (£94.1bn), per capita $2,868 (£1,744)
Defence Exp: Not known
Service Personnel: 406,000 active, plus 107,250 reserves

MYRANMAR NAVY

While Burma became independent of the UK in 1948, a small Navy of Burma was formed in 1940 and played an active role with the Royal Navy against the Japanese during the Second World War, mainly on coastal and minesweeping operations. In late 1947, on the eve of independence, the Union of Burma Navy was formed with 700 personnel and a number of small ships transferred from the RN. The largest ship was a River-class frigate, and four landing craft gun (medium) each armed with two 25-pounder and two 2-pounder guns, which provided support for gunboats.

The initial fleet was enlarged in 1950-51 by the transfer of ten ex-United States Coast Guard cutters under MDAP, the US Mutual Defense Assistance Program (sic). At the time, the Union of Burma Navy was engaged in supporting the army in counter-insurgency operations against groups anxious to destabilise the Union, protecting river and coastal convoys, carrying supplies and troops, and providing fire support. It helped relieve the port of Moulmein, captured by Karen rebels in 1948, although one of its patrol craft defected to the insurgents, and the town of Bassein in the Irrawaddy Delta. During 1956-57, five Dark-class motor torpedo and gunboats were acquired from the UK, followed in 1958 by an Algerine-class minesweeper transferred from the RN and river gunboats bought from Yugoslavia. Further US patrol craft followed in the 1960s.

Yugoslav assistance starting in 1960 enabled Burma to establish a small shipbuilding industry, providing small patrol and landing craft, as well as two Nawarat-class corvettes. Additional corvettes were transferred from the USN.

During the following decade, new or donated surplus vessels did not keep pace with the loss or increasing obsolescence of older ships. By the late 1970s, the UBN had two frigates, both ex-RN, and four corvettes, two of which were ex-USN and two built locally, while there were more than seventy smaller patrol boats and twelve auxiliaries and landing craft. A programme was initiated to modernise the UBN, with six Australian-built Carpentaria-class inshore patrol boats, three Swift-class coastal patrol boats from Singapore and three Osprey-class offshore patrol boats from Denmark. Locally-built patrol boats were also provided.

In 1989, the country changed its name to Myanmar and the navy's title changed as well.

The country became a military dictatorship spurned by the West, and procurement reflected this with missile-armed patrol craft and corvettes from Communist China.

In May 2008, Burma was hit by Tropical Cyclone Nargis and, while no official figures are available, the Network for Democracy and Development in Thailand claims that 289 officers and men were declared missing and as many as twenty-five naval vessels were sunk, while the IISS suggests the figure could be nearer to thirty vessels.

Today, the Myanmar Navy has about 16,000 personnel. It has three Anawrahta-class corvettes, each with a 76mm gun; six Housin-class guided missile patrol craft with 'Styx' AShM, which also arms nine Myanmar-class patrol boats; while another sixty or so patrol boats carry cannon or heavy machine gun armament. There are eighteen medium and small landing craft, as well as ten auxiliaries. There are no aircraft and any air support is provided by the Myanmar Air Force, although this does not have an MR or ASW capability.

The bases are at Rangoon's Monkey Point, Bassein, Mergui, Moulmein, Seikyi and Sittwe.

Despite claims that the objective is a blue water navy, the MN is still very much a brown water navy engaged in coastal and riverine operations. Sales of timber to countries in what once would have been described as the 'Eastern Bloc' enable the country to sustain its armed forces with equipment purchased from the same sources, but major expansion is unlikely to be affordable.

NAMIBIA

Population: 2.2 million
Land Area: 318,261 square miles (824,296 sq.km.)
GDP: $120bn (£77.9bn), per capita $5,439 (£3,531)
Defence Exp: $408m (£264.9m)
Service Personnel: 9,200 active, plus 6,000 paramilitary

NAMIBIA NAVY

A former German colony, South-West Africa, Namibia was mandated to South Africa until 1989, when the country became independent and adopted its current name. While an army was created after independence, with continuing internal unrest, the Namibia Navy was not established until 2004, with considerable aid from Brazil, which has trained personnel and also conducted marine surveys, including one defining the limits of the coastal shelf.

Currently there are about 200 personnel, although some accounts suggest the figure could be much higher as the fleet consists of five Brazilian-built Brendan Simbwaye-class offshore patrol craft, the first of which was delivered in 2011; two coastal patrol craft and two smaller patrol boats, although more are supposed to be on order. In 2004, South Africa donated two Namacurra harbour patrol boats. The main base is at Walvis Bay.

NETHERLANDS

Population: 16.7 million
Land Area: 13,959 square miles (36,175 sq.km.)
GDP: $780bn (£506.5bn), per capita $46,822 (£30,403)
Defence Exp: $11.3bn (£7.3bn)
Service Personnel: 37,368 active, plus 3,189 reserves

The Royal Netherlands Navy's destroyer *Zeven Provincien* at speed. She is the class leader and there are three other ships of the same type. (Royal Netherlands Navy)

ROYAL NETHERLANDS NAVY

Although the Netherlands is part of Europe and is a small country, it is a maritime power and has a long naval history, which officially dates from 1488, pre-dating the modern Dutch state as at the time the country was under the control of the Habsburgs north of the Rhine, while south of it the remaining four out of the eleven provinces were controlled by Spain. Like many of the older navies, in the early days it was largely comprised of merchantmen whose owners had armed them as protection against pirates. In wartime, the government granted these ships letters of marque, effectively making them privateers and allowing their captains to engage enemy ships and if possible seize them and their cargo. This was a difficult operation to control and in 1488, the Emperor Maximilian of Austria founded the predecessor of the modern Netherlands Navy, appointing an admiral. Even this did not resolve the problem completely as many of the provinces continued to sponsor small navies of their own.

It was not until 1581 that the foundations of the modern state were laid when the northern provinces declared their independence, after the Dutch revolt, which lasted from 1568 to 1648. The new state was initially a republic and acted quickly to impose a new command structure on the navy, with no fewer than five admiralties established at de Maze, Amsterdam,

153

Zeeland, the Noorderkwartier and Friesland. Initially, Spain was the enemy. In 1607, Dutch warships sank most of a Spanish fleet building at Gibraltar. This period saw a blockade of the port of Antwerp to aid the Flemish uprising against Spain and also escorting Dutch merchantmen in the North Sea and Baltic.

The years that followed saw the new country grow in power and take the first steps towards colonial expansion. Tensions rose with neighbouring countries and especially England, leading to the First Anglo-Dutch War, which saw English privateers acting against Dutch merchantmen. In 1652, the Dutch Admiral Maarten Tromp, won the Battle of Dungeness to ensure Dutch ships could use the English Channel. The Second Anglo-Dutch War saw no fewer than five battles, including the Battle of Chatham, 1667, which saw the English suffer a major defeat. After this, the Third Dutch Naval War saw an alliance between England and France, plus the German states of Cologne and Munster. At this time, the Dutch fleet was the world's largest, but the alliance between England and France reversed the position, but Dutch Admiral Michiel de Ruyter inflicted so much damage on the allies in three battles off the Dutch coast that the threat of invasion by the Anglo-French-German alliance evaporated. The Anglo-Dutch wars ended with the Treaty of Westminster in 1674, but when a fresh Anglo-French alliance seemed likely in 1688, William of Orange sailed to England and landed at Brixham in Devon, and force-marched his troops to London to depose his father-in-law, James II, and was proclaimed King William III, although this 'Glorious Reviolution' was the only time in British history when the monarchy was shared, this time with his wife, Mary II. This marked a change in the pattern of European alliances with the Dutch and English allied against France, but warfare continued until the end of the War of the Spanish succession in 1713.

Throughout this period, the Dutch fleet had continued to grow. No fewer than sixty ships had been ordered in 1653 and this order was repeated just ten years later. The flagship *De Zeven Provincien* had ninety-six guns, just eight fewer than the British *Victory*, built more than 100 years later. The service during this period had about 4,000 personnel, not enough for such a large fleet, but worked on the basis of a permanent cadre of professional sailors, including ships' captains who were on long-term contracts and in times of crisis authorised to recruit sufficient men to take their ships to sea. From 1665, troops were deployed aboard the warships and these became the predecessors of the Dutch marines.

The eighteenth century saw the service's fortunes reversed and despite a fresh shipbuilding programme starting in 1780, the Fourth Anglo-Dutch War, 1780-1784, saw the Royal Navy emerge as the world's leading sea power, a position it retained for more than 130 years. The clumsy decentralised command, with no fewer than five admiralties, ended after the Batavian Revolution in 1795, which led to greater unity throughout the country and its institutions. Nevertheless, the new service, based on The Hague, suffered the surrender of a squadron near Saldanha Bay, 1796, and defeat at the hands of the Royal Navy at Camperdown, 1797. For three years, the Netherlands were occupied as a part of France, but independence was regained and in December 1813, the navy was resurrected. Despite the country becoming a monarchy, the prefix 'Royal' was not granted until 1905.

The nineteenth century saw the number of personnel double from 5,000 in 1850 to more than 10,000 in 1900, largely by recruitment from the country's far-flung colonies, which stretched from the Caribbean to the East Indies. The latter region became a major preoccupation after the bankruptcy of the Dutch East India Company, so that eventually some 60 per cent of the active fleet was based on the East Indies.

Neutral during the First World War, the service introduced its first aircraft in 1917, six Martin seaplanes and three Farman F-22s.

The inter-war years saw the service reduced in size with a vocal pacifist movement in the Netherlands, and at the outbreak of the Second World War in Europe in September 1939, the country once again expected to remain neutral. Even so, an attempt to re-arm had started in 1938. After the German invasion of May 1940, such ships as were in the Netherlands escaped to British ports and continued the war fighting alongside the Royal Navy. In the Far East, the Japanese invasion of the Netherlands East Indies led to fighting and the creation of ABDA, an American British Dutch Australian command, which nevertheless had no time to exercise and no effective communications system, resulting in its defeat in the Battle of the Java Sea, where the combined fleet was under the command of the Dutchman, Rear Admiral Karel van Doorman, who went down with his flagship, the light cruiser *De Ruyter*, sunk along with another Dutch light cruiser, the *Java*. The few remaining Dutch warships in the East were based on Sydney in Australia and in Ceylon, now Sri Lanka. A notable contribution to the protection of Allied convoys in the North Atlantic was made by the merchant aircraft carriers or MAC-ships, tankers and grain carriers converted to carry Swordfish ASW aircraft, of which several were manned by Dutch crews and a Dutch naval air squadron was formed within the Royal Navy's Fleet Air Arm as No.860 NAS.

Post-war, the Royal Netherlands Navy received its first aircraft carrier, an escort carrier, HMS *Nairana*, donated by the Royal Navy and renamed *Karel Doorman* in Dutch service. She was one of the few British-built escort carriers. This was replaced by the Colossus-class light fleet carrier *Venerable*, which was commissioned on 28 May 1948, also as *Karel Doorman*. These ships initially operated Firefly fighter-bombers, but aboard the second *Karel Doorman* these were replaced by Sea Fury fighters and eventually by Seahawk jet fighters as well as Avenger ASW aircraft, themselves later replaced by Trackers, of which there were at one time three squadrons, with two at any one time shore-based. The Netherlands post-war was no longer neutral but became a member of NATO in 1952.

The immediate post-war period was far from peaceful; it took four years of war for the Netherlands to re-establish its authority over the East Indies as the Republic of Indonesia was declared just two days after the Japanese surrender in August 1945. The fighting ended with the Dutch recognising Indonesian independence, but Dutch units remained in Western New Guinea until 1962, when that was also handed over to Indonesia.

The period immediately after the Second World War saw most of the re-armament effort devoted to ground and air forces, but this changed both with NATO membership and the Korean war, 1950-1953. This prompted the Dutch government to concentrate on building a balanced fleet with the aircraft carrier, two de Ruyter-class cruisers, twelve destroyers, eight submarines, six van Speijk-class general-purpose frigates (based on the successful British Leander-class) and a substantial force of minesweepers. The van Speijk-class introduced helicopters to smaller warships with the Wasp ASW helicopter. The van Speijk-class ships were modernised in the late 1970s and then joined, and eventually replaced, by the Kortenaer-class gas turbine-powered guided missile frigates with each carrying two Lynx helicopters. The service provided a regular contribution to NATO's Standing Force Atlantic. The Kortenaer-class have in recent years been sold to a number of other navies, with most going to the Hellenic Navy.

The *Karel Doorman* was withdrawn and sold to the Argentine Navy in 1970. Since then, the service, which had operated Harpoon and then Neptune ASW aircraft, which were replaced by Atlantique aircraft in 1970, has withdrawn from fixed-wing aviation entirely.

The fall of the Berlin Wall, the collapse of the Warsaw Pact and the break-up of the Soviet Union saw a substantial reduction in the size of the Royal Netherlands Navy along with the country's other armed forces. The service became more involved in supporting UN peacekeeping operations, and the role became one of expeditionary peacekeeping and enforcement.

Today, the RNN has 8,500 personnel, including 2,654 marines. It has four Zeven Provincien-guided missile destroyers, each with 127mm gun, Harpoon AshM, SM-2MR/ESSM VLS SAM, two twin ASTT, and capable of accommodating either a Lynx or an NH-90 ASW helicopter. There are two Karel Doorman-class frigates, each with a 76mm gun, Harpoon AShM, Sea Sparrow VLS SAM, two twin ASTT and capable of accommodating either a Lynx or an NH-90 ASW helicopter. Amphibious warfare remains important and the fleet includes the *Rotterdam* and *John de Witt* LPDs, each capable of carrying either six Lynx or four NH-90 or Cougar helicopters, landing craft and with up to 538 troops in the former and 700 in the latter. There are seventeen landing craft of various kinds. There are four Walrus-class conventional submarines, each with four torpedo tubes capable, also, of launching Harpoon AshM. There are ten Alkmaar-class (Tripartite-class)

Largest ship in the Royal Netherlands Navy is the LDH *Rotterdam*, whose floodable stern dock can be seen clearly here. She is often to be found at NATO amphibious exercises. (Royal Netherlands Navy)

MCMV. The logistics fleet includes the *Amsterdam* and *Zuiderkruis*, replenishment tankers with accommodation for four Lynx or two NH-90 in the former and two Lynx or an NH-90 in the latter. Another fourteen vessels include training, survey vessels and tugs. The main base is at Den Helder, with a naval air station at De Kooy, and fleet units are based at Willemstad in the Netherlands Antilles.

NEW ZEALAND

Population: 4.3 million
Land Area: 103,736 square miles (268,676 sq.km.)
GDP: $141bn (£91.6bn), per capita $32,654 (£21,203)
Defence Exp: $1.59bn (£1.03bn)
Service Personnel: 9,673 active, plus 2,314 reserves

ROYAL NEW ZEALAND NAVY

As the least populated of the dominions, self-governing countries within the British Empire, New Zealand relied on the Royal Navy for security, although the population did buy a gunboat as early as 1846, and spare torpedo boats were bought by the government in 1884, while in 1887 it contributed ships to an Australasian Naval Squadron. Although still without its own navy, New Zealand paid for the construction of the battle-cruiser HMS *New Zealand*, which saw action at the Battle of Jutland in 1916. Before this, the New Zealand Naval Forces had been created in 1913 and the cruiser HMS *Philomel* was transferred to it. Nevertheless, in 1921, the force became the New Zealand Division of the Royal Navy, with two cruisers and a minesweeper.

The Royal New Zealand Navy dates from 1 October 1941, recognising that by this time the service was largely self-sufficient. Before this, the New Zealand-manned HMS *Achilles* played an important role in the Battle of the River Plate in December 1939, supporting the heavy cruiser *Exeter* and the light cruiser *Ajax*, helping in the action that ended in the scuttling of the German *Panzerschiff Admiral Graf Spee*. Another New Zealand-manned light cruiser, *Leander*, escorted the New Zealand Expeditionary Force to the Middle East in 1940. Later in the war, she sank the Italian auxiliary cruiser *Ramb I*, and on returning to the Pacific was present at the sinking of the Japanese cruiser *Jintsu*. Wartime saw the RNZN grow in size to more than sixty ships, but after the fall of Singapore the service operated as part of the US 7th Fleet until the creation of the British Pacific Fleet in November 1944, when most RNZN ships were transferred to the BPF.

Largest ship in the Royal New Zealand Navy is the so-called multi-purpose ship HMNZS *Canterbury*, intended to provide force projection and also disaster relief. There have been criticisms of the ship as her design is based on that of an Irish Sea ferry and is not best suited to the Pacific Ocean. (RNZN)

Naturally enough, the return of peace saw the service cut back dramatically, but even so the RNZN was able to deploy six British-built Loch-class frigates during the Korean War, 1950-1953. Later, New Zealand became a member of the South East Asia Treaty Organisation (SEATO), which was a British and US-led alliance to counter the spread of communism. SEATO never fulfilled its promise and, unlike NATO, lacked a formal command structure. As with Australia, New Zealand then came to rely on a tripartite alliance with the USA, ANZUS. Nevertheless, this relationship was placed under strain because of resistance to visits by nuclear-powered and nuclear-armed US warships to New Zealand.

Throughout this period, New Zealand continued to buy British warships and the RNZN settled at a force of four frigates, mainly Leander-class, and four offshore patrol boats. A small air arm was established, which peaked at seven Wasp helicopters for operation from frigates, but it was decided that this small force was not viable and responsibility for shipboard aviation passed to the RNZAF.

New Zealand joined Australian forces in the occupation of East Timor after Indonesian forces withdrew in 1999.

In recent years, the RNZN has been reduced further, and now has just two frigates, added to an Australian order for Anzac-class ships, each of

One of two Anzac-class frigates, a joint Australian and New Zealand venture. In the RNZN is HMNZS *Te Mana*, seen here leaving port. (RNZN)

which has a 127mm gun, vertical launch SAM and a Phalanx CIWS gun, as well as two triple torpedo tubes and a Super Seasprite helicopter. A recent addition to the fleet intended to assist in force projection, troop transport and crisis relief has been the multi-role vessel HMNZS *Canterbury*, built in the Netherlands to a commercial ferry design, but this ship has been criticised as its design was for the Irish Sea and it has shortcomings when operating in the Pacific. Two Otago-class patrol craft can also operate Seasprite helicopters, while there are also four offshore patrol craft of the Rotoiti-class. There is a tanker and a survey ship. There are 2,161 personnel and the fleet is based on Auckland.

NICARAGUA

Population: 5.8 million
Land Area: 57,143 square miles (148,006 sq.km.)
GDP: $6.4bn (£4.2bn), per capita $1,100 (£714)
Defence Exp: $38m (£24.7m)
Service Personnel: 12,000 active.

NICARAGUAN NAVY

Nicaragua became independent from Spain in 1821 and, until 1838, was part of the Central American Federation before becoming fully independent. For most of the next century, the country suffered from repeated conflict between conservative and liberal groups, until in 1927, under a 'Good Neighbour' policy, the United States sent in the US Marines and established a National Guard.

Although the country has Pacific and Caribbean coastlines, maritime matters were not to the forefront. During the Second World War the country was neutral, but allowed the United States to use Corinto as a base and became eligible for US military aid as a result, although this seems to have consisted mainly of aircraft. Post-war, the country joined the Organisation of American States in 1948, but by the late 1970s, its maritime forces consisted of just 200 men and ten small patrol craft.

Between 1979 and 1990, the country fell under the influence of Cuba and was controlled by the Sandinistas. During this period, the armed forces grew to 97,000 and were supplied with Soviet equipment. Over the three years to 1993, manpower fell to about 15,000.

Currently, the Nicaraguan Navy is subject to overall control by the Army, and has 800 personnel. There are seven patrol craft, mainly based on Corinto. There are a number of vessels of Soviet, East European and North Korean origin, but their operational status is doubtful.

NIGERIA

Population: 158 million
Land Area: 356,669 square miles (923,773 sq.km.)
GDP: $207bn (£134bn), per capita $1,311 (£851)
Defence Exp: $1.55bn (£1.0bn)
Service Personnel: 80,000 active, plus 82,000 paramilitary

NIGERIAN NAVY

While the Federation of Nigeria dates from independence from the UK in 1960, the Nigerian Navy dates its history back to the formation of the paramilitary Lagos Marine in 1887, which not only became the port authority but undertook policing of waterways and what would today be regarded as the EEZ. Later, this became the Nigeria Marine Department of the British Royal Navy, formally becoming the Nigeria Marine when Northern and Southern Nigeria were united in 1914. The Nigerian Navy was founded before independence in 1956, later changing its name to the Nigerian Defence Force and then, in May 1958, to the Royal Nigerian Navy. The following year, a British Algerine-class minesweeper was transferred to the RNN and commissioned as HMNS *Nigeria*. The 'Royal' prefix was dropped in 1963, when the country became a republic.

The Nigerian Navy was not directly involved in or affected by the civil war that affected Nigeria during the 1960s. By the late 1970s, it had 4,500 personnel. The largest ship at the time was a new *Nigeria*, a Dutch-built frigate delivered in 1965, while there were also four British-built corvettes, six missile-armed fast attack craft, and twelve patrol craft, as well as tankers, survey ships and training vessels.

The Nigerian Navy has some 8,000 personnel today, including members of the Coast Guard. The largest warship is the *Aradu*, a German-built MEKO 360, fitted with Otomat AShM, Aspide SAM, two triple ASTT and a 127mm gun, as well as accommodation for an ASW helicopter. A British-built corvette remains in service, with Sea Cat SAM, anti-submarine mortar and a 76mm gun. There are a number of patrol craft, including four Balsam-class, which are ex-US buoy tenders; a French-built Combattante-class missile attack craft with Exocet AShM and a 76mm gun, while another two of this class are not serviceable; three German-built patrol craft each have a 76mm gun, while there are another eleven smaller patrol craft with four more on order. There are two Italian-built MCMV. A landing ship can accommodate five tanks and up to 220 men, while there is a survey ship and four tugs.

Naval aviation includes two Lynx helicopters that are no longer operational, and two AB-139.

In addition to a headquarters, there is a Western Command based on Apapa, an Eastern Command at Port Harcourt, and additional bases at Calabar and Warri.

NORWAY

Population: 4.9 million
Land Area: 125,379 square miles (322,600 sq.km.)
GDP: $418bn (£271.4bn), per capita $86,082 (£55,897)
Defence Exp: $5.77bn (£3.75bn)
Service Personnel: 26,450 active

ROYAL NORWEGIAN NAVY AND COAST GUARD

Although not an island, Norway has a long and heavily indented coastline with offshore islands, of which the most notable are Spitsbergen, a major archipelago to the north of Norway, and the Lofoten Islands off the north-west coast. The limited areas of agricultural land have meant that fishing is an important industry, augmented these days by offshore energy. Norway has also developed a substantial merchant fleet over many centuries. For many years Norway was united with Denmark, and a combined fleet was created in 1509. Over the next 200 years, the common fleet had the then high number of 15,000 personnel, of whom about two-thirds were estimated to have been Norwegian.

The modern Royal Norwegian Navy traces its beginnings to 1814, at the time when the country separated from Denmark and entered a union with Sweden, but by this time the size of the service had dwindled and Norway's share of the former combined fleet amounted to just seven brigs, a schooner-brig and eight schooners, as well as a number of small vessels, including gun barges. An admiralty was created the following year. Even though Norway remained united with Sweden until 1905, a separate navy was retained and, as nationalist sentiment increased, the fleet was enlarged to ensure Norwegian independence. By 1900, the fleet consisted of two British-built coastal defence ships, each of about 3,500 tons, about the size of a cruiser of the day, four monitors, three gunships, twelve larger gun-boats and sixteen small gunboats, as well as twenty-seven torpedo-boats. Personnel numbers stood at 816 officers and men.

Although the country remained neutral during the First World War, the armed forces were mobilised to ensure that neutrality was not infringed, but on the high seas the merchant marine took heavy losses from German U-boats and commerce raiders.

In 1939, on the eve of the outbreak of the Second World War in Europe, the RNN had four small, elderly battleships, none of which displaced more than 4,200 tons, and six small destroyers, and although half of these dated from the mid-1930s, their size was that of pre-WWI destroyers and they were all smaller than the sloop *Fridtjof Nansen*, 1,300 tons, used for fisheries protection. There were seventeen torpedo boats and seven small torpedo boats, also classed as patrol boats, nine small coastal submarines and four minelayers, as well as a number of small craft, mainly pre-1900. The country was once again expecting to be allowed to remain neutral and protested strongly both to the UK and to Germany when the *Altmark*, supply ship for the German *Panzerschiff Graf Spee*, was intercepted by the Royal Navy in early 1940.

The hopes for continued neutrality were dashed on 8 April 1940, when German forces invaded both Denmark and Norway. The invasion opened with the sinking of a guard ship, while in a battle off Narvik two elderly ships were torpedoed and sunk. Shore-based artillery damaged the German heavy cruiser *Blucher*, which was subsequently sunk, delaying the German invasion sufficiently for resistance to be organised and an Anglo-French force to be landed. It enabled the royal family and the government to seek refuge in the UK. As the Anglo-French expeditionary force was withdrawn to boost the crumbling defences in France, on 7 June, thirteen ships, five aircraft and 500 men escaped to the UK, where they continued to fight as part of the Royal Navy, with their numbers swelled by expatriate Norwegians and others who had escaped after the German invasion. By the time of the Normandy landings, there were ten Norwegian warships and 1,000 men present, but overall, during the war years, the Royal Norwegian Navy grew in size to fifty-eight ships and 7,500 men.

In 1944, the RNN gave up its own air arm to merge with that of the army to form the Royal Norwegian Air Force (*Kongelige Norske Luftforsvaret*).

Post-war, with the start of the Cold War and with Norway on the front-line, the country abandoned neutrality and became a member of NATO, thus qualifying for US military aid. By 1979, it had 9,000 personnel, while the fleet included five Oslo-class frigates and two Sleipner-class corvettes, as well as fifteen Type 207 coastal submarines, and forty fast missile-armed attack craft, while the country had developed its own AShM, the Penguin. The primary role was defined as coastal protection against invasion.

The end of the Cold War has seen a move to operating fewer but larger warships. Today the RNN has 3,750 personnel, of whom 1,450 are conscripts. There are five Fridjof Nansen-class guided missile destroyers, each with a 76mm gun, NSM AShM, ESSM VLS SAM, two twin ASTT, and accommodation for an NH-90 helicopter. There are six Ula-class conventional submarines, each with eight torpedo tubes. The guided missile patrol force is now down to six Skjold-class vessels, each with a 76mm gun, NSM AShM and Mistral SAM. There are six MCMV, of which three each

The Royal Norwegian Navy's destroyer *Fridjof Nansen*, the lead ship of a class of five well-armed destroyers. (Royal Norwegian Navy)

are Alta-class and Oksoy-class. There are twelve landing craft. The thirteen-strong logistics and support fleet consists of three auxiliaries, a royal yacht and two training vessels as well as a number of tugs.

The main base is at Bergen, but there are also bases at Ramsund and Trondenes.

Maritime-reconnaissance and shipboard helicopters are provided by the Royal Norwegian Air Force, which has a force of six P-3C Orion aircraft.

The Norwegian Coast Guard has fourteen patrol craft, of which eight have helicopter landing platforms. The main base is at Sortland.

OMAN

Population: 2.9 million
Land Area: 82,000 square miles (212,380 sq.km.)
GDP: $53.8bn (£34.9bn), per capita $18,513 (£12,021)
Defence Exp: $4.02bn (£2.61bn)
Service Personnel: 42,600 active, plus 4,400 paramilitary

ROYAL NAVY OF OMAN

The Royal Navy of Oman (RMO) was formed during the 1950s initially as a coastal defence force, although by the late 1970s, it had 900 personnel and the fleet included three corvettes, one of which was originally the Sultan's yacht but was fitted with a 40mm Bofors guns. At the time, there were also eleven British-built patrol craft and three smaller patrol boats as well as three landing craft.

Today, the RMO has 4,200 personnel. There are three British-built Khareef-class corvettes that have recently been added to the fleet but few details are known about these and whether they will replace the two Qahir Al Amwaj-class corvettes, both with Exocet AShM, two triple ASTT, Crotale SAM and a 76mm gun as well as a landing platform for helicopters. There are also three Dhofar-class fast patrol craft that also have Exocet AShM and a 76mm; plus another four patrol craft and four small patrol boats. The LST *Nasr el Bahr* can carry seven tanks and up to 240 troops, and also has a helicopter landing platform, while there are five landing craft. There are five auxiliaries.

Headquarters is at Widam A'Sahil and the main base is at Seeb, or Muaskar al Murtafaia.

QATAR

Population: 1.5 million
Land Area: 4,000 square miles (10,360 sq.km.)
GDP: $127bn (£82.5bn), per capita $83,880 (£54,467)
Defence Exp: $2.5bn (£1.6bn)
Service Personnel: 11,800 active

QATAR EMIRI NAVY

Qatar has developed a small navy, which collaborates with the other members of the Gulf Co-operation Council, Bahrain, Kuwait, Oman, Saudi Arabia and the UAE, and also has US support for training, while the armed forces also have British and American personnel as advisers, and there are a number of foreign, mainly Pakistani, personnel.

The Qatar Emiri Navy has grown since 1990, and today has 1,800 personnel, some of whom are Marine Police. There are four UK-built Barzan-class patrol craft, each with Exocet AShM and Mistral SAM as well as a 76mm gun, while four other patrol craft are operated by the Marine Police, as are another ten small patrol boats. There is an LCT. The main base is at Doha and there is another base at Halul Island.

PAKISTAN

Population: 184.8 million
Land Area: 310,403 square miles (803,944 sq.km.)
GDP: $172bn (£111.69bn), per capita $933 (£606)
Defence Exp: $5.2bn (£3.37bn)
Service Personnel: 617,000 active, plus 513,000 reserves

To describe Pakistan as a failed state on a par with Somalia or Yemen, and even Afghanistan once Allied forces leave, would be unfair and an exaggeration. Nevertheless, the writ of Islamabad does not run throughout the entire country and much of the north-west is wild and lawless and provides a training ground for Taliban and even Al-Qaeda terrorists. Pakistan has not been immune from terrorist attacks itself, and attempts by the Army to penetrate the more lawless areas have met with stiff resistance. On the other hand, there is the widely held belief that many army officers, especially in the intelligence services, have provided covert support for the Taliban and Al-Qaeda.

Given the country's geographical position, it is not surprising that the main emphasis is on the army, which accounts for about 90 per cent of all service personnel, and the Pakistani Air Force is next.

For most of the period since independence, the main defence priority has been the country's uneasy relationship with India and, while this seemed to improve in recent years, a major terrorist atrocity in Mumbai had its origins in groups sheltering within Pakistan. While India has tended to look at various sources for its equipment and has an increasing ability to provide its own, but has had Russia as its main supplier, Pakistan originally looked to the USA and France and then to Communist China. The country has been much slower to industrialise, and development of defence equipment has gone no further than a collaborative trainer aircraft with China.

Pakistan is now a nuclear-armed state, although all of its warships are conventionally powered. As with India, possession of nuclear weapons has changed the structure of Pakistan's defence, with a National Command Authority (NCA) created to oversee their development and deployment. The mainstay of Pakistan's nuclear deterrent lies in ballistic and tactical missile systems, but the Pakistan Air Force could also be tasked with delivery of these weapons. For the foreseeable future, the 'enemy' against which such weapons would be used appears to be India. That being so, it is all the more important that Pakistan has Western help in its own battle against extremists for the prospect of the country being taken over by extreme Islamists is not too incredible, and the thought of a nuclear-armed

A joint exercise between the Pakistan Navy and the United States Navy, with the former UK Amazon-class frigate, now Tariq-class, *Shah Jahan*, and the US guided missile cruiser USS *Mobile Bay* in the background. (USN)

extreme Islamic state is one that should concern strategists and policy-makers in the democracies.

PAKISTAN NAVY

The history of the Pakistan Navy prior to independence and partition of what had been the British Dominion of India on 15 August 1947 was, of course, that of India. On partition, an Armed Forces Reconstitution Committee divided the military assets of India between the two new states, with the Royal Pakistan Navy being given two frigates, two sloops, four minesweepers and two armed trawlers as well as four harbour launches. The initial personnel strength was just 358, which was insufficient for the warships provided.

Pakistan became a republic in 1956, but like India remained in the British Commonwealth. The Royal prefix was dropped and the service simply became the Pakistan Navy. Ships were no longer Her Majesty's Pakistani Ship (HMPS), but simply Pakistan Naval Ship (PNS). Royal Navy officers continued to serve on secondment and that same year, the Royal Navy transferred a cruiser and four destroyers to strengthen the Pakistan Navy. When the country joined the two anti-Communist alliances, the Baghdad Pact (later renamed the Central Treaty Organisation, CENTO, after a revolution in Iraq) and the South East Asia treaty Organisation (SEATO), the country began to benefit from the US Military Assistance Programme, and between 1956 and 1963, it received two destroyers, a submarine, eight coastal minesweepers and a fleet oiler.

Despite the unrest and outbreaks of fighting between India and Pakistan, the PN was not involved until the Indo-Pakistani War of 1965. Pakistani warships bombarded the Indian town of Dwarka.

A far higher level of intensity occurred when the two countries went to war again in late 1971. On 4 December, the IN attacked the PN's main base at Karachi, using three OSA-class missile boats using 'Styx' anti-shipping missiles, sinking two Pakistani ships and badly damaging another. A French-built submarine, the *Hangor*, sank the Indian frigate *Khukri* off Gujarat on 8 December, and also damaged the *Kirpan*. Later that same day, after dark, a further IN raid on Karachi was made by a missile boat and two frigates, sinking a Panamanian merchantman and damaging another while also damaging a Pakistani warship as well as the port's fuel storage depot. With East Pakistan blockaded by the IN, that part of the country took the opportunity to become the independent state of Bangladesh. Overall, the PN lost two destroyers, seven gunboats, three coastguard patrol craft, a minesweeper, and eighteen support vessels. Three merchantmen and ten small civilian ships were captured by the IN, while 1,900 personnel were lost and another 1,413 captured. The IN lost a frigate, another was damaged, and the PAF shot down an Alize ASW aircraft.

Re-equipping after the war was made more difficult by a US arms embargo that stopped sales to both India and Pakistan. Nevertheless, this eventually ended and in 1982, US arms supplies resumed. During the 1980s, the fleet doubled from eight to sixteen warships, including the loan of eight Brooke and Garcia-class frigates from the USN, which also supplied a depot ship. The situation reversed in the 1990s as the leased ships became due for return. The PN started to diversify its arms orders amongst other states. The PN was rapidly overwhelmed during the Kargil War in 1999.

By this time, the PN had developed a naval air arm, having operated Sikorsky H-19 helicopters since the late 1950s, and later adding Alouette III helicopters and two Fokker F-27 Friendships for maritime-reconnaissance and transport. Westland Lynx helicopters were acquired for shipboard use while four Atlantique and three P-3C Orion aircraft were also acquired for MR, but operated with mixed PN and PAF crews. In 1999, an Orion was lost in an accident and an Atlantique was shot down by the Indian Air Force on 10 August whilst flying over disputed territory.

Warships were deployed by both sides during the 2001-2002 naval stand-off. In 2004, the PN collaborated with the USN at the start of Operation Enduring Freedom, the invasion of Iraq. By this time, the PN had a massive modernisation of its frigate strength with the addition of the six surviving Amazon-class all-gas turbine-powered frigates from the Royal Navy.

Following the tsunami on 26 December 2004, the PN sent four ships to aid the inhabitants of the Maldives, Bangladesh and Sri Lanka. Relief operations were needed in Pakistan itself in 2010, when the country suffered severe flooding, with the PN rescuing more than 350,000 people.

Today, the PN has 22,000 personnel, including 1,400 marines and 2,000 maritime security agency paramilitary troops. The principal surface vessels are the six Tariq-class (ex-UK Amazon) guided missile frigates, each with two triple ASTT, a 114mm gun and accommodation for a Lynx or Alouette III helicopter. Four of the ships have Harpoon AShM and two have Aspide SAM launchers. Another three frigates are Chinese-built Sword-class, each with a 76mm gun, YJ-83 SAM, an octuple HQ-7 SAM and two triple ASTT as well as accommodation for a light helicopter. There are eight submarines, of which five are French supplied, including two Hashmai-class (French Agosta 70) and three Khalid-class (French Agosta 90B), all of which have four torpedo tubes, while the former can fire Harpoon AShM and the latter Exocet AShM. Special forces use three MG110 submarines, each with two torpedo tubes. A number of new submarines are on order from Communist China. There are ten offshore patrol craft, of which six – two each of the Zarrar, Jalalat and Jurrat-classes – are fitted with AShM. There are three French-built Munsif-class MCMV. There are four landing craft, and a fleet train of eleven vessels includes two replenishment tankers, with one having a Sea King and the other an Alouette III helicopter, as well as three other oilers, a survey ship and five tugs. There are five Sea King helicopters, which are being joined by Chinese-built Z-9s, and four Alouette III.

The main base is at Karachi and there are two smaller bases at Ormara and Gwadar.

There is a small paramilitary coastguard, with five patrol craft.

PANAMA

Population: 3.5 million
Land Area: 28,575 square miles (74,009 sq.km.), excluding Canal Zone
GDP: $27.2bn (£17.5bn), per capita $7,752 (£5,001)
Defence Exp: $230m (£148.4m)
Paramilitary Personnel: 12,000 active

PANAMA NATIONAL MARITIME SERVICE

Panama became independent from Spain in 1821 and briefly joined a federation of Colombia, Ecuador and Venezuela until 1830, before becoming a province of Colombia. When Colombia refused to allow the United States to construct a canal across the isthmus, Panama declared its independence in 1903. The Panama Canal opened in 1914, and brought great economic benefits to the country, although nationalist opinion demanded control of the Canal Zone and this has only been granted in recent years because of the importance of the canal to shipping generally but especially to the USN, cutting the passage between the Atlantic and the Pacific by 9,000 miles. By the outbreak of the Second World War, the canal was heavily defended by US forces.

Although Panama had a small paramilitary National Guard, it was not until 1964 that the National Navy (*Marina Nacional*) was formed, although initially known as the Department of Marine Operations. At first, coastal patrols were mounted using small craft, but during the late 1980s, two large patrol craft and two coastal patrol boats were added, with small patrol and harbour craft and three ex-USN amphibious landing ships. The large patrol craft were built in the UK and armed with two 20mm guns. Later, two US-built large patrol craft were added.

Subsequently, the service became known as the National Maritime Service and remains a paramilitary organisation with 600 personnel at present. It has the *Independencia*, a US Balsam-class patrol craft, as well as another seventeen smaller vessels, including the UK-built large patrol craft mentioned above. It has three bases, at Amador, Balboa and Colon.

PAPAU NEW GUINEA

Population: 6.9 million
Land Area: 183,590 square miles (461,693 sq.km.)
GDP: $9.1bn (£5.9bn), per capita $1,318 (£855)
Defence Exp: $43m (£27.9m)
Service Personnel: 3,100 active

PAPUA NEW GUINEA DEFENCE FORCE MARITIME ELEMENT

Administered by Australia until independence in 1975, a Papua New Guinea Defence Force was established to maintain internal security in 1973, just before independence. Personnel strength on independence totalled 3,750, plus 465 Australian personnel on secondment. While the force is small, it takes an estimated 4 per cent of GDP and attempts to reduce its size have been hampered by fierce resistance, including a mutiny by the Army element in 2001.

The Maritime Operations Element consists of four Pacific-class patrol boats and two Balikpapan-class landing craft. The service is small, with just

400 personnel, and there are doubts about training and professional standards, although help continues to be provided by Australia, New Zealand and the United States.

The main base is at Port Moresby, with other bases at Alotau, Kieta and Lombrun, on Manus Island.

PARAGUAY

Population: 6.5 million
Land Area: 157,047 square miles (406,630 sq.km.)
GDP: $16.9bn (£11bn), per capita $2,618 (£1,700)
Defence Exp: $142m (£92.2m)
Service Personnel: 10,650 active, plus 164,500 reserves and 14,800 paramilitary

PARAGUAYAN NAVY

Landlocked Paraguay does have access to the Atlantic Ocean through the Paraguay–Paraná Rivers and maintains a small navy, which even in recent years has been known for the age of some of its ships, which as late as 1990 included patrol craft commissioned as early as 1930. In 1939, there were just six ships, of which the two largest were 750 tons displacement, and the other four, small patrol craft, and these ships were still in commission during the late 1970s.

Today, the Paraguayan Navy has 1,950 personnel, of whom 850 are conscripts serving two years, and this includes 100 personnel engaged in naval aviation and 700 marines. There are twenty patrol and coastal craft, although the serviceability of the largest remains in doubt, while there are three landing craft and an auxiliary that doubles as a river transport. Most of the aircraft are Cessna light aircraft but there are also Ecureuil and Bell 47 helicopters. There are bases at Puerto Sajonia, near Asuncion, Bahia Negra and Cuidad Del Este.

PERU

Population: 29.5 million
Land Area: 496,093 square miles (1,249,048 sq.km.)
GDP: $152bn (£98bn), per capita $5,160 (£3,329)
Defence Exp: $1.11bn (£716m)
Service Personnel: 115,000 active, plus 188,000 reserves and 77,000 paramilitary, with 7,000 reserves

PERUVIAN NAVY

Peru gained independence from Spain in 1821, although fighting continued for another three years, during which the Peruvian Navy (*Marina de Guerra del Perú*, MGP) fought using captured Spanish ships. A new war broke out in 1828 between Colombia and Peru, which saw the MGP blockading the port of Guayaquil before the war ended in 1829. There were a number of other conflicts in the years that followed, including with Spain during the Chincha Islands War, 1866.

The outbreak of the War of the Pacific, 1879-1883, saw the service unprepared and weaker than the rival Chilean Navy. It suffered defeat at the Battle of Angamos, 1879, during which the Peruvian *Huascar*, which had been conducting hit-and-run raids, was forced to surrender after a valiant ninety-minute battle with the Chilean armoured ships *Almirante Cochrane* and *Blanco Encalada*. The remaining years of the nineteenth century saw the navy being rebuilt, but by 1900 it still had only a cruiser, a screw-driven steamer and ten smaller ships of doubtful value. It was not until 1907 that reconstruction gained pace, with the acquisition of two protected cruisers from the UK, followed in 1911 by two submarines from France. Border conflicts with Colombia in 1911 and 1932, and a war with Ecuador in 1941, saw Peruvian warships involved in minor engagements and also acting in support of ground forces. In 1920, the Naval Ministry was formed and the Naval Aviation Corps.

In 1939, the fleet consisted of the *Almirante Villar*, 1,550 tons and fitted with 4.4-inch guns, originally built for Russia in 1918, but was put into the Estonian fleet until transferred to Peru in 1933; a torpedo boat; four US-built submarines; seven river gunboats and a depot ship. While Peru remained neutral throughout most of the Second World War, not declaring war until 1945, patrols were maintained against possible incursions by the Imperial Japanese Navy.

Post-war, Peru joined the Organisation of American States in 1948 and became eligible for US military aid. Ships were also obtained from the UK and Italy, so that during the late 1970s, the fleet included two ex-British Ceylon-class cruisers and two ex-Dutch De Ruyter-class cruisers; two ex-British Daring-class destroyers, modified to operate helicopters, and two ex-US Fletcher-class destroyers; four Italian-built Lupo-class frigates and two ex-US Cannon-class frigates; ten submarines, including four German-built Type 209 and two ex-US Guppy submarines; sixteen patrol craft and four amphibious warfare vessels, as well as twenty-six auxiliaries and support ships. This period, continuing into the 1980s, saw the MGP enjoy considerable investment in new ships, but this had to be scaled back due to an economic crisis that led to the decommissioning of several ships and an inability to ensure adequate maintenance of those still in service. In more recent years, there has been some improvement, although the MGP is not back to its strength of the early 1980s.

Today, the MGP has 24,000 personnel, including 1,000 members of the Coast Guard and 800 involved in naval aviation, as well as 4,000 marines. The largest ship is the *Almirante Grau*, the surviving De Ruyter-class ship, with four twin 152mm guns and Otomat AShM; eight frigates include four Aguirre-class (Italian Lupo) with Otomat AShM, Aspide SAM, two triple ASTT, a 127mm gun, and accommodation for either a Bell 212 or a SH-3D Sea King helicopter, as well as four Carvajal-class (modified Lupo), with similar armament but Sea Sparrow SAM. Corvettes include six French-built Velarde-class with Exocet AShM and a 76mm gun. There are also six patrol craft and three smaller patrol boats. Amphibious vessels include four Paita-class able to accommodate 395 troops, while there are eleven logistics and support ships including a fleet oiler.

Aircraft include a maritime patrol squadron with Beech 200T, Fokker F-27 Friendship, SH-3D Sea King and Bell 212 aircraft and helicopters, while there is an An-32B 'Cline' transport flight.

The main base is at Callao, with further ocean bases at Talara, Paita and San Lorenzo Island, a lake base at Puno and two river bases at Puerto Maldonaldo and Iquitos.

PHILIPPINES

Population: 38.05 million
Land Area: 120,733 square miles (311,700 sq.km.)
GDP: $188bn (£122bn), per capita $2,009 (£1,304)
Defence Exp: $2.13bn (£1.38bn)
Service Personnel: 125,000 active, plus 131,000 reserves

PHILIPPINE NAVY

Although the Philippine Navy officially dates from 1898, armed ships were used by Filipino revolutionaries at the start of the uprising against Spanish colonial rule in 1896. Nevertheless, tensions with the United States after the fall of Manila led to a naval blockade and by 1901, the service was moribund and a period of American colonial rule began. During this period, Filipinos were eligible to serve in the United States Navy, while the Philippine Coast Guard was formed on the lines of the USCG. The Americans reopened the former Spanish colonial *Escuela Náutica de Manila*, which was renamed the Philippine Nautical School, adopting the methods of the United States Naval Academy at Annapolis. Despite this, legislation passed by the Philippine government in 1935 placed the emphasis on the army, largely comprised of reserve personnel, and the control of the country's waters was left to the Philippine Offshore Patrol with a few small patrol and torpedo boats, and security maintained by the US Asiatic Fleet, which was badly damaged in a Japanese attack following Pearl Harbor. Japanese forces invaded the Philippines and after fierce fighting by US troops, the country was occupied until liberated by US forces in 1944, with landings on Luzon and US victory in the Battle of Leyte Gulf.

The Offshore Patrol was revived in 1945 and strengthened in 1947, being renamed the Philippine Naval Patrol. Communist guerrilla activity began at about this time, leading to the formation of a Philippine Marine Battalion in 1950. The following year, the service was officially named as the Philippine Navy. Over the next decade, the service received new equipment and was organised for expansion, but during the 1970s, the service was neglected once again in the face of a renewed Communist guerrilla movement and its role was reduced to providing blockade and bombardment of Communist positions as well as transporting troops.

By the late 1970s, the Philippine Navy had 20,000 personnel, of whom 7,000 were marines. Its ships included a Savage-class frigate, which originated with the South Vietnamese Navy before being transferred to the Philippines, as well as four Casco-class frigates that had originally been US seaplane tenders before transfer to the US Coast Guard. Most of the remaining ships, including nine large patrol craft, have also been either USN or USCG craft.

The United States left its bases in the Philippines in 1992, including the major USN base at Subic Bay. This, and the country's proximity to potential flashpoints such as the Korean Peninsula and the Spatly Islands, led to moves to strengthen the Philippine Navy. In addition, the PN is involved in an annual series of bilateral maritime training exercises, Co-operation Afloat Readiness and Training (CARAT), between the US Navy and the armed forces of Singapore, Thailand, Malaysia, Indonesia, Brunei and Philippines.

Today, the PN has 24,000 personnel, of whom 8,300 are marines. There is a frigate, the *Rajah Humabon*, which has three 76mm guns, while there are thirteen offshore patrol craft of the Emilio Jacinto (ex-RN Peacock-class) and Miguel Malvar-classes, each with a 76mm gun, while the Rizal-class has two 76mm guns. There are another fifty-one smaller patrol boats. There are seven landing ships, two of which have helicopter landing platforms, as well as twenty-six landing craft. There are seven auxiliaries, including tankers.

Naval aviation consists of four Defender and two Cessna 177 aircraft, as well as four Bo-105 light helicopters.

The main bases are at Sangley Point on Cavite and at Cebu.

POLAND

Population: 38.05 million
Land Area: 120,733 square miles (311,700 sq.km.)
GDP: $463bn (£300.6bn), per capita $12,163 (£7,898)
Defence Exp: $8.35bn (£5.4bn)
Service Personnel: 100,000 active, plus 223,000 reserves

POLISH NAVY

While the Polish Navy traces its history back to Poland's independence from Russia in 1918 after the Russian Revolution, naval vessels were present on the country's rivers in the fifteenth century and, during the Thirteen Years' War, 1454-1466, these vessels ventured into the open sea. In the centuries that followed, privateers defeated the Teutonic Knights Navy and gave Poland permanent access to the Baltic. Other victories followed against both Russia and Sweden. Although a permanent navy was established in 1625, by 1650, this had virtually disappeared due to a lack of funding. Later attempts to re-establish a navy came to little and the partition of Poland in the late eighteenth century marked an end to attempts to establish Polish sea power, as Poland fell under Prussian control in the west and Russian in the east.

After independence, on 28 November 1918, a Polish Navy was formed, using six former German torpedo boats surrendered to the Royal Navy. An attempt was made during the 1920s and 1930s to expand and modernise the PN, but while plans included buying cruisers and destroyers, the Great Depression limited the funds available and, by 1939, the fleet included just four destroyers, a large minelayer and five submarines, as well as mine-sweepers and support craft. On 30 August 1939, three destroyers were ordered to withdraw to British ports rather than be destroyed, while the remaining ships did their best to harass the much stronger German Navy. Two submarines managed to escape later and the other three were interned in Sweden. All of the other ships were sunk.

A Polish Navy in exile was formed in the UK and provided with British ships, including two cruisers, seven destroyers and three submarines as well as smaller craft. This force fought as part of the Allied navies off Norway, in the North Sea and the Atlantic and the Mediterranean, and was present at the sinking of the German battleship *Bismarck* and the Normandy landings.

German forces were driven out of Poland only to be replaced by those of the Soviet Union. The Polish Navy was resurrected with headquarters in Gdansk in July 1945. Under Communist rule, as part of the Warsaw Pact's armed forces, the PN experienced a massive modernisation and expansion, including the creation of a marine force for amphibious operations. Soviet

175

ships were supplied, including a Kashin-class guided missile destroyer as well as other destroyers, thirteen submarines and seventeen missile patrol craft, while Polish shipyards built landing craft, minesweepers and supply ships.

Even before the collapse of the Soviet Union and the Warsaw Pact, there was considerable unrest within Poland and supplies of Soviet equipment ended in 1989, with Russian forces withdrawing the following year, with the Warsaw Pact folding in 1991. Poland was amongst the first of the former Eastern Bloc nations to join NATO, and Gdansk has become the main base for NATO submarines active in the Baltic. To ensure compatibility with NATO ships and equipment, Poland has been steadily adopting Western ships, such as two ex-USN Oliver Hazard Perry-class frigates, four Kobben-class submarines from Norway, which augmented a surviving Russian-built Kilo-class boat, while Super Seasprite helicopters have also been introduced.

While the defence budget remains limited, the Polish Navy has embarked on a modernisation programme running through to 2018. Nevertheless, this has been subjected to review and cancellations due to the lack of funds, and there are even fears that the fleet might shrink from its present size.

Currently, the PN has 8,000 personnel. The fleet includes two Pulaski-class (US Oliver Hazard Perry-class) frigates, each with a 76mm gun, Harpoon AShM and two triple torpedo tubes, as well as accommodation for two Super Seasprite helicopters. There are five submarines, of which four are Norwegian-supplied Sokol-class and the *Orzel*, a Russian 'Kilo'-class boat. A corvette, the *Kaszub*, has a 76mm gun and two twin torpedo tubes as well as Russian 'Grail' SAM. There are five patrol craft all fitted with one 76mm gun, AShM and SAM, of which three are Orkan-class (ex-East German Sassnitz-class) and two are Tarantul-class. There are twenty MCMW, of which three are Krogulec-class, four Mamry-class and thirteen Goplo-class. There is a substantial amphibious capability for the size of the PN, with five Lublin-class landing ships, each capable of carrying nine tanks and 135 troops, as well as three of the smaller Deba-class. There are thirty-three support ships, including oilers, survey ships and tugs.

In addition to the PN, the Border Guard includes a Maritime Border Guard with almost twenty patrol craft.

PORTUGAL

Population: 10.7 million
Land Area: 34,831 square miles (91,945 sq.km.)
GDP: $226bn (£146.75bn), per capita $21,099 (£13,700)
Defence Exp: $3.19bn (£2.1bn)
Service Personnel: 43,340 active, plus 210,900 reserves.

PORTUGUESE NAVY

The Portuguese Navy (*Marinha Portuguesa*) traces its history to the twelfth century, when in 1180, a Portuguese fleet defeated a Muslim fleet near Cape Espichel during the reign of the country's first king, Alfonso. During the next century, the main enemy remained the Moors, with the Portuguese ships sometimes acting alone, but often jointly with fleets from other Christian countries. Officially, the navy dates from 1312, while in 1317, King Denis decreed a permanent organisation.

The impetus for maintaining a navy came as Portuguese explorers started to provide the country with the beginnings of an empire, and this gathered pace in the fifteenth century with the conquest of Ceuta in Morocco in 1415, followed by Porto Santo in 1419, Madeira the following year and then the Azores in 1427. Brazil was discovered and claimed for Portugal in 1500. The Portuguese presence in the Indian Ocean brought further conflict with Muslim rulers, leading in 1509 to the Battle of Diu, and in 1542, the Portuguese engaged in battle with the Ottoman Empire in the Red Sea.

From 1580, Portugal united with Spain under King Philip, but continued to maintain its own ships and fought against the Barbary pirates in the Mediterranean, but the country's small population could not maintain its growing empire, much of which eventually passed to Spain when the country regained its independence in 1640. Before this, Portuguese ships were included in the Spanish Armada, which sailed against England in 1588. An innovation in 1618 was the first official marine unit, instead of using troops from army units, and this, the *Terço da Armada Real da Coroa de Portugal* (naval infantry of Portugal), was the origin of the current Portuguese Marines.

The break from Spain enabled Portugal to conclude peace agreements with Great Britain, France and the Netherlands, but the following year found the country at war with the Netherlands over the north-east of Brazil, while also retaking Angola in south-west Africa. The alliance with Great Britain was more enduring and in 1705, eight ships of the line were contributed to the British fleet fighting Spain at Gibraltar. In 1717, the Portuguese Navy defeated the Ottoman Navy at Matapan. Later in the eighteenth century, further operations with the Royal Navy included the campaign against the French in Egypt in 1798, and afterwards off Malta. Further operations against the French came during the Napoleonic Wars when Portugal was invaded, and the Royal Family evacuated to Brazil in a fleet that included eight ships of the line. Although the Royal Family returned, the rest of the century saw an unsettled political situation, which only began to be resolved towards the end of the century, with the period before the outbreak of the First World War seeing extensive modernisation with the commissioning of six cruisers, four torpedo boats and three destroyers, as well as thirteen gunships and the PN's first submarine.

The First World War saw the PN protecting Portuguese territorial waters and also escorting troopships to the African colonies as well as those heading towards France. Naval aviation began in 1917, with officers trained to fly in the UK and Fairey Campania seaplanes and Felixstowe flying boats introduced. The destroyer and submarine forces were increased and several merchantmen armed. There were few naval engagements involving the PN, but there was an encounter with a German U-boat, and a Portuguese minesweeper was sunk by a mine off Lisbon.

Post-war, new warships were commissioned, including two cruisers built in the UK, while in 1922, two naval officers flew across the South Atlantic.

Despite the difficult economic situation, the PN started to re-equip between 1933 and 1936, with new destroyers, frigates and submarines, although an ambitious plan for an aircraft carrier was cancelled. When the Second World War came, Portugal was officially neutral, although East Timor was occupied by Japanese forces between 1942 and 1945, while the USN based maritime-reconnaissance aircraft in the Azores.

Post-war, Portugal became a founding member of NATO, by which time the PN had seven frigates, three submarines, four patrol boats, sixteen minesweepers and three survey vessels. The Cold War era saw Portugal engaged in several colonial conflicts as India invaded Goa in December 1961, with the PN having just a sloop, against which the Indian Navy had frigates and an aircraft carrier. The sloop was sunk in a gun battle with two Indian frigates. At Diu, a small patrol boat was attacked by Indian aircraft. At this time, uprisings began in the colonies of Angola, Portuguese Guinea and Mozambique. These saw the PN and the Portuguese Marines heavily stretched, with operations in the Atlantic, Indian Ocean and at Macau, on the coast of mainland China. The fleet changed during this period with new corvettes bought from Germany and Spain.

The pace of operations eased with independence for most of the colonies, leaving Portugal with just the Azores and Madeira. The end of the Cold War also brought further reductions in the PN's strength, although there was still a demand for the service in humanitarian missions, and the independence of some of the colonies also required the PN and PM to assist by evacuating civilians.

The PN sent a logistics ship for the liberation of Kuwait in 1991, and during the wars that followed the break-up of Yugoslavia, a frigate with special forces aboard was deployed to the Adriatic in support of UN and NATO forces. When East Timor, which had been seized by Indonesia, became independent in 1999, two frigates were sent with troops to aid the country. In more recent years, the PN has joined NATO exercises in the Indian Ocean and also maintained anti-piracy patrols off Somalia.

Today, the PN has 10,540 personnel, including 1,430 marines. There are five guided missile frigates, of which three are Vasco da Gama-class, each with a single 100mm gun, Harpoon AShM, Sea Sparrow SAM, and two triple ASTT, as well as accommodation for two Super Lynx ASW helicopters, while the other frigates are two ex-Dutch Karel Doorman-class, with similar armament except that the Sea Sparrow are VLS and the gun is 76mm as well as having accommodation for a single Super Lynx. Of seven corvettes, three are Baptiste de Andrade-class with a 100mm gun, and four are Joao Coutinho-class with a 76mm gun, but all have a helicopter landing platform. There are four offshore patrol craft with helicopter landing platforms and a further fifteen patrol craft. There are two German Type 209 submarines, known as the Trident-class, with eight torpedo tubes. There is a single landing ship as one of the ten logistics, support and training craft – the replenishment tanker *Berrio*, ex-RFA (Royal Fleet Auxiliary) Rover-class – which has a landing platform capable of taking a medium helicopter. There are five Super Lynx helicopters in total while MR is provided by the air force using six P-3P Orions.

The main base is at Lisbon, with a naval air station at Montijo, but there are supporting bases at Leca de Palmeira and Portimao, respectively covering the northern and southern stretches of the coastline, as well as at Madeira and in the Azores at Ponta Delgada.

ROMANIA

Population: 21.2 million
Land Area: 91,961 square miles (237,428 sq.km.)
GDP: $162bn (£105.2bn), per capita $7,627 (£4,952)
Defence Exp: $2.14bn (£1.39bn)
Service Personnel: 71,745 active, plus 45,000 reserves

ROMANIAN NAVY

Romania as a united country dates from 1859, and the following year the predecessor of the Romanian Navy was formed as the Flotilla Corps. During the First World War, Romania supported the allies and post-war was granted the territories of Bessarabia and Transylvania. Immediately after the end of the war, four destroyers were purchased from Italy.

Between the wars, Romania became a dictatorship and allied herself with Germany. During the Second World War, the Romanian Navy was active in the Black Sea from 1941 to 1944, operating four destroyers, six torpedo boats and three submarines as well as five midget submarines, two minelayers and seven small torpedo boats. Two of the more modern destroyers were used to evacuate Axis personnel from the Crimea. Romania surrendered to the advancing Soviet forces in 1944, when the most modern ships were incorporated into the Soviet Black Sea Fleet, although returned in 1951 after Romania became a Communist republic in 1947. Territory was lost to neighbouring states, although Transylvania was later restored to Romania. The country took a more independent line from 1963 and adopted a neutral position when relations between the USSR and Communist China began to deteriorate. Despite this, during the late 1960s, new light forces were supplied by China, while the destroyers were withdrawn leaving the Romanian Navy with nothing larger than three corvettes, although later, three frigates were obtained.

The end of communism took longer in Romania than in the countries of the Warsaw Pact, but was followed by a switch to Western equipment.

Currently, the Romanian Navy has 7,345 personnel, although this is steadily reducing to about 6,800. The largest warships are three guided missile destroyers, including two Regele Ferdinand-class (ex-British Type 22) frigates, each with a 76mm gun rather than the 4.5-inch originally fitted, and capable of accommodating a Puma or two Alouette III helicopters, while the guided missile systems are being changed. The third destroyer is the *Marasesti*, with two twin 76mm guns, 'Styx' AShM, two triple ASTT and accommodation for two Alouette helicopters. There are two Tetal-class and two improved Tetal-class corvettes, with the former having two twin 76mm guns and two twin ASTT, while the latter have a 76mm gun, two twin ASTT and accommodation for an Alouette III helicopter. There are seventeen offshore patrol craft, of which six are used for river patrols. Out of ten MCMV, six are devoted to river operations. There is a minelayer with a capacity of 100 mines. There are twelve logistics and support ships, including five oilers and a survey vessel. There are three Puma helicopters and up to eight Alouette IIIs. There is a marine force, the 307th Marine Battalion (*Batalionul 307 Infanterie Marinã*), which acts as a light infantry and reconnaissance force.

The main base is at Constanta, but there is another important base on the Danube for the river flotilla.

RUSSIA

Population: 140.4 million
Land Area: 6,501,500 square miles (16,838,885 sq.km.)
GDP: $2.11tr (£1.37tr), per capita $10,602 (£6,884)
Defence Exp: $61.8bn (£40.13bn)
Service Personnel: 1,046,000 active, plus 20,000,000 reserves and 449,000 paramilitary

On the break-up of the Union of Soviet Socialist Republics, Russia, the core of the USSR, attempted to tie the other parts of the union to itself by forming the Commonwealth of Independent States (CIS), with varying degrees of success. The collapse of the USSR also brought problems for the military, with the widely spread armed forces having to be brought back to the mother country, which lacked the barracks and other facilities to accommodate them. Greater freedom and the growth of capitalism also meant that the artificial economy created by a closed society and dictator-ship could no longer work, and the cost of such vast armed forces had to be reduced. The sole exception to the homing of the armed forces has been the continuation of a naval base in the Ukraine, which is home to the Baltic Fleet, and dates from Tsarist times, and a base in Syria.

The result was that for more than a decade personnel numbers dropped and equipment serviceability also fell, with much equipment in store, and that still in service becoming increasingly obsolete. In recent years, however, there has been a determined effort to rebuild the armed forces and re-equip them. This was made possible by the rapidly rising price of oil and gas, but the worldwide recession of 2008-2009 saw energy prices fall and this will have made the continued redevelopment of Russia's military might more difficult, but only for a relatively brief period. A warning to the West and to the country's neighbours lies in the fact that the Russian armed forces total 1,046,000 personnel in a country with a population of just over 140 million; a ratio of almost 0.75 per cent against ratios of about 0.33 per cent, reducing to less than 0.25, in the UK, and 0.50 per cent in the United States. Many other countries in the West do far worse than the UK. The loss of its external commitments also means that

The Russian Navy's only operational aircraft carrier is the Kuznetsov-class *Orel*, seen here from above.

the Russian forces are far less stretched than those of the United States, which has a truly global role and on which far too much now depends.

Then there are twenty million personnel in the reserve forces, while those in the West have also been reduced and in some cases have all but disappeared, including those of the British Royal Navy and Royal Air Force.

The question is whether Russia needs this massive strength because of nervousness about the intentions of others, aggravated by the trauma of the German invasion in 1941, or whether it is intended to intimidate. The old Soviet Union has gone, but relationships with neighbouring states are uneasy. For the moment, Russia is using its control of gas supplies to inflict its will on its neighbours, but it is worth remembering that expansion beyond the country's borders started long before communism and the revolution. A policy objective of Vladimir Putin is the creation of a Eurasian Union, which he denies will be another Soviet Union, but it is intended to include all of the USSR's former republics.

RUSSIAN NAVY

Like many of the older navies, the Russian Navy can trace its origins back to early times when merchants or coastal communities would arm vessels for self-protection and, of course, provide the basis of a fleet in wartime. Russia was at the time far from united, and these 'pre-navies' included one established by the citizens of Novgorod on the Baltic and another by the Don Cossacks, who fought against the Ottoman Empire. As naval warfare at the time usually consisted of opposing fleets trying to board each other, it also meant that often soldiers were sent to sea.

The real beginning for the Russian Navy was its creation by Tsar Peter the Great. In 1696, during the Second Azov Campaign, the Russians used for the first time two warships, twenty-three galleys, 1,300 strugs (small boats that could be rowed or sailed) and four fireships against their Ottoman enemies. This led the Dumar (parliament) to pass a decree on 20 October of that year authorising the establishment of a regular navy. Peter the Great had earlier toured Western Europe, especially England and the Netherlands, and seen their navies. The first major ships for the new service were commissioned in 1700 at Voronezh, and included three ships of fifty-eight, seventy and eighty guns.

The initiative was only just in time, as in 1700, the Great Northern War began and lasted until 1721. The Russians created a Baltic Fleet and also the city of St Petersburg, which became the main base for the Baltic Fleet from 1703 to 1723, when the fleet moved to Kronstadt. The Russian Admiralty was established at St Petersburg. Other bases followed, including two in what is now Finland, but then part of Russia. The Black Sea Fleet was next, established during Catherine the Great's wars with Turkey, with its main base at Sevastapol. In 1770, at the Battle of Chesma, the Turkish fleet was destroyed and the Russians gained naval supremacy in the Aegean. A Danube Military Flotilla was created to protect the Danube estuary from the Turks.

An expedition to the Mediterranean in 1799 saw the Imperial Russian Navy create a Greek Republic of Seven Islands, and remove the French occupying forces from Corfu and the Ionian Islands, before blockading French bases in Italy at Genoa and Ancona, as well as attacking Rome and Naples. The Russians took control of the southern Adriatic, blockaded Dubrovnik and, in 1807, destroyed an Ottoman fleet at the Battle of Athos.

Despite these impressive achievements, ashore, Russia lagged behind the rest of Europe and especially in the application of steam power, then the emerging technology. It was not until 1826 that the first armed steamer was built, and during the Crimean War, 1853-1855, steamships were few. While naval mines were used for the first time, defeat followed and the Russians lost the right to maintain a Black Sea Fleet at the Treaty of Paris. New construction centred on steamships from this time onwards while, in 1877, torpedoes were launched in combat for the first time. The Russians also built the world's first icebreaker, the *Yermak*, and used it on two Arctic expeditions, in 1899 and 1901.

By this time, Russia had one of the world's strongest navies, with some sources believing it to have been the third largest. Nevertheless, the Russo-Japanese War of 1904-1905, in which mines were used for the first time, saw defeat at Port Arthur, losing much of the 1st Pacific Squadron to Japanese torpedo attack, while the naval Battle of Tsushima, 27-28 May 1905, saw the loss of all but three of the warships of the Baltic Fleet sent on a long voyage to the Far East.

A programme of naval construction followed, with the emphasis on building modern dreadnought-type battleships, but the Imperial Russian Navy was also entering a period of instability. As early as 1905, ratings aboard the battleship *Potemkin* in the Black Sea mutinied. In 1906, soldiers mutinied and took control of coastal fortifications around Helsinki. The First World War saw little action in the Baltic by the Russians due to heavy offensive mining, but the Black Sea Fleet, now rebuilt, mined the Bosporus and prevented the Ottoman Fleet from entering the Black Sea. Blank shots fired from the cruiser *Aurora* signalled the start of the October 1917 (the Russians still used the old calendar, so in the West this was November) Revolution. The loyal crews of the ships in the Baltic Fleet moved from Helsinki to Kronstadt, and many Black Sea Fleet ships moved to Bizerte in North Africa. Russia was then plunged into civil war, which the Bolshevik forces won, but then faced a rebellion by sailors at Kronstadt, in March 1921.

Post-revolution, what had become the Soviet Navy was accorded a low priority, and it was not until 1930, with the beginning of a programme of industrialisation, that a new shipbuilding programme commenced.

The Russian guided missile cruiser *Kerch* at Sevastopol, the major naval base in the Ukraine maintained by Russia since Tsarist times.

Nevertheless, this did not produce the expected results, and by the outbreak of war in Europe in 1939, the Soviet Navy had no modern battleships. There were just two elderly battleships in the Baltic Fleet, along with the even older cruiser *Aurora*, dating from 1903, although there were eleven large modern destroyers dating from the late 1930s and sometimes referred to as 'destroyer cruisers', as well as another two laid down in 1912 but only completed during the late 1920s, and ten First World War destroyers. There were also eight elderly torpedo boats and about twenty submarines, of which the most modern dated from 1930. In addition, there were ten patrol boats, a gunboat and eight minelayers, with the oldest dating from 1874. The Black Sea Fleet had an elderly battleship of the same class as those in the Baltic, four elderly cruisers, five destroyers, three torpedo boats, and sixteen relatively modern submarines, but only one minelayer. The Caspian Flotilla had three old and very small destroyers and two gunboats. Little information seems to be available on the China Squadron of that time, the precursor of the modern Pacific Fleet, but it mainly consisted of small craft.

The Soviet Union was not immediately involved in the Second World War, although in September 1939, it followed Germany into Poland after that country's resistance had been overcome, and Germany occupied the western part of the country while the USSR seized the east. This was followed in November by an attack on Finland in an attempt to seize at least part of that country's territory. The war lasted until 13 March 1940, ending with Finland ceding some territory after the overwhelming might of the Red Army had failed. The Soviet Navy was not involved in either of these ventures, but the 'Winter War' pushed Finland into the Axis camp and when Germany did attack the Soviet Union in June 1941, Russia's Baltic ports were closed by Finnish and German mines.

The German invasion prompted the United States and United Kingdom to provide military aid to the Soviet Union, but the hazardous Arctic convoys to Archangel and Murmansk were escorted mainly by the Royal Navy with no participation by the Soviet Navy. Despite the Royal Navy donating the battleship HMS *Royal Sovereign*, four submarines and eight of the Town-class destroyers received from the USN under Lend-Lease, the Soviet Navy did little. The one achievement of the Soviet Navy during the war was during the final months as the German *Kriegsmarine* and Merchant Navy attempted to rescue 1.5 million refugees – the biggest evacuation in maritime history – from the eastern provinces in the face of the advancing Red Army, but of these, at least 15,000 lives were lost, mainly in the sinking of just three ships, of which the worst loss of life was on the liner *Wilhelm Gustloff*, when more than 7,000 perished.

Once the war ended, the Cold War came quickly. At first, the Soviet Union continued to treat the service as the poor relation of the air forces and the army, but the Khrushchev-era changed this. The Soviet Navy was quick to exploit nuclear technology for its submarines and at its peak had some 500 submarines of all kinds, more than ten times the number of the German *Kriegsmarine* at the outset of the Second World War. A distinctive feature of many post-war Soviet warships was the widespread fitment of minelaying rails. The surface fleet expanded rapidly under Khrushchev, and set the pace in equipping its ships with a wide variety of missiles and, in particular, large AShM were placed on relatively small and fast missile boats. This aspect of Soviet Naval doctrine was also extended not just to the satellite states, members of the Warsaw Pact, but to the many Soviet client regimes around the world. Nuclear submarines were introduced and many of these were armed not just with ICBMs, as with American, British and French submarines, but with intermediate-range missiles as well, and, later, cruise missiles. The one area in which the Soviet Navy was slow to match the NATO allies was in naval aviation, for while maritime-reconnaissance had a high priority and Kamov helicopters appeared on many different classes of warship, the aircraft carrier was a late arrival. Heavy cruisers such as the Kirov and Slava-classes had considerable missile firepower.

Despite the build-up, the Soviet Navy did little during the Cuban Missile Crisis of 1962.

A somewhat dated image of an Osa-class missile-armed fast attack craft, almost certainly the most common vessel of this type and exported by both the former Soviet Union and Communist China to client states around the world.

By the late 1970s, the Soviet Navy had three Kiev-class aircraft carriers, described officially by the USSR as 'anti-submarine cruisers', while the two earlier Moskva-class helicopter cruisers could accommodate up to eighteen ASW and anti-ship helicopters. There were eight Kara-class, fourteen Kresta-class and four Kynda-class guided missile cruisers; while the twelve Sverdlov-class guided missile cruisers also had a command function. A strong destroyer force included nineteen Krivak, nineteen Kashin, four Kildin, eight Kanin and eight modified Kotin-class guided missile destroyers, while there were another nineteen Kotlin and thirty-six Skory-class destroyers. These ships were supported by 108 frigates of the Mirka, Petya, Riga and Kola-classes, as well as seventeen Nanuchka-class guided missile corvettes, and thirty Grisha and sixty-four Poti-class corvettes. There were also 128 ocean minesweepers. Submarines included (using NATO codenames for many of the classes) twenty-three 'Delta', thirty-four 'Yankee', eight 'Hotel' and twenty-two 'Golf'-class ICBM-carrying submarines; two 'Papa', fifteen 'Charlie', twenty-nine 'Echo II', sixteen 'Juliet', seven 'Whiskey Long-Bin' and three 'Whiskey Twin-Cylinder'-class cruise missile submarines; two 'Alfa', twenty-one 'Victor', thirteen 'November' and five 'Echo'-class attack submarines. There were also a number of conventionally-powered patrol submarines.

Not mentioned in these figures were the large number of 'trawlers', spy ships that had nothing to do with fishing but were equipped with monitoring equipment, and which shadowed the movements of NATO ships, especially during exercises.

The lack of aircraft carriers until the late 1970s was due to the problems of carrier operation not being fully understood, and when carriers were introduced, they depended on Sukhoi V/STOL aircraft incorporating lift jets, a technique discarded by the British in favour of the vectoring nozzle. Soviet technology was also found wanting with their nuclear submarines, which were far noisier and easier to detect than their Western equivalents, and sonar technology also lagged behind. Even so, the Soviet Typhoon-class submarines were, and remain, the world's largest.

The priority for the Soviet Navy during the Cold War was to stop reinforcements from the United States and Canada reaching Western Europe, while also targeting USN carrier battle groups while, as a final option, the ICBM and intermediate missile-carrying submarines would target Western centres of population and industry.

The arms build-up continued almost to the end of the Cold War, so that ships and armament were accorded a higher priority than support facilities. The collapse of the Soviet Union and the Warsaw Pact saw many ships brought home and the older ones hulked to provide much needed accommodation for servicemen who were brought back from first the satellite states as well as South-East Asia, and then from former Soviet territories that had declared independence. The two bases outside Russia that were retained were in the Ukraine at Sevastopol, where about 13,000 Russian naval personnel were stationed, and a base in Syria to support Russian ships in the Mediterranean.

A somewhat battered Oscar-class nuclear-powered submarine of the Russian Navy. Boats of this class have two torpedo tubes for heavy torpedoes and another four reserved for AShM.

The Kiev-class ships were retired early, while the Admiral Kuznetsov-class aircraft carrier *Varyag* was sold to Communist China, leaving just the *Admiral Kuznetsov* herself as the sole Russian aircraft carrier. Three-quarters of the former Soviet Naval Aviation's combat aircraft were withdrawn. Perhaps the decline of the service was most marked when the Oscar II-class submarine *Kursk* was lost during exercises with all hands aboard.

In recent years, with the Russian economy recovering on the back of oil and natural gas revenues, the Russian Navy has seen a revival in its fortunes allied with a determination to project power, including a visit to the Caribbean in 2008 for exercises with the Venezuelan Navy. While there is still a decline in the number of operational ships, new ships are being built and a Mistral-class LHD has been bought from France with plans to build at least two more in Russia. A policy objective of Vladimir Putin, elected president in 2012, is the creation of a Eurasian Union, which he denies will be another Soviet Union, but it is intended to include all of the USSR's former republics.

Today, the Russian Navy has 161,000 personnel, of whom 35,000 are involved in naval aviation and another 9,500 are marines and 2,000 are coastal defence troops. An unusual feature of the Russian Navy compared to many of the world's other leading navies is that ships spend a considerable amount of time in port. There is a single aircraft carrier, the Kuznetsov-class *Orel*, with a capacity of up to twenty-four V/STOL jet fighters, and almost twenty ASW and AEW helicopters, while the ship also

The bulky lines of this Delta III-class nuclear-powered submarine give away the fact that she carries up to sixteen intercontinental ballistic missiles.

A Victor III-class nuclear-powered attack submarine sometimes referred to as 'hunter-killer' or, in UK terms, 'fleet', submarines. These can fire surface-to-surface missiles as well as torpedoes.

has 'Shipwreck' AShM, VLS 'Gauntlet' SAM. There are two Orlan-class nuclear-powered guided missile cruisers, each with 'Shipwreck' AShM, VLS 'Gauntlet', 'Gecko' and 'Grumble' SAM, ten single ASTT, a twin 130mm gun, and two Ka-27 Helix helicopters. A Berkot-B-class guided missile cruiser has 'Stilex' AShM and ASW missiles, 'Goblet' and 'Gecko' SAM, two quintuple ASTT, and can accommodate a Ka-27 Helix helicopter, as well as three Atlanta-class with 'Sandbox' AShM, VLS 'Grumble' SAM, two quintuple ASTT, a twin 130mm gun, which can also accommodate a Ka-27 Helix helicopter. A force of eighteen guided missile destroyers includes eight Sarych-class, each with 'Sunburn' AShM, either 'Grizzly' or 'Gadfly' SAM, two twin ASTT, two twin 130mm guns and can accommodate a Ka-27 Helix helicopter; nine Fregat-class with 'Stilex' AShM/ ASW, VLS 'Gauntlet' SAM, two quadruple ASTT, two 100mm guns and can accommodate two Ka-27 Helix helicopters; and a Komsomolets-class guided missile destroyer with 'Switchblade' AShM, SA-N-1 SAM, five single ASTT and a twin 76mm gun. Frigates include three Jastreb-class with VLS 'Gauntlet' SAM, six single ASTT, a 100mm gun and a Ka-27 Helix helicopter; as well as two Gepard-class and three Burevestnik-class with 'Stilex' AShM/ASW, 'Gecko' SAM, two quadruple ASTT and either 76mm or 100mm guns. There are no fewer than seventy-eight patrol and coastal combatants, many of which are armed with AShM, and fifty MCMW. Amphibious warfare capability includes the new Mistral-class bought from France with at least two more planned; the Project 771, capable of carrying six tanks and 180 troops, as well as nineteen LST and thirteen landing craft.

Submarines include fourteen SSBN of the Kalmar and Delfin-classes based on the Delta series and three Akula or Typhoon-class, while the new Borey-class is entering service and will mean an extra four boats. There are also forty-five tactical submarines, including eight of the Antyey-class, which can carry AShM, ten Schuka-class, nine Victor-class derivatives, with all of these nuclear-powered; while fifteen Paltus and four Varshavyanka-class, derived from the Kilo-class, and the first of at least three Lada-class, are all conventionally-powered.

Naval aviation is divided into four Fleet Air Forces and includes shore-based Tu-22M 'Backfire' bombers; MiG-31 'Foxhound' and Su-27 and Su33 'Flanker' fighters; Be-12 'Mail', Il-142 'Bear' and Il-38 'May' maritime-reconnaissance aircraft; ship-based Ka-27 'Helix' and Mi-14 'Haze' ASW helicopters; as well as attack and rescue helicopters, transport and training aircraft.

The Russian Navy is based on a Northern Fleet, based on Severomorsk and Murmansk; Pacific Fleet, based on Vladivostok; Baltic Fleet based on Baltiysk and Kronstadt; and Black Sea Fleet, based on Sevastopol; as well as a Caspian Sea Flotilla based on Astrakhan.

SAUDI ARABIA

Population: 26.2 million
Land Area: 927,000 square miles (2,400,930 sq.km.)
GDP: $434bn (£281bn), per capita $16,531 (£10,734)
Defence Exp: $45.24bn (£29.37bn)
Service Personnel: 233,500 active, plus 15,500 paramilitary

ROYAL SAUDI NAVY

Saudi Arabia came into being in 1926 with the merger of the Nejd and Hejaz, but it was not until 1960 that the Royal Saudi Navy was formed. During the 1970s, expansion began in earnest with US assistance, with the intention that the Royal Saudi Navy should be a counter to the growing Imperial Iranian Navy, and this assistance intensified after the Iranian Revolution overthrew the Shah of Iran in 1979. At the time, the RSN had nine small corvettes, essentially Al Siddiq-class patrol boats built in the US, and four fast attack craft armed with missiles, while another three had torpedoes, and there were a large number of smaller patrol craft and four coastal minesweepers as well as eight British-built SRN-6 hovercraft. French assistance also followed the revolution and warships were purchased from the UK and France as well as the US, with a US defence contractor also designing and integrating the service's own integrated command, control and communications system.

As the country lacks a shipbuilding industry, it is dependent on foreign production of warships. Between 1981 and 1983, four Badr-class corvettes were bought from the US. Later, these were joined by French-built frigates and British-built MCMV.

The RSN supported the Coalition Forces liberating Kuwait from Iraqi control in 1991.

Today, the RSN has 13,500 personnel, of whom 3,000 are marines. Reports that the RSN would buy two British Type 45 destroyers have proved groundless and as the construction of these ships is drawing to a close, a US purchase seems more likely. There are three Al Riyadh-class (modified French La Fayette-class) guided missile destroyers, each with Exocet AShM, VLS Aster SAM, four single ASTT and a 76mm gun as well as accommodation for a Dauphin helicopter; four Medina-class (French F-2000) guided missile frigates each have Otomat AShM, Crotale SAM, for single ASTT, a 100mm gun and accommodation for a Dauphin helicopter; four Badr-class (US Tacoma-class) corvettes each have Harpoon AShM, two triple ASTT and a 76mm gun; nine Al Siddiq-class corvettes are

The Royal Saudi Navy's French-built guided missile frigate *Al Makkah*. (Royal Saudi Navy)

effectively large patrol craft but also have Harpoon AShM and a 76mm gun. There are seventeen smaller patrol boats. MCMV include three Al Jawf-class (UK Sandown-class) and four Addriyah-class (US MSC-322), while amphibious warfare ships are four LCU and four LCM. There are five fleet support ships, of which two are Boraida-class (modified French Durance-class) replenishment ships capable of accommodating two Dauphin or a single Super Puma helicopter.

Naval aviation, for which manpower details are not available, includes six Dauphin 2, fifteen AS-565 with anti-shipping missiles and thirteen Bell 406CS, with Super Puma helicopters for transport.

The HQ is at Riyadh, while, given the country's Red Sea and Gulf coastlines, there is a Western Fleet with its HQ at Jeddah and an Eastern Fleet with its HQ at Jubail, with additional bases at Damman, Al Wajh, Ras al Mishab and Ras al Ghar.

SENEGAL

Population: 12.9 million
Land Area: 76,104 square miles (197,109 sq.km.)
GDP: $12.8bn (£8.3bn), per capita $996 (£646)
Defence Exp: $199m (£129m)
Service Personnel: 13,620 active, plus 5,000 paramilitary

SENEGAL NAVY

The Senegal Navy was formed after independence from France in 1965. It is a coastal or brown water navy, and since the late 1970s, it has grown from 350 personnel to the present 950. The current fleet includes four patrol craft, of which one is ex-Danish and another ex-French, while another two are not operational. There are also five smaller patrol boats and two landing craft.

There are bases at Dakar and Casamance.

SERBIA

Population: 9.9 million
Land Area: 34,107 square miles (88,337 sq.km.)
GDP: $40.2bn (£26.1bn), per capita $4,081 (£2,650)
Defence Exp: $918m (£596m)
Service Personnel: 29,125 active, plus 50,171 reserves

SERBIAN ARMY RIVER FLOTILLA

Until 2006, Serbia was in union with Montenegro after the break-up of the former Republic of Yugoslavia. Prior to the First World War, the country had a long history of independence, although part of the Ottoman Empire for some 500 years.

The Serbian Army maintains a river flotilla on the River Danube, originally shared with Montenegro but retained by Serbia when the two states separated. There is no breakdown of the number of the Serbian Army's 12,260 serving personnel who are attached to the flotilla, but it has five small patrol craft, four MCMV and four logistics and support craft.

SEYCHELLES

Population: 84,600
Land Area: 140 square miles (404 sq.km.)
GDP: $935m (£607m), per capita $11,049 (£7,174)
Defence Exp: $87m (£56.5m)
Service Personnel: 200 active, plus 450 paramilitary

SEYCHELLES COAST GUARD

The Seychelles consists of more than a hundred small islands in the Indian Ocean. Its paramilitary Coast Guard has 200 personnel, including eighty marines. There are two patrol craft and three smaller patrol boats. A landing craft is operated by a civilian crew. The main base is at Port Victoria.

SIERRA LEONE

Population: 5.8 million
Land Area: 27,925 square miles (72,326 sq.km.)
GDP: $1.93bn (£1.25bn), per capita $331 (£215)
Defence Exp: $13m (£8.44m)
Service Personnel: 10,500 active

REPUBLIC OF SIERRA LEONE NAVY

This West African Republic became independent of the UK in 1961 and did not have armed forces until 1973, when these were founded with assistance from Sweden. From 1991 to 2002, the country suffered a prolonged civil war, following which the armed forces were reduced in size and then rebuilt, mainly with British assistance.

Today, the Republic of Sierra Leone Navy has about 200 personnel and a Shanghai III-type patrol boat, based at Freetown.

SINGAPORE

Population: 4.8 million
Land Area: 225 square miles (580 sq.km.)
GDP: $218bn (£141.5bn), per capita $45,071 (£29,266)
Defence Exp: $8.34bn (£5.4bn)
Service Personnel: 72,500 active, plus 312,500 reserves and 75,100 para-military, with 44,000 reserves

REPUBLIC OF SINGAPORE NAVY

As with neighbouring Malaysia, Singapore traces its naval history to the formation of the Straits Settlement Volunteer Naval Reserve (SSNVR) in the 1930s. The SSNVR was formed to assist the Royal Navy in the defence of Singapore, where a major naval base was being constructed. Singapore was regarded vital to the defence of the Malay Peninsula as a whole and the intention was to establish a 'Gibraltar of the East', with a naval base capable of supporting and sustaining a large fleet. An Acacia-class sloop was transferred from the Royal Navy to serve as a headquarters and drill ship.

Japan's aggressive intentions were already clear, so when the Second World War broke out in Europe, members of the SSNVR were mobilised and recruitment of local personnel intensified in order to support the hard-pressed Royal Navy. By the time Japan entered the war on 7 December 1941, the SSNVR had 1,450 men, including 400 men of the Royal Navy Malay Section, and the combined force became known officially as the Malay Navy. The sloop was sunk early in 1942 as Japanese forces swept south through Malaya to take Singapore, but personnel from the Malay Navy served with the Allies in the Indian and Pacific Oceans. By the time of Japanese surrender in August 1945, just 600 personnel had survived.

The Malay Navy was disbanded in 1947 due to financial constraints, but reactivated in December 1948 at the start of the Malayan Emergency as communist-backed guerrillas attempted to overthrow the colonial government. Its main role was coastal patrols to prevent supplies for the guerrillas being smuggled into Malaya by sea and also guarding the approaches to Singapore. In 1952, the Malay Navy became the Malayan Royal Naval Volunteer Reserve and was organised with a Singapore Division and a Federation (that is, Malayan) Division. A River-class frigate was transferred from the Royal Navy for training, and by 1950, the fleet also included an abandoned Japanese minelayer, an LST, a motor fishing vessel and a torpedo recovery vessel as well as seaward defence launches. A further change of title came in 1952, with the creation of the Royal Malayan Navy.

Preparations for independence centred around the creation of a Federation of Malaysia, with Singapore becoming one of its states in September 1963. The new Federation was strongly opposed by Indonesia and confrontation occurred with the Federation supported by the UK and Australia. During this period, the service was renamed the Royal Malaysian Navy, while Singapore was home to the Singapore Volunteer Force. Frictions within the Federation led to Singapore seceding in August 1965 to become an independent nation within the British Commonwealth, with the maritime element of the new state's armed forces becoming the Singapore Naval Volunteer Force in January 1966, with two wooden coastal vessels. It was soon renamed the People's Defence Force (Sea), and then became the

Despite the country's small size, the importance of sea-going trade has meant that Singapore has a blue water navy and includes ships as large as this Endurance-class LPD, capable of carrying eighteen tanks and 350 troops. (Republic of Singapore Navy)

Maritime Command in 1968. It was not until April 1975 that the country's armed forces were formally organised into three distinct services and the Republic of Singapore Navy was established.

Singapore regards itself as a maritime nation and acts as an entrepôt port for many countries, so from the outset the long-term aim was the creation of a blue water navy, although in the initial stages it was the protection of coastal waters that had to be given priority.

By the late 1970s, the RSN had 3,000 personnel and consisted of light and patrol forces. There were four German-built fast attack craft with Gabriel SSM, and six fast attack craft, of which the lead ship was built in the UK and the remaining five in Singapore. The fleet was completed with two coastal minesweepers and twelve landing craft.

The RSN obtained four submarines, known locally as the Challenger-class, from Sweden in 1995, for training and ASW exercises, and followed these in 2005 with an order for another two ex-Swedish submarines, which updated the force. These boats have all had to be extensively refitted and modified for tropical conditions.

Meanwhile, the RSN supported the Western Allies in their intervention in Iraq and has also conducted anti-piracy patrols in the Gulf of Aden and provided relief for the tsunami disaster in the Indian Ocean in December 2004. In addition, the RSN is involved in an annual series of bilateral maritime training exercises, Co-operation Afloat Readiness and Training (CARAT), between the US Navy and the armed forces of Singapore, Thailand, Malaysia, Indonesia, Brunei and Philippines.

Today, the RSN has grown to 9,000 personnel, of whom 1,000 are conscript and another 5,000 or so are active reservists. The RSN now has many Singapore-built ships, including frigates, corvettes and LPDs as well as smaller vessels. In addition to the six submarines mentioned above, with the Challenger-class each having four torpedo tubes and the Archer-class six, there are six Formidable-class frigates, each with Harpoon AShM, VLS Aster SAM, two triple ASTT, a 76mm gun and accommodation for an S-70B ASW helicopter; six Victory-class corvettes, each have Harpoon AShM, Barak SAM, two triple ASTT and a 76mm gun; eleven Fearless-class offshore patrol craft have Mistral SAM, and there are another eighteen patrol craft and four Bedok-class MCMV. A strong amphibious warfare force is centred on four Endurance-class LPDs, each with Mistral SAM, 76mm gun and capacity for two medium helicopters, as well as four landing craft, eighteen tanks and up to 350 troops, and which are supported by more than 100 landing craft. There is a single repair ship and a training vessel.

Helicopters are provided by a squadron of the RSAF, although mission crew are provided by the RSN.

The main base is at Changi, with a smaller base at Tuas.

Singapore also has strong coastal forces, typical of which are these three fast patrol craft. (Republic of Singapore Navy)

SLOVENIA

Population: 2 million
Land Area: 7,796 square miles (20,269 sq.km.)
GDP: $47bn (£30.5bn), per capita $23,216 (£15,075)
Defence Exp: $672m (£436.4m)
Service Personnel: 7,600 active, plus 1,700 reserves

SLOVENIAN ARMY MARITIME ELEMENT

Slovenia became independent on the break-up of Yugoslavia in 1991. Initially there was no provision for any kind of maritime force but a small diving unit was formed within the army, which had to use commercial sport diving equipment because of a UN arms embargo against the former Yugoslav republics. The embargo was not lifted until 1996, when an Israeli-built Super Dvora Mk2 patrol boat was purchased and this has since been complemented by a Russian Project 10412 patrol boat. There are just forty-seven personnel in the SAME, which is based at Koper.

SOMALIA/SOMALILAND

Population: 9.4 million
Land Area: 246,000 square miles (637,658 sq.km.)
GDP: Figures not available
Defence Exp: Figures not available
Service Personnel: Nil

SOMALILAND COAST GUARD

In 1960, the protectorate of British Somaliland and the Italian Trust Territory of Somalia became independent at the same time and amalgamated to form the present state. In 1991, a revolution split the country into fiefdoms dominated by rival clans and, despite United Nations attempts to restore peace and provide aid, largely with US and Italian assistance, to ward off the effects of a severe famine, the forces had to be withdrawn as the situation made a military presence virtually impossible. Somalia is now a failed state with as many as ten different groups fighting while extreme Islamic groups and pirates have used the country as a base.

Two statelets have broken away, Somaliland and Puntland, with the former maintaining the small Coast Guard, which uses small commercial speed boats as there is an arms embargo covering the whole of Somalia. There is a main base at Berbera, with smaller bases at Zeylac and Mait.

SOUTH AFRICA

Population: 50.5 million
Land Area: 471,445 square miles (1,224,254 sq.km.)
GDP: $362bn (£235.1bn), per capita $7,166 (£4,653)
Defence Exp: $4.15bn (£2.7bn)
Service Personnel: 62,082 active, plus 15,071 reserves

SOUTH AFRICAN NAVY

Although the South African Navy was originally formed as the South African Naval Service on 1 April 1922, earlier naval service was provided by the Natal Naval Volunteers, formed at Durban in 1885 and the Cape Naval Volunteers, formed at Cape Town in 1905. On 1 July 1933, these two volunteer groups were merged and became the South African Division of the Royal Naval Volunteer Reserve. When the South African Naval Service

(SANS) was formed in 1922, it had just three ships, a hydrographical survey vessel and two minesweeping trawlers. A change of name came in January 1940, when it became the Seaward Defence Force, and was primarily concerned with minesweeping and anti-submarine warfare. The Seaward Defence Force was merged with the South African RNVR in 1942 to create the South African Naval Forces (SANF).

It was not until 1951 that the SANF officially became the South African Navy, and the following year the prefix of His Majesty's South African Ship, HMSAS, was dropped and the title simply became South African Ship (SAS). The changes and the replacing of the crown in the cap badge by the Lion of Nassau in 1959 all took place before the country became a republic in 1961. On 27 April 1994, the SAN became part of the South African National Defence Force (SANDFG), along with the Army and South African Air Force.

Throughout most of the post-war period up to 1994, South Africa had applied a policy of apartheid, sometimes referred to as 'separate development', with a colour bar, and international isolation had followed. This kept the SAN short of modern warships and its mainstay was a small number of ex-British warships, including Second World War destroyers. Before sanctions were applied fully, three Rothesay-class frigates were

Although South Africa has operated ships as large as destroyers and frigates in the past, the country has never been a maritime power despite its important position on the Cape route, and today the largest ships are corvettes such as *Mendi*, seen here. (South African Navy)

obtained and in SAN service these became the President-class, while three Daphne-class submarines were obtained from France. Sanctions prevented the delivery of more modern submarines of the Agosta-class.

The end of apartheid saw ships with names connected to the era renamed with either geographical names or those of less controversial figures.

The size of the SAN has been reduced in recent years and the size of the fleet cut by a fifth, so that only one corvette and its supporting replenishment ship can be at sea at any one time. The SAN has not been able to afford to assist in the campaign against piracy off Somalia.

Today there are 6,244 personnel. There are four German-built Valour-class corvettes (MEKO A200), each with a 76mm gun, VLS SAM and upgraded Exocet AShM, as well as a Super Lynx helicopter. Three Heroine-class submarines have eight torpedo tubes each. Two Israeli-built offshore patrol boats and three German-built River-class MCMV complete the active fleet. There are six landing craft and a single oiler, which can accommodate a helicopter. A hydrographic vessel is used for Antarctic surveys and is operated by a private contractor, while there is also an ex-British survey ship. Bases include Durban, Port Elizabeth, Pretoria and Simon's Town.

SPAIN

Population: 45.3 million
Land Area: 194,945 square miles (504,747 sq.km.)
GDP: $1.39tr (£0.9tr), per capita $30,708 (£19,940)
Defence Exp: $10.2bn (£6.62bn)
Service Personnel: 142,212 active, plus 319,000 reserves

SPANISH NAVY

One of the oldest navies in the world, the Spanish Navy (*Armada Española*), maintains that it predates the unification that created modern Spain. The two main kingdoms, Aragon and Castile, which came together to form Spain, had powerful fleets as early as the thirteenth century, and over the next two centuries this enabled Aragon to control much of the Mediterranean, including not just the Balearic Islands, but also Sardinia, Sicily, southern Italy and even Athens. Castile seized Cadiz in 1232 and allied itself with France during the Hundred Years' War, while the Canary Islands were colonised in 1402. Further north, Spain acquired territory in the Low Countries.

The Spanish Navy provided support for the colonisation of a number of islands in the Caribbean in the sixteenth century, followed by present-day Mexico and Peru, as well as what is now Florida and Texas. In 1565, the

Seen entering the naval base at Ferrol, the new Spanish LHD *San Carlos* is unusual in that she can also be used to operate V/STOL aircraft such as the Harrier or, in future, the F-35B, with the upwards sweep to the flight deck. The Royal Australian Navy is buying two of these versatile ships. (Armada Española)

Philippines began to be settled as the Spanish East Indies. When Spain was united under the Hapsburgs, the service was organised as what amounted to a Mediterranean fleet of galleys, successor to the navy of Aragon, and as an Atlantic fleet of larger sailing ships for worldwide operation, successor to the Castilian navy, while the Kingdom of Granada was annexed in 1492. Territory was gained in North Africa, including Melilla, but eventually lost many of the gains to the expanding Ottoman Empire, which became a major foe for several decades until defeated at the Battle of Lepanto in 1571. The distinctions between the two fleets gradually disappeared in the seventeenth century as galleys became obsolete and a single large fleet of sailing ships was used in the Mediterranean and elsewhere.

During the 1570s, the Dutch uprising led to the creation of a strong Dutch fleet, which contested Spain's occupation of part of the Low Countries, and in 1607 the Battle of Gibraltar saw a Spanish fleet destroyed by a Dutch naval squadron. To counter the Dutch threat, Spain encouraged privateers to seize and attack Dutch merchantmen and fishing vessels. The conflicts with the Dutch drew England into war with Spain, and this and a dispute over the English crown led to an attempt to invade England in 1588, defeated by strong English resistance and bad weather. The half-century or so that followed saw Spain at the peak of its imperial glory, but a number of conflicts, including the Thirty Years' War, marked the start of a slow decline and by the late seventeenth century the country could no longer fund adequate naval forces. The Dutch took control of the smaller Caribbean islands, England took Jamaica and France the western areas of Santo Domingo, although Spain managed to retain Cuba and Puerto Rico.

The War of the Spanish Succession saw the Habsburgs replaced by the Bourbons, an offshoot of the ruling French royal family, but Spain lost many of its Mediterranean territories, including Minorca, as well as the Spanish Netherlands. Attempts to regain Sicily and Sardinia during the War of the Quadruple Alliance failed, prompting renewed interest in sea power and a ministry was established to oversee the reconstruction and organisation of both the navy and the army. Warship design became more standardised and the emphasis changed from escort duties to battle. A permanent force was established in Havana, with a major base and its own dockyard. By the 1750s, the Spanish Navy was third behind those of Great Britain and France. Allied with France during the Seven Years' War, 1756-1763, Spain retook Minorca but failed to regain Gibraltar.

Alliances changed again during the French Revolutionary Wars, 1792-1802, with Spain opposed to France, but changed again in 1796, when Spain allied herself with France against Great Britain, but was defeated at the Battle of Cape St Vincent in February 1797.

The Spanish Empire went into a steep decline during the nineteenth century, leading to reductions in the size of the fleet. In October 1805, the

The Spanish aircraft carrier *Principe de Asturias* is based on the design of the American Sea Control Ship, something never adopted by the USN itself. (Armada Española)

Battle of Trafalgar saw the Royal Navy defeat a larger combined Franco-Spanish fleet, with Spain losing nine of its fifteen ships participating in the battle. This was a small part of the overall fleet, which at the time stood at 150 ships, of which forty-five were ships of the line, but many were stuck in harbour, blockaded until Spain changed sides and joined the Anti-Napoleonic Coalition in 1808. In the years that followed, the Spanish Navy was once again neglected, while Spain had lost most of her colonies in the Americas. During the Spanish-American War in 1898, a Spanish fleet was defeated in the Battle of Manila Bay, the first major engagement of the war, and another was defeated in that same year in the Battle of Santiago de Cuba as it tried to break a powerful American blockade.

The twentieth century saw Spain on the sidelines for the first quarter, with neutrality during the First World War, and it was not until the Rif War in Morocco that any major operation was mounted, with the Alhucemas Landing in 1925, believed to be the first combined air and naval landing.

During the Spanish Civil War, 1936-1939, the navy, in common with the other services, was divided between the warring factions, but lost two coastal battleships, a heavy cruiser and a large destroyer, as well as a number of submarines and supply vessels.

Exhausted by the strain of the Spanish Civil War, Spain remained neutral during the Second World War. The country also lacked its current industrial base at the time and would have had difficulty meeting its armaments needs. In 1939, the Spanish navy had just a battleship, one heavy and five light cruisers, some twenty destroyers, many of which were very small and old, about eighteen submarines, and a number of gunboats, minelayers and torpedo boats. Some of the submarines and destroyers had been purchased from Italy.

Post-war, the country received military aid from the United States in return for the use of Spanish ports and air bases, but it was not until after the restoration of the monarchy in 1975 that Spain joined NATO. By this time the fleet included a light aircraft carrier, *Daedalo,* formerly the USS *Cabot*, an Independence-class ship of Second World War vintage used as a helicopter carrier, while other ex-USN ships included a Gearing and five Fletcher-class destroyers, while there were also three Spanish-built destroyers, five Baleares and eight F30-class guided missile frigates, an Audaz-class frigate and two remaining members of the Churruca-class, originally consisting of twenty-two ships, as well as two modernised Pizarro-class frigates and four Altrevida-class frigates. There were eleven conventional submarines, with four Agosta-class, four Daphne-class and three S30-class, ex-US Guppy-class. These ships were augmented by a number of patrol craft. The *Daedalo* was originally loaned to the *Armada Espanola* by the USN in 1967, but sold to Spain in 1973. The Baleares-class frigates were based on the USN's Knox-class and reflected a growing tendency for the AE to follow USN practice.

The *Alvaro de Bazan* is the first in a new class of Spanish destroyer. (Armada Española)

The *Daedalo* was replaced by a Spanish-built aircraft carrier in 1985, the *Principe de Asturias*, based on the American concept of a sea control ship that dated from 1974 and which is designed to operate with V/STOL aircraft and helicopters. Rather than use Sea Harriers, BAe/Boeing AV-8B Harris IIs were ordered for the ship, which can accommodate eight AV-8Bs and ten helicopters. The new Juan Carlos-class LHD, almost twice the tonnage of the *Asturias*, while primarily designed to carry helicopters and up to 700 troops, has a flight deck suitable for launching V/STOL aircraft and can be used to augment the *Asturias*. Overall, the AE has become structured primarily for amphibious warfare.

Today, the AE has 21,606 personnel, of whom 5,300 are marines and another 814 are involved in naval aviation. There is still just a single aircraft carrier, the *Principe de Asturias* but, as mentioned above, she is augmented by the LPH *Juan Carlos*, which in addition to up to eighteen aircraft and 700 troops, can also carry up to forty-six tanks, while there are another two Galicia-class LPD that can accommodate six Bell 212 or four Sea King helicopters, and 450 troops and up to thirty-three tanks. There are four Alvaro de Bazan guided missile destroyers, each with a 127mm gun, Harpoon AShM, VLS Sea Sparrow SAM, two twin ASTT, and capable of accommodating a Sea Hawk helicopter, as well as six Santa Maria-class guided missile frigates, each with a 76mm gun, Harpoon AShM, SAM and two triple ASTT, with accommodation for two Sea hawk helicopters. There are four Galerna-class conventional submarines, each with four torpedo tubes. A 'Maritime Action Force' consists of twenty-four patrol craft, of which three Alboran-class and three Meteoro-class have helicopter landing platforms, while there are seven MCMV. There are two Pizarro-class landing ships, one of which is in reserve, and fourteen landing craft. The AE has three replenishment ships, of which two carry helicopters, while the Maritime Action Force has twenty-nine logistics and support craft, of which two have ice-strengthened hulls for Antarctic research.

The submarine *Tramontana* is one of the Spanish Navy's small force of four Galerna-class conventional submarines. (Armada Española)

Aircraft include sixteen AV-8B Harrier IIs and II Plus, as well as a TAV-8B on loan from the USMC. While the Spanish Air Force has a maritime-reconnaissance force of six P-3 Orions, the AE also has seven of these aircraft as well eight Sea King and twelve Seas Hawk helicopters for ASW, and another three Sea Kings for AEW. There are also light aircraft and small helicopters for training and communications duties.

Although the HQ is in Madrid, the fleet HQ is at Rota, and other bases include El Ferrol, Cadiz, Cartagena, Mahon in Menorca and Porto Pi in Mallorca, as well as Las Palmas in the Canary Islands.

SRI LANKA

Population: 20.4 million
Land Area: 24,959 square miles (65,610 sq.km.)
GDP: $48.5bn (£31.5bn), per capita $2,376 (£1,542)
Defence Exp: $1.44bn (£935m)
Service Personnel: 160,900 active, with 5,500 reserves and 62,200 para-
   military, with 30,400 paramilitary reserves

SRI LANKAN NAVY

Originally known as Ceylon, the country became independent within the British Commonwealth in 1948, and became a republic in 1956, and adopted its present title in 1972.

The Sri Lankan Navy predates independence with the formation of the Ceylon Naval Volunteer Force in 1937, which was absorbed into the Royal Navy as the Ceylon Royal Naval Volunteer Reserve during the Second World War, when its operations included coastal patrols and mine-sweeping with converted trawlers. After independence, the service was revived as the Royal Ceylon Navy in 1950, using the Ceylon Royal Naval Volunteer Reserve as a cadre from which to expand. The first warship for the new navy was an Algerine-class minesweeper transferred from the Royal Navy. A second Algerine followed and the fleet was then augmented with patrol boats and tugs before two ex-Royal Canadian Navy River-class frigates were added. Progress was interrupted in 1962, when the Royal Ceylon Navy's commanding officer was relieved of his command as he was implicated in a planned coup. The rest of the decade saw the service neglected, with officer recruitment stopped and ships sold off or scrapped. The service had not been involved in the civil war between Tamils and Singhalese between 1956 and 1963, but when another insurrection followed in 1971, it was not able to help the government forces.

In 1972, the country became the Democratic Socialist Republic of Sri Lanka, and the Sri Lankan Navy started to be rebuilt, initially with the gift of Shershen-class torpedo boats from the Soviet Union and Shanghai-class fast gunboats from Communist China. These small craft enabled the SLN to control its coastal waters and prevent smuggling, especially of arms.

By the late 1970s, the SLN had a single River-class frigate and five ex-Chinese gunboats, but just a single Russian torpedo boat remained, although up to twenty small British-built patrol craft were also in service. Once again, the story was one of expansion followed by neglect, and when a fresh civil war broke out in the 1980s, the service was at first poorly equipped until new fast patrol boats were introduced, including locally-built Jayasagara-class offshore patrol craft. During the early 1990s, the SLN mounted its first amphibious operation landing troops. A Chetak helicopter was bought from India to be flown from new offshore patrol vessels. There were a number of engagements between the SLN and arms runners during the civil war until it ended in 2009.

Following the end of the civil war, some of the SLN's duties were passed to a new paramilitary coastguard.

Today, the SLN has 15,000 personnel, of whom 2,400 are reservists on recall. Despite claims to be a blue water navy, its largest ship is an ex-Indian Navy Sayura-class (Indian Vigraha-class) offshore patrol vessel, although this has a helicopter landing platform, while there are two Israeli-built patrol craft with Gabriel AShM and a 76mm gun each. The remaining 130 or so patrol craft are mainly small and include semi-inflatables. There is a landing ship capable of carrying two tanks and 250 troops, while there are also eight landing craft. Overall headquarters and Western Command HQT is at Colombo, while the main base is at Trincomalee, which is also the HQ for Eastern Command; Northern Command is at Kankesanthurai; Southern Command is at Galle; North Central Command is at Medawachiya.

SUDAN

Population: 43.2 million.
Land Area (including South Sudan): 967,500 square miles (2,530,430 sq.km.)
GDP: $66.1bn (£42.9bn), per capita $1,531 (£994)
Defence Exp: estimated at $696m (£452m)
Service Personnel: 109,300 active, plus 85,000 paramilitary

SUDANESE NAVY

Until 1958, the Sudan was administered jointly by the United Kingdom and Egypt. The country's history has been one of insurrection and in 2011 the population of the mainly Christian south voted to have an independent state, South Sudan, free from domination from the largely Islamic north. It is the north that retains the title of Sudan and has established armed forces.

The Sudanese Navy was not established until 1962, with a presence on both the Red Sea and the river Nile. By the late 1970s, the SN consisted mainly of patrol craft for coastal and riverine use, with fifteen vessels at most, plus a landing craft and two DUKW amphibious vehicles, and 600 personnel.

Today, the service has 1,300 personnel with two ex-Iranian large patrol craft, four Kurmuk-class river patrol craft, as many as ten other patrol boats, and a number of landing craft as well as two supply ships. The head-quarters is at Port Sudan with a base at Flamingo Bay on the Red Sea and another at Khartoum on the Nile.

SURINAM

Population: 524,345
Land Area: 70,087 square miles (161,875 sq.km.)
GDP: $3.4bn (£2.2bn), per capita $6,464 (£4,197)
Defence Exp: $49m (£31.8m)
Service Personnel: 1,840 active

SURINAMESE ARMY MARITIME WING

Surinam gained independence from the Netherlands in 1975, when the locally-raised Forces in Surinam (*Troepenmacht in Suriname*, TRIS), became the Surinamese Armed Forces (*Surinaamse Krijgsmacht*, SKM). On 25 February 1980, a group of junior officers mutinied and overthrew the government. A democratic government was elected in 1991, after which military assistance was provided by the Netherlands, the United States, Brazil and, in the late 1990s, the People's Republic of China.

Although army-based, the service includes a maritime wing with three coastal patrol craft and another five for river patrols. There are some 240 personnel and the base is at Paramaribo.

SWEDEN

Population: 9.3 million
Land Area: 173,620 square miles (449,792 sq.km.)
GDP: $450bn (£292bn), per capita $48,427 (£31,446)
Defence Exp: $5.54bn (£3.6bn)
Service Personnel: 21,070 active, plus 200,000 reserves

SWEDISH NAVY

Although from the ninth to the fourteenth centuries, a coastal protection force known as the *ledungen* existed, with compulsory service for coastal dwellers, this system gradually fell into disuse. Swedish warships were involved in the Battle of Oresund, 1427, against the Hanseatic League, along with Danish and Norwegian ships, as the three countries were combined in the Kalmar Union, but little is known about the organisation and whether the ships were true warships or armed merchantmen. Sweden left the Kalmar Union in 1521, and the then sovereign bought a number of ships from the Hanseatic port of Lubeck in 1522, which the Swedish Navy (*Marinen*) takes as the year of its formation, although at the time it was known as the Royal Swedish Navy (*Kungliga Flottan*). A seventeenth century ship, the *Vasa*, survives in preservation in Stockholm.

An 'Amphibious Corps' was founded in 1902 as well as a Coastal Artillery force, and at this time the current name of *Marinen* was first used. The doctrine of the service was to prevent hostile forces landing on Swedish territory.

Sweden remained neutral in both world wars. In 1939, it had eight coastal battleships, of which the largest were the Drottning Victoria-class of 7,000 tons and fitted with 11-inch guns. There were two cruisers, one of which, the *Gotland*, was designated as a 'cruiser aircraft carrier' with a long flight deck aft of the second funnel and which could accommodate eleven aircraft, while there was also a seaplane carrier and a minelayer, as well as thirty patrol boats. There were sixteen destroyers, ranging between 300 tons and 1,000 tons and dating from the First World War or earlier, seven torpedo boats, and sixteen coastal submarines. Support was provided by five depot ships.

Neutrality continued after the Second World War and the country did not join NATO when it was formed. Initially, the service structured itself around three light cruiser squadrons but the last of these was sold in 1970 and by the late 1970s it consisted largely of light forces and mine warfare. There were six frigates, fourteen coastal submarines, and sixty-two patrol boats, many of which were very small, as well as three minelayers, forty-five small or coastal minelayers, and thirty-six minesweepers. The service had been amongst the first navies to experiment with missiles, prompted by the recovery of a V-2 rocket in 1944. Anti-submarine warfare rockets were developed. Helicopters were first introduced in the late 1950s and early 1960s. In 1972 the government decided that it would no longer protect merchant shipping and started to move to a lighter fleet.

In 1998 the helicopters of all three Swedish armed forces were combined into a Helicopter Wing (*Helikopterflottij*). Coastal fortifications were abandoned in the 1990s and the Amphibious Corps organised as a Marine Corps, known as the *Amfibiekaren* (Swedish Amphibious Corps).

The Royal Swedish Navy has operated cruisers in the past, but today has concentrated on patrol craft such as those seen here. (Royal Swedish Navy)

In recent years, the service has participated in UN peacekeeping missions, reaching as far afield as the Lebanon.

Today, the *Marinen* has 3,423 personnel, of whom 1,083 are conscripts. There are five Visby-class corvettes, each of which has a helicopter landing platform and RBS-15 AShM, as well as four individual torpedo tubes. There are sixteen patrol craft of various types and six MCMV, but more than 160 landing craft. There are three Gotland-class and two Sodermanland-class coastal submarines, each of which has six torpedo tubes. There are seventeen logistics and support craft, including training vessels.

The main bases are at Karlskrona and Musko.

SWITZERLAND

Population: 7.6 million
Land Area: 15,941 square miles (41,310 sq.km.)
GDP: $526bn (£341.6bn), per capita $69,294 (£44,996)
Defence Exp: $4.57bn (£2.97bn)
Service Personnel: 25,620 active, plus 171,891 reserves

SWISS ARMY

Landlocked Switzerland does not have a navy but the army deploys seven small patrol craft for operations on lakes and rivers.

SYRIA

Population: 22.5 million
Land Area: 71,210 square miles (184,434 sq.km.)
GDP: $58.3bn (£37.9bn), per capita $2,592 (£1,683)
Defence Exp: $1.89bn (£1.23bn)
Service Personnel: 295,000 active, plus 314,000 reserves and 108,000 para-
  military

SYRIAN ARAB NAVY

Syria was part of the Ottoman Empire until the end of the First World War,
when the country was mandated to France. During the Second World
War, British and American troops invaded and overthrew the Vichy French
administration. Post-war, the country became independent, but did not
form a navy until 1950, initially using a few ex-French warships manned
by soldiers who had been sent to France for naval training.

Syria briefly united with Egypt in the United Arab Republic, but left in
1961, following a military *coup d'état.*

The Syrian Arab Navy's main experience of combat was during the
Yom Kippur War, 6-25 October 1973, which was also known as the Fourth
Arab-Israeli War. After the Israeli Navy sank five Syrian ships in a battle
off Latakia, the remainder spent the rest of the war in port. In addition to
its own fleet, since 1971, what was the Soviet Navy, now the Russian Navy,
has been allowed to use the port of Tartus, which, since 2008, has been
converted into a permanent Mediterranean base for Russian warships and

A more up to date image of an Osa-class missile-armed fast attack craft, in service
with the Syrian Arab Navy, and fitted with launchers for Termit AShM.

has been dredged to allow access for the largest Russian warships as well as having been completely refurbished and modernised. In return, Russia cancelled 75 per cent of Syria's outstanding Soviet-era debts for military equipment.

During the riots of 2011, the SAN was accused of shelling dissidents.

The Syrian Arab Navy has just 5,000 men, with a further 4,000 in reserve. The largest ships are two Petya-class corvettes, although sometimes described as frigates, transferred from the Soviet Union in 1975, each with a triple ASTT and RBU 2500 rockets as well as two twin 76mm guns. There are sixteen Osa-class patrol craft with SS-N-2C Styx AShM and six Tir-class with SS-N-8 AShM, five MCMV, three landing ships and a training vessel.

Naval aircraft are manned by the Syrian Arab Air Force and include thirteen Ka-28 and eleven Mi-14 helicopters.

The main base is at Latakia, but there are also bases at Tartus and Minet el-Beida.

TAIWAN

Population: 23 million
Land Area: 13,890 square miles (35,975 sq.km.)
GDP: $433bn (£281.2bn), per capita $18,853 (£12,242)
Defence Exp: $9.3bn (£6.0bn)
Service Personnel: 290,000 active, plus 1,657,000 reserves and 17,000 para-
  military

Taiwan is one of the potential flashpoints for a major war. The People's Republic of China has successfully and peacefully reclaimed Macao from Portugal and Hong Kong from the United Kingdom, the latter largely because part of the colony was only leased from China and when that ended, what was left would not have been viable. Since the establishment, or, depending on one's viewpoint, the continuation of the Republic of China on Taiwan in 1949, the People's Republic has not only laid claim to it, but underlined its claim by occasional bouts of artillery fire and fleet manoeuvres offshore.

During the Cold War, a NATO rapprochement with the People's Republic came earlier than with the USSR and the Warsaw Pact, largely to deprive the USSR of an ally. Western and especially United States attempts to court China have often been at the disadvantage of Taiwan. Arms supplies have depended to a great extent on the state of Sino-American relations. Officially, the USA has a 'Two Chinas' policy, but from time to time words appear not to be supported by actions. Fortunately, Taiwan has become

An artist's impression of the *Kang Ding*, the class leader of six guided missile frigates in the Republic of China, or Taiwanese, Navy. (ROCN)

one of the world's major shipbuilders, and can supply ships, or if one wants to use the modern term, platforms, but while the country's technological capabilities have also moved forward, it is still dependent on the West for the most sophisticated weaponry.

China's growing naval and industrial strength and the desire of many in Europe and the US to integrate the country's low-cost manufacturing base into that of American and European industry have meant that, increasingly, the People's Republic appears to have the whip hand. Yet, weakness over the future state of Taiwan could be misinterpreted and encourage the People's Republic to believe that an invasion would not be opposed by the countries that Taiwan should be able to regard as allies. This is how conflict starts.

REPUBLIC OF CHINA NAVY

Although the Republic of China Navy dates from the foundation of the new republic in Taiwan in 1949 after the Communist take-over of mainland China, it is also the inheritor of the old Republic of China Navy, dating from 1911, and itself the successor to the former Chinese Imperial Navy.

The period between the two world wars were difficult for the country as war lords took power in many parts of the country and the authority of the central government was weak. The ROCN, however, remained loyal to the Kuomintang government both at this time and during the civil war with the Communists. The period also saw Japanese forces invade Manchuria and as the ROCN was no match for the well-equipped and far larger Imperial Japanese Navy, most of the service's activities were confined to riverine operations. Post-war, with the surrender of Japan, a number of

US and surviving former warships were transferred to the ROCN. As the Communist advance continued, towards the end, efficiency and fighting effectiveness was compromised by defections to the Communists.

The Kuomintang government was forced to flee to Formosa, now Taiwan, Chinese islands, where a new government was established and the ROCN re-established itself. The ROCN played a major role in helping troops loyal to the government to escape to Taiwan and also mounted commando operations to stop attempts by the Communists to mount an invasion against Taiwan. For many years, commando raids were also mounted against Chinese artillery positions used to shell Taiwanese territory while the People's Republic maintained, and continues to maintain, its claim that Taiwan is an integral part of the PRC.

Given the 'Cold War' between the two countries, it is not surprising that the role of the Republic of China Navy has evolved into one of patrolling the Taiwan Strait to ensure that there are no Communist incursions, and also creating a fleet that would be able to counter any attempt by the People's Republic to enforce a blockade.

After the initial transfer of ex-Japanese and US ships to Taiwan to rebuild the Republic of China Navy, the next large influx of former US ships came in the early 1970s. By the end of the decade, the ROCN had 35,000 personnel on active service and 45,000 in reserve. The fleet consisted of nine ex-USN Gearing-class destroyers with another ship converted to a radar picket; eight Allen M Sumner-class destroyers modified to carry guided missiles and fitted with a helicopter landing platform; four Fletcher-class destroyers; ten APD 37 and APD 87 frigates, and two Guppy II-class submarines. There were also three Auk-class frigates, more than twenty light patrol craft as well as a similar number of minesweepers and twenty-four landing ships and twenty-six landing craft.

This is primarily a fleet designed to repel an invasion and break a blockade, a brown water navy rather than the blue water navy being created by the PRC, which nurtures global ambitions.

Today the ROCN has 45,000 personnel with another 67,000 in reserve, and includes 15,000 marines, although no figure is available for the number engaged in naval aviation. The largest ships are four Keelung-class (ex-USN Kidd-class) guided missile cruisers, each equipped with Harpoon AShM, SM-2MR SAM, ASROC and two 127mm guns, as well as accommodation for two helicopters. There are twenty-two frigates, of which eight are Cheng Kung-class, each with Hsiung Feng AShM, SM-1MR SAM, two triple ASTT, a 76mm gun and accommodation for two S-70 ASW helicopters; six modified Chin Yang-class, each with ASROC and Harpoon AShM, SM-1 MR SAM, two twin ASTT, a 127mm gun and room for a small helicopter such as the MD-500; six Kang Din, each with Hsiung Feng AShM, Sea Chapperal SAM, two triple ASTT, a 76mm gun and accommodation for an S-70 ASW helicopter; two Chin Yang-class, each with

A Kang Din-class frigate with a Sikorsky S-70C Seahawk helicopter. (ROCN)

ASROC and Harpoon AShM, two twin ASTT, a 127mm gun and room for a small helicopter such as the MD-500. These ships are augmented by no fewer than seventy-three patrol and coastal craft and twelve MCMV, a command ship, two LSD and thirteen landing ships, as well as 288 landing craft of all kinds. There are four conventional submarines, of which two are Hai Lung-class with six torpedo tubes and the other two are Hai Shih-class used for training and have ten torpedo tubes, six forward and four aft.

Naval aviation consists of three squadrons with the S-70 Seahawk ASW helicopter and two shore-based maritime patrol squadrons with thirty-two S-2E/G Tracker fixed-wing aircraft.

The ROCN is divided into three districts with an ASW HQ at Hualein, a Fleet HQ at Tsoying and a new East Coast Fleet. Other bases are at Makung, Keeling and Suo.

TANZANIA

Population: 45 million
Land Area: 361,800 square miles (939,706 sq.km.)
GDP: $27.7bn (£17.9bn), per capita $504 (£327)
Defence Exp: estimated at $247m (£160.4m)
Service Personnel: 27,000 active, with 80,000 reserves and 1,400 paramilitary

TANZANIA PEOPLE'S DEFENCE FORCE NAVAL COMMAND

Tanzania was formed on the federation of two former British colonies, Tanganyika and Zanzibar, in 1964. The new state quickly came under Communist Chinese influence and also sought military assistance from the then East Germany.

Part of an integrated defence force, today the Tanzania People's Defence Force Naval Command has about 1,000 personnel and has a fleet of eight Chinese-built patrol craft, two of which are fitted with torpedo tubes. There are also two landing craft. The main base is at Dar es Salaam, with a further base at Zanzibar and a base at Mwanza, on Lake Victoria.

THAILAND

Population: 68.1 million
Land Area: 198,250 square miles (519,083 sq.km.)
GDP: $314bn (£202.6bn), per capita $4,602 (£2,969)
Defence Exp: $4.81bn (£3.1bn)
Service Personnel: 305,860 active, with 200,000 reserves and 113,700 active paramilitary, with 45,000 reserves

The only other ship to follow the pattern of the USN's Sea Control Ship is the Thai aircraft carrier *Chakri Naruebet*, built in Spain but smaller than the *Asturias*. (Royal Thai Navy)

ROYAL THAI NAVY

Thailand, formerly Siam, was created out of the remains of the Khmer Empire, which was centred on present day Cambodia, and suffered numerous invasion attempts by first her neighbours, then the British and finally the French as the country fought off nineteenth century European colonialism. The Thai response was to create the Royal Siamese Army in 1852, which adopted the European model and, by 1887, had a series of commands. The Royal Siamese Navy followed in 1900. On the outbreak of the First World War, Thailand was allied to the Entente Powers (the Allies).

The country was renamed Thailand in 1939, by which time it was a military dictatorship. It was occupied by Japan from 1942 until the Japanese surrender in 1945.

Post-war, Thailand resumed her alliance with the Western Powers, contributing forces to the Korean War, becoming a member of the South East Asia Treaty Organisation, which also made the country eligible for US military aid, and also supporting the US in the Vietnam War in operations inside Laos. Nevertheless, the Communist victory in Vietnam emboldened Communist dissidents within the country and the 1970s saw an insurgency, which was mainly suppressed by the Royal Thai Army.

By the late 1970s, the Royal Thai Navy had six frigates, including a UK-built light frigate and five ex-USN ships, as well as four large patrol craft dating from the late 1930s, and about forty patrol craft; sixteen minesweepers and a depot ship; five landing ships and forty landing craft, as well as three training ships and a number of small auxiliaries.

The country already had naval aviation, albeit all shore-based for many years, with ASW S-2F Trackers and SAR Albatross amphibians. This force was modernised during the early 1990s with P-3 Orion maritime-reconnaissance aircraft, and later S-70 helicopters.

While SEATO was eventually wound down, never having had the standing structures and organisation of NATO, through its membership of the Association of South-East Asian Countries (ASEAN) Thailand has maintained military and naval collaboration with her neighbours. In addition, there is an annual series of bilateral maritime training exercises, Co-operation Afloat Readiness and Training (CARAT), between the US Navy and the armed forces of Singapore, Thailand, Malaysia, Indonesia, Brunei and the Philippines. The RTN became the first in South East Asia to operate an aircraft carrier, but financial difficulties delayed her entry into service.

Today, the RTN has almost 70,000 personnel, of whom 25,850 are conscripts, with 23,000 of the total being marines and 1,200 are engaged in naval aviation. The aircraft carrier *Chakri Naruebet* is based on the US concept of a sea control ship and was built in Spain, but is smaller than the *Asturias*; she can accommodate nine AV-8A Harrier and six S-70B helicopters. Frigates include two Naresuan-class, each with Harpoon AShM, VLS Sea

217

Sparrow SAM, two triple ASTT, a 127mm gun and accommodation for a Super Lynx helicopter; two Chao Phraya, each with 'Styx' AShM, CSA-N-2 SAM (which is believed to be non-operational), RBU 1200 rockets and a twin 100mm gun; two Kraburi-class, each have 'Styx' AShM, CSA-N-2 SAM, RBU 1200 rockets, a twin 100mm gun and a helicopter landing platform; two Phuttha Yotfa Chulalok, leased from the USN, each have Harpoon AShM/ASROC, two twin ASTT, one 127mm gun and accommodation for a Bell 212 helicopter; another older frigate has two triple ASTT and two 114mm guns while there is also a frigate with six single ASTT and three 76mm guns that is used for training, Corvettes include two Rattanakosin-class, each with Harpoon AShM, Aspide SAM, two triple ASTT and a 76mm gun; three Khamronsin-class, each with two triple ASTT and a 76mm gun; two Tapi-class, each with six single ASTT and a 76mm gun; three missile-armed patrol craft have Gabriel AShM and another three have Exocet AShM; fourteen patrol craft have a 76mm gun each; in addition there are more than fifty smaller patrol boats. Mine warfare is provided by twenty MCMV and a depot ship. There are six LSTs, two landing ships, and sixteen landing craft. There are fourteen auxiliaries and support ships, including a training vessel.

Naval aviation includes seven Harrier II and two twin-seat Harrier conversion trainers; eighteen Corsair IIs; three P-3A Orion MR aircraft; three F-27-200 MPA maritime patrol aircraft; nine Sentry reconnaissance

The Thai guided missile frigate *Naresuan* during a courtesy visit to Hong Kong. (Royal Thai Navy)

aircraft; and about a dozen light transports. Helicopters include four Super Lynx and six S-70B Seahawk; Bell 214ST and 212, and four S-76B.

The Fleet HQ is at Sattahip while the Mekong River Operating Unit is based at Nakhon Phanom.

TIMOR LESTE

See East Timor

TRINIDAD AND TOBAGO

Population: 1.3 million
Land Area: 1,980 square miles (5,128 sq.km.)
GDP: $21.2bn (£13.8bn), per capita $15,794 (£10,255)
Defence Exp: $172m (£111.7m)
Service Personnel: 4,063 active

TRINIDAD AND TOBAGO DEFENCE FORCE COAST GUARD

Formerly a British colony, Trinidad was a member of the Federation of the West Indies from 1958 until 1962, when it became completely independent and formed its own integrated Trinidad and Tobago Defence Force, of which the Coast Guard accounts for about a quarter of the personnel.

A fleet of about twenty small patrol craft is maintained, of which the largest is a former Royal Navy Island-class fisheries protection vessel, the *Nelson*, and there are another eighteen or nineteen small patrol craft. Plans for three British-built patrol craft were abandoned as the ships were too large for Trinidad's needs, and have been sold to Brazil. The bases are at Staubles Bay, Hart's Cut, Point Portin, Tobago and Galeota. There are 1,063 personnel.

TOGO

Population: 6.8 million
Land Area: 22,000 square miles (54,960 sq.km.)
GDP: $3.15bn (£2.04bn), per capita $464 (£301)
Defence Exp: estimated at $67m (£43.5m)
Service Personnel: 8,550 active, with 750 paramilitary

TOGOLESE NAVY

Although the former French colony of Togo became independent in 1960, it was not until 1976 that the Togolese Navy was established as a coastal force to cover some 35 miles of coastline and the port of Lomé, its only base. Today, it has about 200 personnel and two patrol boats with SS12M AShM.

TUNISIA

Population: 10.4 million
Land Area: 63,362 square miles (164,108 sq.km.)
GDP: $45.4bn (£29.5bn), per capita $4,376 (£2,841)
Defence Exp: $532m (£345m)
Service Personnel: 35,800 active, plus 12,000 paramilitary

TUNISIAN NAVY

Tunisia was a French protectorate from 1881 to 1956, and although an army was created on independence from Tunisian units in the French Army, a navy was not established until 1959. By the late 1970s, it was largely a coastal defence force with 2,500 men and its largest ship was the frigate *President Bourguiba*, a US Edsall-class destroyer escort transferred in 1973, while there were sixteen patrol craft and two coastal minesweepers.

Today, the Tunisian Navy has about 4,800 men. While the frigate *President Bourguiba* is believed to still exist, she is no longer in service. The largest warships are three La Galite-class (French Combattante III-class) fast attack craft, each armed with Exocet AShM and a 76mm gun, while there are also three French-built Bizerte-class attack craft with SS 12M AShM, as well as six German-built Albatros-class torpedo boats with two single tubes each. There are thirteen patrol boats, of which at least three have been supplied by Communist China. There are six support ships, including tankers.

The main base is at Bizerta, with other bases at Sfax and Kelibia.

TURKEY

Population: 75.7 million
Land Area: 301,302 square miles (780,579 sq.km.)
GDP: $737bn (£475.5bn), per capita $9,730 (£6,318)
Defence Exp: $10.5bn (£6.8bn)
Service Personnel: 510,600 active, plus 378,700 reserves

Once the power in the Middle East, Turkey is again emerging as a leading regional power, and that includes a stronger navy. This is the German-built Type 209 submarine *Preveze*, surfacing. (Turkish Navy)

Turkey has long been NATO's eastern bulwark, an especially important strategic role during the Cold War when the country had one of the world's largest armies. Large armed forces have traditionally also existed because of rivalry with neighbouring Greece, which has led to interruptions to arms supplies with both countries heavily dependent on US generosity for the supply of modern weapons. While the relationship with Greece has become much easier in recent years, the strong Islamic character of the current government, despite Turkey's twentieth century tradition of secularism, has created fresh tensions, not least with Israel, whose defence industry has enjoyed considerable business with Turkey in recent years.

The country now seems to be attempting to create a role for itself as the dominant military power in the Middle East. Friction with Israel over the Palestinian territories has injected a level of uncertainty. Turkey does not have the wealth to afford well-equipped armed forces, but it does have the manpower with substantial numbers of conscripts who serve fifteen months and remain in reserve until they reach the age of forty-one.

It remains to be seen whether the country reverts to the secular tradition introduced by Ataturk, or whether there could be a military takeover in the future, or even if a resurgent Russia drives Turkey closer to its NATO allies.

TURKISH NAVY

Turkey was at the heart of the Ottoman Empire, which at one time included much of Eastern Europe and the Arab world, and which engaged in battle with the fleets of the Christian Western European nations on a number of occasions. Even before the outbreak of the First World War, during which the country allied with the Central Powers, the Ottoman Empire was contracting under pressure from the West and from Arab nationalism. The Turkish fleet during the First World War was strengthened by a German battleship, the *Goeben*, and a heavy cruiser, *Breslau*, both of which transferred to the Turkish fleet and changed their names to *Sultan Jawus Selim* and *Midilli* respectively, but retained their German crews until put out of action.

Officially, the service claims to date from 1018, but the Ottoman Navy effectively ceased to exist on 3 November 1918, and all flags were struck on ships lying in the Golden Horn. The surviving warships of the Ottoman fleet were rendered inactive by the Allies under the Armistice of Mudros and were disarmed at the end of December. To provide what was effectively a coastguard service, a small number of smaller vessels were released from internment in late February 1919.

Civil war, known as the Turkish War of Independence, followed, and two gunboats that had returned to active service were placed under the command of the liberation forces led by Mustafa Kemal, now known as Kemal Ataturk, the founder of modern Turkey. Even before the Sultanate was abolished and a republic declared in 1923, a Directorate of Naval Affairs had been established in Ankara in mid-1920. Under Ataturk, a rapid programme of westernisation was started, but initially the fleet consisted of former Ottoman warships, including two cruisers, a destroyer, four gunboats, a minelayer, a yacht and a number of tugs and motor launches. A far larger force was out of service and needing repairs, including two battleships, two cruisers, four destroyers, six torpedo boats and a gunboat. A floating dock had to be bought from Germany, as several of the larger ships could not move under their own power and were even unseaworthy. The Treaty of Lausanne, 1923, called for the demilitarisation of the Turkish straits and resulted in the forces on the Bosporus and Sea of Mamara being transferred to Golcuk, which became the navy's main base, and by 1932 was actually building ships.

The attempts to reconstruct the navy were undermined by scandal and maladministration, resulting in a reorganisation in early 1928 with the navy put under the command of the Turkish General Staff. A Naval War College opened in late 1930.

The Montreaux Convention, 1936, finally recognised Turkish sovereignty over the Turkish Straits and the country was able to assign naval commands to the Bosporus and the Dardanelles.

By 1939, the Turkish Navy consisted of a pre-First World war battle-cruiser, the *Yavuz*, two small cruisers dating from the early years of the century, four destroyers, ten torpedo boats and gunboats, three elderly submarines with four under construction, and six minelayers. The country remained neutral throughout the Second World War. In 1949, there was a further reorganisation with the creation of a Turkish Naval Forces Command.

The start of the Cold War and the formation of the Warsaw Pact put Turkey on the frontline, defending southern Europe and, in February 1952, the country became a member of NATO. The armed forces became eligible for US military aid, although this was sometimes limited because of the continuing tension between Turkey and Greece. In 1961, four major subordinate commands were created: Turkish Fleet Command; Turkish Northern Sea Area Command; Turkish Southern Sea Area Command; and Turkish Naval Training Command.

By the late 1970s, the Turkish Navy had 45,000 personnel. The mainstays of the fleet were twelve destroyers, all ex-USN and mainly Fletcher or Gearing-class ships, as well as two Turkish-built Berk-class frigates. The most modern submarines were four German-built Type 209s, while another twelve were ex-USN boats. There were also thirteen guided missile patrol craft. A naval air arm was formed with Grumman Trackers, all shore-based, but in 1975 these were transferred to the air force, although the navy retained control over their deployment. Later, frigates capable of carrying helicopters were introduced.

Before this, in 1973, the Turkish Navy played a major role in the invasion of the northern coast of Cyprus, where a Turkish minority community was opposed to the mainly Greek government of the island. Little naval action was seen as the location of Cyprus meant that it was difficult for Hellenic naval forces to intervene.

Today, the Turkish Navy has 48,600 personnel, including 3,100 marines and 2,200 Coast Guard personnel and, of the total, 34,500 are conscripts. There are seventeen guided missiles frigates, including eight Gaziantep-class (ex-USN Oliver Hazard Perry-class), each with one 127mm gun, Harpoon AShM, SAM, and two triple ASTT, as well as accommodation for an AB-212 helicopter. There is also the *Muavenet*, a former US Knox-class frigate, with similar armament but without SAM. The remaining ships are all variants of the German MEKO 200 with a 127mm gun, Harpoon AShM, VLS Aspide SAM and two triple ASTT, as well as accommodation for an AB-212 helicopter. There are fifty-two patrol and coastal craft, including six Burak-class (French d'Estienne d'Orves), each with a single 100mm gun, Exocet AShM, Mistral SAM and four single ASTT. The smaller craft include twenty-six Gogan (German Lurssen-57), Kartal (German Jaguar) Kilic and Yildiz-class missile armed patrol craft with 76mm guns and generally fitted with Harpoon AShM except for the Kartal-class, which have

The German-built MEKO 200 frigate *Kemal Reis* of the Turkish Navy. (Turkish Navy)

Penguin AShM. There are also twenty smaller patrol craft. Conventional submarines include six Atilay-class (German Type 209/1200) with eight single torpedo tubes and eight Preveze-class (German Type 209/1400) also with eight single torpedo tubes, but capable of firing Harpoon AShM. Amphibious forces include the *Osman Gazi*, capable of carrying four landing craft, seventeen tanks and 980 troops; two Ertugrul-class (ex-US Terrebonne Parish-class) capable of carrying eighteen tanks and 400 troops, and two Sarucabey-class capable of carrying eleven tanks and 600 troops. There are also forty-one landing craft. The logistics and support fleet includes forty-nine ships, including two replenishment ships capable of carrying helicopters, and a number of smaller replenishment ships, training and survey vessels and tugs.

While the Bell and Agusta-Bell 212 predominates in naval aviation, there are also Sea Hawks and six CN-235s plus two ATR-72s for transport.

The main bases are at Golcuk, Erdek, Canakkale, Eregli, Bartin, Izmir, Istanbul, Antalya and Mersin.

TURKMENISTAN

Population: 5.2 million
Land Area: 188,400 square miles (491,072 sq.km.)
GDP: $19.9bn (£12.9bn), per capita $3,849 (£2,499)
Defence Exp: $261m (£169bn)
Service Personnel: 22,000 active

TURKEMNISTAN NAVY/COAST GUARD

Landlocked Turkmenistan's defences rest mainly on a small army and even smaller air force, but a combined navy and coastguard has been formed for patrols on the Caspian Sea, operating jointly with Russian and Kazakhstan forces. It currently has 500 personnel and six small patrol boats, with a small base at Turkmenbashy.

UGANDA

Population: 33.8 million
Land Area: 93,981 square miles (235,887 sq.km.)
GDP: $16.2bn (£10.5bn), per capita $479 (£311)
Defence Exp: $230m (£149m)
Service Personnel: 45,000 active, plus 1,800 paramilitary

UGANDA PEOPLE'S DEFENCE FORCE WATER WING

Sometimes referred to as the 'Marines', the Uganda People's Defence Force Water Wing is part of an integrated defence force, which is 98 per cent army. It has about 400 personnel and is based on Kampala, with a fleet of eight small riverine craft.

UKRAINE

Population: 45.4 million
Land Area: 231,990 square miles (582,750 sq.km.)
GDP: $137bn (£88.9bn), per capita $3,005 (£1,951)
Defence Exp: $1.43bn (£0.93bn)
Service Personnel: 129,925 active, plus 1,000,000 reserves

UKRAINIAN NAVAL FORCES

Although the current Ukrainian Navy dates from 1992, the country briefly seized its independence from Russia in 1917, during the Russian Revolution, and a substantial navy was established using ships from the former Imperial Russian Navy's Black Sea Fleet lying in Ukrainian ports. A naval ministry was established in Kiev. A period of civil unrest followed, during which the country became a socialist republic and in 1923, it became part of the newly formed Union of Soviet Socialist Republics (USSR).

History repeated itself to some extent when the current service was created officially in August 1992, using ships from the former Soviet Navy's Black Sea Fleet, but it was not until 1997 that Russia and the Ukraine formally divided the Black Sea Fleet's assets between the two countries. The title of Black Sea Fleet remained with the Russians, who were also allowed to retain bases in the Ukraine, including a naval flying school at Saki, a special forces base at Ochakiv and a fleet HQ at Sevastopol. Nevertheless, the period that followed was difficult for the Ukrainian fleet so that by 2009 only one frigate was capable of sustained operations. There have also been recurring differences between the two navies over bases and operating areas.

Today, the Ukrainian Naval Forces have 13,932 personnel, including 3,000 naval infantry and about 2,500 engaged in naval aviation, while the total includes 2,000 conscripts. There is just one frigate, the *Hetman Sagaidachny*, a former Russian Krivak III-class ship, with a 100mm gun, Osa-M SAM, two quadruple ASTT, and accommodation for a Ka-27 ASW helicopter. There are ten corvettes and coastal patrol ships, all of which have a 76mm gun, including three Grisha-class corvettes with Osa-M SAM and two twin ASTT, while four of the patrol craft have Styx AShM. There are five MCMV, two landing ships and a landing craft, as well as twenty-nine logistics and support ships, including training and yard craft.

Naval aviation includes ten Be-12 'Mail' flying boats, as well as sixteen transports, mainly of Antonov manufacture but with a Tu-134 and an Ilyushin Il-18. There are seventy-two ASW helicopters, including twenty-eight Ka-25 'Hormone' and forty-two Mi-14 'Haze'.

Operability of the ships and aircraft is uncertain, but the personnel numbers for naval aviation suggest that most aircraft are either in store or inactive.

UNITED ARAB EMIRATES

Population: 4.7 million
Land Area: 32,300 square miles (82,880 sq.km.)
GDP: $240bn (£156bn), per capita $50,910 (£33,058)
Defence Exp: $7.96bn (£5.16bn)
Service Personnel: 51,000

UNITED ARAB EMIRATES NAVY

In defence, as in other fields, the countries that make up the Emirates collaborate yet, on occasion, also maintain forces of their own. The present UAE armed forces date from 1976, when the Defence Union Forces merged with those of the UAE, which comprises Abu Dhabi, Dubai, Ras al-Khaimah, Fujairah, Ajman, Umm al-Quwain and Sharjah. Dubai is the most obvious example of a member state maintaining forces of its own.

Initially, the emphasis was on coastal forces and by the late 1970s, there were 600 personnel and seventeen patrol craft, many of them very small. Since that time, the UAEN has grown to about 2,500 personnel. A total of seven guided missile frigates of the Abu Dhabi and Baynunah-classes are entering service, starting in 2012 and continuing until 2014. Meanwhile, ships include German-built corvettes, including two Muray Job-class with Exocet AShM, Crotale SAM and a 76mm gun, which also have a helicopter landing platform; two Mubarraz-class with Exocet AShM, Mistral SAM and a 76mm gun; two Ben Yas-class with Exocet AShM and a 76mm gun. There are six British-built Ardhana-class patrol boats, two MCMV; twenty-eight landing craft and three harbour tugs.

Naval aviation includes two Learjets, seven Super Puma, seven Panther and four Alouette III helicopters.

The main base is at Abu Dhabi, but there are bases in each of the Emirates.

UNITED KINGDOM OF GREAT BRITAIN AND NORTHERN IRELAND

Population: 61.9 million
Land Area: 92,000 square miles (242,880 sq.km.)
GDP: $2.25tr (£1.46tr), per capita $36,427 (£26,538)
Defence Exp: $59.1bn (£37.8bn)
Service Personnel: 178,470 active, plus 82,274 reserves

Once the world's most powerful maritime nation with a navy maintained at twice the size of any navy into which it was likely to come into conflict, today's Royal Navy is a shadow of its former self. The United Kingdom has a long history of wide-ranging and almost global defence commitments, but from the late 1960s onwards, moves were made to refocus defence on Europe and the North Atlantic, with successive governments intent on withdrawing from 'east of Suez'. That this plan was short-sighted was soon exposed by first the Falklands campaign, which saw substantial forces deployed to the South Atlantic in 1982, and then later by the need to join the so-called 'Coalition' to liberate Kuwait from Iraqi occupation, and then

The Royal Navy LPD HMS *Albion* entering Portsmouth. She is one of two ships, with her sister *Bulwark*, but only one is actually in service at any one time. (BAE Systems)

by fresh commitments east of Suez in Afghanistan and Iraq, as well as anti-piracy patrols off the coast of Somalia.

Despite these commitments, Britain's armed forces were scaled back to what many regarded as dangerously low levels, placing considerable strain on service personnel, while also exposing serious deficiencies in equipment and defence procurement. The percentage of GNP devoted to defence halved between 1990 and 2010 to 2.2 per cent, and this continued a process that started even before the collapse of the Soviet Bloc, with an illusory chase at what was seen as the average proportion of GNP devoted to defence for NATO nations, and was followed by the decision to reap the so-called peace dividend immediately the Soviet Union broke up. A Labour government that took office in 1997 instigated a wide-ranging defence review that planned armed forces capable of mounting expeditionary warfare, with the capability of conducting two medium intensity conflicts at any one time. At no point were the resources made available for the armed forces to be able to meet this commitment and, despite having two medium intensity conflicts in Afghanistan and Iraq, force reductions continued. The British have extricated themselves from the latter operation, probably too early, although a Royal Navy team remained afterwards to complete the training of the new Iraqi Navy.

The situation has been made worse since 2000 by the introduction of 'Resource Based Accounting', which meant that the armed forces were charged rental for equipment and facilities being used, even though these had been paid for already. The net result of this is that equipment once withdrawn is either scrapped or sold as quickly as possible to reduce the strain on the defence budget. No longer does the Royal Navy have a number of recently withdrawn ships to fall back on as it was able to do at the time of the Falklands campaign, when one of the assault ships was brought hastily out of reserve.

One outcome has been that the Royal Navy has fallen behind that of France, the *Marine Nationale,* which pursues an active east of Suez policy, underlined by the opening of a new naval base in the Gulf.

The Royal Navy lost its Sea Harriers in 2006, leaving the Fleet without fighter defences, and this was followed in late 2010 by the withdrawal of the Joint Force Harrier, a force of combined RAF and Fleet Air Arm Harriers for ground attack duties. The aircraft carrier *Ark Royal* was withdrawn and the remaining Invincible-class carrier, *Illustrious*, re-designated as a helicopter carrier, taking turns with the helicopter carrier *Ocean*, with only one ship actually operational at any one time. Meanwhile, ashore, the fleet of new Nimrod MR4 maritime-reconnaissance aircraft operated by the RAF was scrapped without entering service, leaving the Royal Navy without reconnaissance to protect its only nuclear submarine base at Faslane on the Clyde, in the west of Scotland.

A Type 45 Daring-class air defence destroyer HMS *Dragon* entering Portsmouth. The 'dragon' symbol on her bows was only allowed for her first year in commission. (BAE Systems)

The folly of these decisions was highlighted by the decision in early 2011 to support the Libyan uprising against the Gaddafi regime, with the RAF having to use bases in Italy. When strikes were mounted from *Ocean*, it was by just four Army Air Corps Apache helicopters, and these had to fire their weapons while still offshore for fear of providing easy targets for Libyan surface-to-air missiles.

ROYAL NAVY AND ROYAL MARINES

The origins of the Royal Navy are hard to define. Its continuous history really dates from the restoration of the monarchy in 1660, and the reign of Charles II (1660-1685). Nevertheless, many maintain that the Royal Navy was established by King Alfred (871-901), some years after England became a united kingdom in 827, but still many centuries before the creation of the United Kingdom itself in 1800. At first, the ruling monarch maintained a fleet of ships on the same basis that he would also maintain a small army, effectively just a royal guard, at his own expense, while noblemen would also have their own small private armies. Ethelred II in the tenth century built a substantial fleet financed by a tax on land. After the Danish conquest in 1017, a substantial fleet was also maintained by taxation. This continued after the creation of the Saxon kingdom in 1042, and Edward the Confessor maintained a substantial fleet.

After the Norman Conquest in 1066, English maritime power dwindled, and English fleets, as elsewhere, were usually merchant ships taken up from trade, augmented at times by a few ships owned by the sovereign. Having absorbed the Norman invaders who took London as their capital, England effectively gained a substantial area of northern France and throughout the twelfth and thirteenth centuries, conflict with France was largely confined to the borders of this area. This changed in the following century when a French plan to invade England was foiled by Edward III's (1327-1377) victory, destroying the French fleet at the Battle of Sluys on 24 June 1340, when more than 200 French ships were sunk or captured. After this, once again the fighting was on French soil, although the south coast of England was raided by the French and by their allies, the Genoese and Castilians. During this period, the main role of the navy was to transport troops and supplies across the English Channel.

The Tudor period saw the creation of a permanent Navy Royal in the reign of Henry VIII (1509-1547). His younger daughter, Elizabeth I (1558-1603), reigned while naval warfare was waged against Spain and the small standing Navy Royal was augmented by the actions of privateers, effectively licensed pirates, against Spanish ships and colonies. Philip II of Spain despatched the Spanish Armada against England in 1588, partly to depose her as a protestant monarch and also to end her support for Dutch rebels. The intention was that the Armada would escort an invasion force from the Spanish Netherlands, but a rapid English response, poor planning and increasing bad weather led to the Armada being forced to flee north around Scotland and Ireland to get back to Spain, suffering heavy losses.

In the aftermath, English sea power was neglected. Increasingly bold raids by the Barbary Corsairs from North Africa encouraged Charles I (1625-1653) to strengthen the navy once again, but the extension of the tax, known as 'ship money', intended to raise funds from the inland counties was one of the underlying causes of the English Civil War, which ended with the creation of a 'Commonwealth' or republic, under first Oliver Cromwell (1653-1658) and then his son Richard (1658-1659). Ironically, the Commonwealth saw the rapid expansion of the navy as war arose with the Netherlands as a result of the Navigation Acts that dictated that all goods shipped to and from England or her colonies must be carried in English ships.

Initially, superior Dutch tactics in the First Anglo-Dutch War of 1652-1654 outweighed the larger English fleet. English tactics improved, and in 1653 a series of victories was achieved at Portland, the Gabbard and Scheveningen. Unlike earlier wars, the English fleet consisted of purpose-built warships owned by the state. Next, the Dutch reformed their navy, copying the English model, and after the restoration of the English monarchy, the Second Anglo-Dutch Naval War of 1665 to 1667 was more balanced, with an English victory at the Battle of Lowestoft in 1665, followed by a Dutch victory in the Four Days' Battle of 1666. The following year, financial difficulties saw the English fleet laid up, allowing the Dutch to raid the Medway and break into the Royal Dockyard at Chatham, capturing or destroying many of the largest English ships.

After rebuilding the fleet, Charles II and Louis XIV of France mounted the Third Anglo-Dutch War between 1672 and 1674, but despite the alliance, the combined fleet's battles with the Dutch were inconclusive and a French invasion overland was also fought off.

Nevertheless, the importance of maritime power was clear and under Samuel Pepys, as Chief Secretary to the Admiralty under both Charles II and James II (1685-1689), important reforms were made in the administration of the Royal Navy and in ensuring the professionalism of its officers and men. The financial support for what had become the Royal Navy were put on a sound permanent footing and a fleet of purpose-built warships replaced the earlier semi-professional Navy Royal with its reliance on ships taken up from trade.

During this period, a major task was to confront the Barbary Corsairs, and a series of defeats ensured that the North African pirate states concluded peace treaties, although these were not to be as permanent as many believed at the time. England joined the European coalition against King Louis XIV in the War of the Grand Alliance, from 1688 to 1697, by this time in alliance with the Netherlands. Defeat at Beachy Head in 1690 was followed by a victory at Barfleur-La Hogue the following year. The Act of Union in 1707 also saw the creation of the United Kingdom, incorporating Scotland and its three-ship navy.

By this time, the Royal Navy had become the largest in the world, but until 1805 was still liable to be matched or outnumbered when Britain's enemies entered alliances. Warship construction improved and so too did tactics and logistical support. Recruitment onto the lower deck remained a problem for many years, with Parliament permitting the enforced conscription of men by the press gangs that roamed ports and coastal areas seeking likely candidates, ideally with merchant navy or fishing experience.

The War of the Spanish Succession, 1702-1714, once again found the Royal Navy in alliance with the Dutch, fighting the combined navies of France and Spain. An enduring alliance with Portugal was concluded in 1703, and the following year Gibraltar, on the southernmost tip of the Iberian Peninsula, was seized, followed by the Mediterranean island of Minorca in 1708. Ashore, another ally was Austria. Initially, the Anglo-Dutch alliance suffered severe losses amongst its merchant shipping, but in 1702 the combined French and Spanish navies suffered a major defeat in the Battle of Vigo Bay, which was followed by further successes and the scuttling of the entire French Mediterranean Fleet at Toulon in 1707. Further afield, the Royal Navy participated in the seizure of the French colonies of Nova Scotia and Newfoundland. Warfare with Spain continued with the War of the Quadruple Alliance, with the Royal Navy countering Spain's attempts to regain Sicily and Sardinia, with a Spanish fleet defeated at Cape Passaro. Conflict continued into the 1720s, when Spain attempted to regain Gibraltar and Minorca.

Competition between the UK and Spain in the Caribbean culminated in what later became known as the War of Jenkins' Ear, 1739-1742, with the Royal Navy being defeated at the Battle of Cartagena de Indias in 1741, but the Kingdom of the Two Sicilies was forced to withdraw in 1742, when a small British squadron threatened to bombard Naples.

France once again became the enemy with the War of the Austrian Succession, 1744-1748, which, while naval operations were inconclusive, included significant engagements in the Indian Ocean for the first time and an abortive French attempt to invade England in 1744. This was soon followed by the Seven Years' War, 1755-1863, with amphibious operations ending the French presence in Canada and India. A further French attempt to invade England was ended by the Battle of Quiberon Bay, fought in 1759 during a gale. Even before the war ended, hostilities against Spain resumed in the Caribbean and in the Far East, with Britain capturing Havana in Cuba and the Spanish fleet based there, as well as Manila in the Philippines.

The American Revolution saw the colonists create a small 'Continental Navy' of frigates, but this was wiped out by the Royal Navy. The situation changed abruptly after France, Spain and the Netherlands supported the rebels, and while a number of battles in the Atlantic and Caribbean were indecisive, the supply lines for British forces were not secured and attempts to cut off the supply lines providing support for the rebels failed. In 1781, the Royal Navy failed to lift the French blockade stopping supplies from reaching Lord Cornwallis's army in the Battle of Chesapeake Bay and this led directly to his defeat in the Battle of Yorktown. The end of the American War of Independence did not bring peace, as the Royal Navy continued to engage the French in the Caribbean, although in 1782, it was the victor in the Battle of the Saintes, and later that year, relieved Gibraltar. At the same time, the Royal Navy also managed to prevent the French from re-establishing a presence in India.

Throughout this period, more naval personnel had died from diseases such as scurvy than enemy action. The Seven Years' War saw the Royal Navy with 184,899 conscripts, of whom 133,708 died of disease or went missing. A cure had been proposed, but it was not until the 1790s that the Sick and Hurt Board persuaded the Admiralty to supply fresh lemons as a remedy – a solution soon copied by other navies. Lemons were soon replaced by limes, which were more readily available from the Caribbean colonies, and which led to the American term for referring to Britons, initially sailors, but later the population as a whole, as 'Limeys'.

The French Revolution lent an extra edge to the seemingly eternal enmity between the UK and France. By this time, the Royal Navy was already the dominant force. An early victory during the Wars of the French Revolution, 1793-1801, was the brief occupation of the port of Toulouse in 1793, destroying or capturing most of the French Mediterranean Fleet, and this was followed by the Glorious First of June, 1794, while many smaller victories followed as the service sought to support the French Royalists regain control of France. Both Spain and the Netherlands joined France in the wars, but the victory over the Dutch at the Battle of Camperdown, 1797, and the surrender of the remaining Dutch ships after landings at Den Helder in 1799, ended Dutch participation. Mutinies at Spithead and the Nore in 1797 temporarily left the Channel and North Sea fleets unable to function, but were soon resolved, removing the danger of invasion. While Rear Admiral Sir Horatio Nelson's British Mediterranean Fleet failed to stop Napoleon Bonaparte's invasion of Egypt in 1798, the French fleet was destroyed at the Battle of the Nile on 1 August and this paved the way for the British to aid the Maltese in evicting the French from the islands the following year and the start of a long association with the island. A Baltic coalition supporting the French emerged, but Nelson forced the Danes into battle by sending frigates into their harbour at Copenhagen, and in the resulting battle in 1801, the country lost most of its fleet and negotiated terms with the British.

Amphibious operations enabled the Royal Navy to capture most of the French colonies in the Caribbean and the Dutch colonies at the Cape of

Good Hope, Ceylon (now Sri Lanka) and the Netherlands East Indies, only for most to be lost under the Peace of Amiens, 1802, with Great Britain allowed to keep only Ceylon and Trinidad. The peace was short-lived as fighting began again in 1803, with the start of the Napoleonic Wars, 1803-1815. Napoleon started to rebuild the French fleet and with the support of the Spanish fleet planned to invade England, but these plans were foiled by the Royal Navy, which then met the combined French and Spanish fleets at the Battle of Trafalgar on 21 October 1805. Almost two-thirds of the combined Franco-Spanish fleet was destroyed or captured, but at the cost of the life of Vice-Admiral Viscount Nelson after being shot on his flag-ship, HMS *Victory*, by a French sniper. While this did not mark the end of the war, which continued on land until 1815, it was the end of the war at sea and the start of more than a century of British naval dominance. The remaining French squadrons were hunted down and destroyed, while amphibious operations restored to the UK many of the colonies ceded at Amiens as well as the Indian Ocean island of Mauritius. Learning of French plans to seize the Danish Navy, the Royal Navy attacked using artillery rockets and destroyed the entire Danish fleet.

During this period, American ships were stopped and boarded by the Royal Navy, which also pressed British and American sailors from these ships into the Royal Navy, and this led to the Anglo-American Naval War, 1812-1814, with one of the American war aims being the acquisition of Canada. Most of the engagements were minor with the exception of the action on Lake Champlain, when an American flotilla defeated a British flotilla, and although the Americans did not gain Canada, they did never-theless secure their northern frontier. The Congress of Vienna, 1814-1815, confirmed British dominance over the Cape colonies and Ceylon, as well as Malta. Napoleon's return led to his defeat at Waterloo in 1815, but there were no further naval actions.

Up to this time, the Royal Navy had been organised in three colour squadrons, red, white and blue, with each flying its respective ensign. As Nelson had been 'Admiral of the White', one of the three colour squadrons of the Royal Navy, Trafalgar was the first battle fought under the white ensign. In 1854, the white ensign was reserved exclusively for warships, with the blue ensign reserved for the reserves and what became the Royal Fleet Auxiliary, the Royal Navy's civilian-manned fleet train, and the red ensign was for merchant ships and all other vessels not in state ownership.

In 1816, a combined British, American and Dutch naval squadron finally routed the Barbary pirates in North Africa, with a combined Anglo-Dutch squadron bombarding Algiers.

The period between 1816 and 1914 saw little significant action as the Royal Navy was by this time the world's dominant navy. It was a period of significant technological change, however, and the ships of 1900 bore little resemblance to those of 1800. The last major naval battle to be fought completely under sail was during the Greek War of Independence at Navarino in 1827, which arose by accident when one Allied ship's boat was fired on by mistake by Turkish troops who mistook it for a boarding party, one of the British ships fired a cannon shot, and a battle then ensued, in which most of the Turkish fleet was destroyed. Although many ships were steam-powered at the time of the Crimean War, the Royal Navy's main role was to help transport part of an Anglo-French expeditionary force of 60,000 men in 1853, while the following year, ships of the line were towed by tugs for the bombardment of Sevastopol.

The first steam-powered ship of the line appeared in 1848, and the changes in propulsion were accompanied by changes in armament. First, rifling of cannon improved accuracy, and then in 1821, the Frenchman, Paixhans, invented the explosive shell, which was so devastating against wooden hulls that there was a rush to introduce armoured plating, initially over the wooden hulls. By this time, despite its numerical strength, the Royal Navy was lagging behind in technology.

These developments could not conceal the fact that the Royal Navy spent most of the nineteenth century on the sidelines, a massive instrument of power. It could be argued that the policy of maintaining a fleet that was the equal of any two others was the ultimate deterrent, and the long Victorian era that was largely peaceful was the result of this policy. The American Civil War, 1861-1865, did not affect the Royal Navy directly. Changes were also taking place that would influence the deployment of the Royal Navy during the following century. The opening of the Suez Canal in 1869 meant that the Mediterranean, which had become something of a backwater following the battle of Lepanto in 1571, once again assumed strategic importance. Indeed, it became a vital thoroughfare, more important than at any time since the end of the crusades, or perhaps even the fall of the Roman Empire. Almost overnight, Gibraltar, Malta and Alexandria became important for the Royal Navy.

Torpedo development continued apace as it became clear that in most cases, warfare at sea would have opposing fleets further apart and that close contact with the enemy would no longer be desirable, or indeed possible as the range of naval artillery increased. Mine warfare also began to make an impact. At first, the Royal Navy had little success with breech-loading guns, and after some accidents returned to muzzle-loading. Captain Coles, one of the leading British advocates of the turret system, was allowed to design HMS *Captain*, a turret ship for the Royal Navy, but she proved to be top-heavy and capsized in the Atlantic on 7 September 1870. Nevertheless, the Admiralty's own design, HMS *Monarch*, proved to be more successful. It was not until HMS *Devastation* entered service in 1873 that the Royal Navy received its first major warship without sails and with turrets, and it served successfully with the fleet until the early twentieth century. A number of experimental designs entered service with the Royal

Navy during the late nineteenth century, including HMS *Agamemnon* in 1883, later followed by what was the largest warship of its day, HMS *Inflexible*, 11,000 tons, with four 16-inch muzzle-loaded guns, and capable of 15 knots. She saw action in 1882, when the Mediterranean Fleet bombarded Alexandria in Egypt after a number of Europeans had been massacred. One further significant invention was to appear before the century closed. This was the steam turbine, which its inventor Sir Charles Parsons had used when building a small fast craft, *Turbina*, which gatecrashed the Naval Review of 1897, demonstrating beyond all doubt its superiority over the reciprocating engines then in use.

In October 1904, Admiral Sir John Fisher became First Sea Lord, an aggressive, fighting admiral, who saw no point in low speeds or light-weight armaments. Fisher inherited a service that had lost its edge since its victories a hundred years or so earlier. The end result of his thinking was HMS *Dreadnought*, the ship that made all other battleships obsolete and subsequently all such vessels would be divided into 'pre-dreadnoughts' and 'dreadnoughts'. After the Imperial German Navy received its first dreadnought, the Nassau-class, in 1907, this proved to be the start of a desperate Anglo-German naval race.

Other changes were taking place. The fear of the torpedo boat had resulted in a countermeasure, the torpedo boat destroyer, and before the First World War broke out, this was already evolving into a larger category of escort vessel, the destroyer. Even though the Admiralty was conserva-tive, by 1900, the Royal Navy did have submarines, with five Holland-type boats in service. Nevertheless, much of the surface fleet was very old, and as late as 1890, the training cruiser was a sailing ship. Fisher incurred the wrath of many senior officers by bringing home from the various fleets, squadrons and overseas stations many older ships, which, in his words, 'could neither fight nor run away.' A sign of the future, however, as the start of the First World War approached, was that the Queen Elizabeth-class ships were oil-fired from the start, speeding refuelling.

When the First World War started, the bulk of the Royal Navy's strength was already gathered in home waters in what was termed the Grand Fleet, which lay ready to face the German High Seas Fleet. There were a number of indecisive clashes between elements of the two fleets, culminating in the Battle of Jutland in 1916, judged a tactical victory for the Germans who inflicted heavier losses on their opponents, but a strategic victory for the Royal Navy in that it continued to dominate the seas and was eventually able to apply an effective naval blockade of German ports. A major weak-ness proved to be the British approach to the design of battleships and, even more so, battlecruisers, with the emphasis on speed and firepower rather than strength under fire. While the Royal Navy hunted down the handful of German surface raiders at large, the failure to introduce a convoy system until late in the war left merchant shipping at the mercy of an effective German submarine campaign, even though hampered at first by the imposition of prize rules. During the Dardanelles Campaign against the Ottoman Empire in 1915, the Royal Navy suffered serious losses during a failed attempt to break through the system of minefields and shore batteries defending the straits, and these have been allowed to overlook the successes of British submariners who managed to penetrate the Dardanelles and attack Turkish shipping and land targets in the Sea of Marmara and the Bosporus. The successes of British submariners in the Baltic against German shipping were brought to a halt by the Russian Revolution, which denied them the bases they needed.

The Royal Naval Air Service was given the task of providing air defence of the UK, and also mounted attacks on the German airship sheds from seaplane carriers, which were largely packet steamers taken up from trade. They also attacked German Zeppelin airships, over Belgium as well as England, and RNAS semi-rigid airships acted as escorts for coastal convoys. Nevertheless, by the time the world's first aircraft carrier, the converted light battlecruiser HMS *Furious*, was ready for service and attacked the German airship sheds at Tondern on 19 July 1918, the RNAS, along with the Royal Flying Corps, had been absorbed into the new Royal Air Force, formed on 1 April 1918. Thus, the Royal Navy ended the war with two aircraft carriers, with two more following in 1922, but no aircraft of its own other than those flown from battleships and cruisers.

The Washington Naval Treaty of 1922 ended any pretence that the Royal Navy could be the world's largest and most powerful, setting limits that ensured that it could be no larger than the United States Navy with a maximum of 525,000 tons of warships apiece. There were also limitations on the size of the various categories of warships, while British governments seemed anxious to tighten these standards still further. A low point was the Invergordon Mutiny in 1932, prompted by plans for a 25 per cent pay cut, which was eventually reduced to 10 per cent. At this time, senior officers could still be sent ashore on half pay until a posting became available. An arms race began in the mid-1930s, and by 1938, the Washington Treaty limits were being ignored, as were those of the two London naval treaties. Although two 16-inch main armament battleships were commissioned in the late 1920s, new construction of the King George V-class was for 14-inch main armament, making them undergunned. On the plus side, greater attention was paid to anti-aircraft armament and older battleships and cruisers being extensively modernised, although as war drew closer, not all of this work could be completed. The Royal Navy led the world in the development of ASDIC, now known as sonar, as an effective submarine detection system, and in the development of ship-borne radar, although again many major warships still did not have this on the outbreak of war. A new warship commissioned in 1938 was the aircraft carrier HMS *Ark Royal*, although the desire to have two hangar decks and a large complement of aircraft reduced her armoured protection dangerously. More promising was the start of work on four, later increased to six, large, fast, armoured aircraft carriers, starting with HMS *Illustrious*, initially intended to replace the original four aircraft carriers, but these were retained as war became increasingly likely. The decision was taken to return the Fleet Air Arm to Admiralty control in 1937, but this did not take effect until spring 1939. The RAF retained responsibility for shore-based maritime-reconnaissance.

Meanwhile, a European war was narrowly avoided in 1935, after Italy invaded Abyssinia, present-day Ethiopia, but French resistance to action meant that the opportunity to counter Italy's ambitions at an early stage was missed. Nevertheless, plans laid at this time included one for an attack on the Italian fleet at Taranto.

On the eve of the Second World War in 1939, the RN had twelve battleships, of which only two dated from after the First World War, and another nine under construction; three battlecruisers; twenty heavy cruisers and another two being built; forty-three light cruisers and seventeen building; seven aircraft carriers and another seven on order or under construction; three seaplane carriers; nineteen destroyer flotilla leaders and

The Royal Navy added a fourth River-class patrol vessel, HMS *Clyde*, with modifications for operations off the Falkland Islands and South Georgia. She is seen here on a visit to South Georgia. (BAE Systems)

another three building; 143 destroyers and thirty-seven building; fifty-two submarines and eighteen building; more than seventy sloops and mine-sweepers; twenty-one river gunboats and thirteen motor torpedo boats with another ten on order.

The battlecruisers included HMS *Hood*, when launched in the 1920s, the world's largest warship. Some of the 'heavy' cruisers were ships of the Town-class, described by the RN as heavy and having twelve guns in triple mountings, but actually had only 6-inch guns, which officially, under the Washington Treaty definitions, meant that they were light cruisers.

It can be seen that the Royal Navy on the outbreak of war on 3 September 1939 was a far more balanced fleet than in 1914. It still outnumbered its two most likely foes, Germany and Italy, but the threat of conflict with Japan meant that it was more widely dispersed than in 1914. Weaknesses included the inferior main armament of new capital ships and the poor performance of carrier-borne aircraft compared to those of the United States and Japan. As it happened, Italy did not enter the war until June 1940, as France was falling, and Japan did not follow until December 1941. This time, there was no delay in instituting a convoy system while an early priority was to protect the movement of the British Expeditionary Force across the English Channel to France and troops to reinforce the main bases in the Mediterranean. Once again, ships were deployed looking for German commerce raiders, especially in the Atlantic and the Indian Ocean, through which much-needed reinforcements could come from Australia and New Zealand.

Accounts of the first months of the Second World War often refer to the 'Phoney War', as there was no action between ground forces. At sea, however, there was no phoney war and on 17 September 1939, the aircraft carrier *Courageous* was torpedoed and sunk. Later, the battleship *Royal Oak* was also torpedoed and sunk in the supposedly secure anchorage of Scapa Flow, in Orkney, to the north of Scotland. The year ended well with victory over the German pocket battleship, or *Panzerschiff*, *Graf Spee*, in the Battle of the River Plate, even though she outgunned the British heavy cruiser *Exeter* and the two light cruisers *Ajax* and *Achilles*, the latter, part of the Royal New Zealand Navy.

To augment the warships on certain duties, especially convoy protection, ocean liners were taken up from trade and armed to act as auxiliary cruisers, but these proved no match for German warships and many were lost. More successful was the conversion of trawlers and paddle steamers as minesweepers.

The Royal Navy provided support for the Anglo-French landings in Norway to support Norwegian resistance to the German invasion. The German light cruiser *Konigsberg* became the first major operational war-ship to be sunk by aircraft, with Fleet Air Arm Skua fighter-bombers flying from a shore base in Orkney, while in two battles of Narvik in April

1940, ten German destroyers were sunk. The aircraft carriers *Furious* and *Glorious* transported aircraft to Norway. During the withdrawal, the carrier *Glorious* was sunk by gunfire from the German battlecruisers *Sharnhorst* and *Gneisenau*, as were the carrier's two escorting destroyers. The irony was that British and French troops were withdrawn from Norway to reinforce units in the Battle of France, but within two months the Royal Navy found itself covering the evacuation of the BEF and other Allied units from France.

The fall of France not only left the British without an ally in the Mediterranean, but also led to attempts to force the French to surrender their ships at Alexandria, where the French ships were peacefully neutralised, and at Mers-el-Kébir, Oran and Dakar, where naval engagements ensued with much loss of life amongst French naval personnel.

The outstanding success of the early years of the war was the attack on the Italian fleet at Taranto, the first naval engagement conducted solely by the use of aircraft. Using just twenty-two obsolescent Swordfish biplanes flying from the aircraft carrier *Illustrious*, after the other carrier, *Eagle*, was out of action due to damage, three of the Italian Navy's six battleships were put out of action, while other ships and shore installations were damaged. The action brought the *Luftwaffe* to Sicily and the Axis air operations against Malta intensified. The island was deemed impossible to defend by the RAF and the army, but had been retained as a naval base for submarines and light forces. Even so, when Italy entered the war, Malta had no fighter defences and had to rely on three Sea Gladiators flown by RAF flying-boat pilots.

Serious damage was taken by the British Mediterranean Fleet during first the evacuation from Greece and then the evacuation from Crete. Despite this catalogue of failure, at no time did the Royal Navy lose control of the seas, even when Germany had aerial supremacy, and one of the largely forgotten successes of the war was that of British submarines in the west and centre of the Mediterranean, which, combined with aerial attack, made it difficult for the Axis powers to support their forces in North Africa.

The Royal Navy continued to suffer serious losses throughout this period, including the battlecruiser *Hood*, with the loss of all but three of a ship's company of 1,418. Shortly afterwards, the German battleship *Bismarck* was lost in a long-running battle with units of both the Home Fleet and Force H, based on Gibraltar, with aircraft from the carrier *Ark Royal* playing a significant part in crippling the German ship. Once Japan entered the war, *Prince of Wales* and *Repulse* were lost off Singapore, while other ships falling prey to the Japanese were the heavy cruisers *Cornwall*, *Dorsetshire* and *Exeter*, as well as the small aircraft carrier *Hermes*, the first carrier to have been designed as such, off Ceylon, present day Sri Lanka.

The Royal Navy covered the invasions of the Faeroes and Iceland, both of which would have helped the German war effort considerably had they been invaded after the fall of Denmark and, later, the Vichy French colony of Madagascar. Malta, which was besieged by the Axis forces and to which few supply ships got through, was relieved on 13 August 1942 by the convoy Operation Pedestal, judged a success, although only five out of fourteen merchantmen reached the island, and the losses included the aircraft carrier *Eagle*, one of four carriers with the convoy, although one, *Furious*, was being used as an aircraft transport. On 26 December 1943, the German battlecruiser *Scharnhorst* was sunk in the Battle of the North Cape by the battleship HMS *Duke of York* and three cruisers, leaving just thirty-six survivors from her crew. Meanwhile, the convoy war was also being won, first with the provision of anti-submarine air cover from merchant aircraft carriers (MAC-ships), which were oil tankers and grain carriers with a flight deck built over their holds, and then with escort carriers carrying fighters and anti-submarine aircraft. The German invasion of the Soviet Union meant that a further task for the Royal Navy was the escort of the Arctic convoys from Iceland and Scotland to Murmansk and Archangel, under constant attack from German aircraft and fleet units based in Norway, except when the weather was so bad that it became the major threat.

Joint operations with the United States Navy included Operation Torch, the invasion of Vichy-French North Africa, on 8 November 1942, followed by the invasion of first Sicily and then mainland Italy and finally, the south of France. The Royal Navy provided heavy bombardment, minesweeping and protection of the landing force's flanks for the invasion of Normandy in June 1944. This saw the tempo of operations in Europe begin to ease.

After the early failures following Japan's entry into the war, the Royal Navy started to devote increasing resources to the war in the Far East. Apart from a raid by miniature submarines on Diego Suarez in Madagascar, Japanese forces did not venture west of Ceylon and increasingly the emphasis was on attacks on Japanese oilfields and refineries in the Netherlands East Indies, initially with US support so that the RN became used to co-ordinated mass aerial attacks from several carriers. A British Pacific Fleet was created to operate alongside the US Navy, usually designated as Task Force 37 or 57, depending on whether the US fleet was designated the Third Fleet or Fifth Fleet, as this changed as the US commanders were alternated between their frontline command role and their planning duties. This was the strongest and most balanced fleet ever sent to sea by the Royal Navy, with up to six aircraft carriers as well as the necessary supporting battleships, cruisers and destroyers. Sydney in Australia was used as a major base. During this time, the Royal Fleet Auxiliary also benefitted from the adoption of US methods, especially for refuelling underway. The fast armoured carriers of the Royal Navy proved their worth under attack by Japanese *Kamikaze* suicide attacks.

The end of the war saw the Royal Navy at its strongest ever, with no fewer than fifty-two aircraft carriers of all kinds, while personnel numbers had grown from the 180,000 of the mobilised regulars and reserves in 1939 to 783,000 in 1945.

Peacetime brought fresh challenges as the friction with the Soviet Union that had been apparent even during the Second World War became more open and much of Eastern Europe was occupied by the Soviet armed forces. The Royal Navy became heavily involved in the Korean War, 1950-1953, and as the RAF was heavily committed elsewhere, this meant that the UK's share of the air war devolved onto the Fleet Air Arm and its new Colossus-class light fleet carriers. A development of the Colossus-class was the Majestic-class, slightly larger, and examples of these classes were sold to the Netherlands, France, Canada, Australia, India, Argentina and Brazil. Inevitably, the size of the fleet was substantially reduced after the Second World War, but while just one battleship was commissioned at the end of the war, plans were laid for two new classes of aircraft carriers, the Centaur-class of four ships and later, the larger Eagle-class of two ships, although originally four had been planned, which became Britain's largest war-ships with a displacement of more than 40,000 tons light load. HMS *Eagle* and *Ark Royal* were developments of the Implacable-class and were fast, armoured carriers. One surviving Illustrious-class ship, *Victorious*, was extensively converted with half-angled flight deck and 3-D radar, rejoining the fleet in 1958.

Many of the refinements that enabled larger and faster jet aircraft to operate safely and efficiently from carriers were British inventions, including the steam catapult, the mirror deck landing system and the angled flight deck that removed once and for all the hazard of aircraft landing and rolling into others parked on the flight deck by enabling pilots to go around.

Egypt's nationalisation of the Suez Canal in 1956 led to a crisis in which the Royal Navy and the French *Marine Nationale* came together for an assault on the Canal Zone. This involved two British carriers, *Ocean* and *Thesus*, in the first heli-borne assault. While the operation, codenamed Musketeer, was a tactical success, politically it was a disaster and the impact on the French and British economies led to a ceasefire and eventual withdrawal.

Two of the Centaur-class carriers, *Albion* and *Bulwark*, were converted to become commando carriers. Other changes that followed were the Royal Navy's first nuclear-powered submarine, *Dreadnought*, while the service's amphibious capability was enhanced by the introduction of two assault ships, *Fearless* and *Intrepid*, with stern landing docks for assault craft. A class of guided missile destroyers, the County-class, with hangars and landing platforms for helicopters, was also introduced, while frigates ceased to be classed as anti-aircraft or anti-submarine and instead became general-purpose frigates with light helicopters, and of these the most successful was the Leander-class of twenty-six ships. Less successful was the conversion of two of the three Tiger-class cruisers as helicopter cruisers with accommodation for up to four anti-submarine medium helicopters. The Royal Navy was to the forefront in work on gas turbine propulsion, and this was included in the County-class destroyers and the Tribal-class frigates, combined with steam propulsion in a system known as COSAG.

Cancellation of the Skybolt missile, which was meant to continue the operation of the RAF's 'V' bombers in delivering Britain's nuclear deterrent led to the role passing to the Royal Navy, which introduced four Resolution-class nuclear-powered submarines to carry the US Polaris ICBM, with the first commissioned in 1967. Nevertheless, by this time a class of two large aircraft carriers of more than 60,000 tons was also cancelled, heralding the end of fixed-wing flying in the Royal Navy once *Eagle* and *Ark Royal* were withdrawn.

Operations throughout this period included helping to restore order after an army mutiny in Kenya, and then, almost immediately, positioning *Victorious* off Kuwait in 1961 to forestall a threatened Iraqi invasion. As the decade continued, the Royal Navy was heavily involved with the Royal Marines resisting Indonesian attempts to wreck the Federation of Malaysia and Singapore. When Iceland extended her territorial waters unilaterally, the Royal Navy provided protection for British trawlers threatened by Icelandic patrol craft in the so-called Cod Wars. Another task was maintaining the so-called Beira Patrol during Rhodesia's Unilateral Declaration of Independence (UDI), between 1965 and 1980, a task that usually required the presence of an aircraft carrier to prevent ships carrying oil and other vital supplies from breaking the blockade, as supplies entered the landlocked country through the port of Beira, in Mozambique.

The withdrawal of *Ark Royal* in 1979, with her Buccaneer bombers and F-4K Phantom fighters transferred to the RAF, did not mark the end of fixed-wing naval aviation as expected as the advent of the Sea Harrier V/STOL fighter and the Invincible-class 'through deck cruisers', in effect, light aircraft carriers, saw fixed-wing naval aviation continue. While *Invincible* was awaited, *Hermes*, having been converted from an aircraft carrier to a commando carrier, was converted back and equipped with a ski-jump so that Sea Harriers could be flown off the ship.

While awaiting the first of three Invincible-class light fleet carriers capable of handling the Sea Harrier V/STOL fighter, in addition to *Hermes*, the late 1970s saw the Royal Navy operating two Tiger-class helicopter cruisers, conversions from conventional cruisers; a solitary Type 82 guided missile destroyer, HMS *Bristol*, and seven County-class guided missile destroyers, each of which could accommodate a single helicopter and all eight were

The Type 23 Duke-class general purpose frigate HMS *Lancaster* entering dry dock at Portsmouth. (BAE Systems)

often described as 'cruisers' because of their tonnage and despite having just a 4.5-inch gun; the first six of fourteen Sheffield-class anti-aircraft guided missile destroyers; eight Type 21 Amazon-class guided missile frigates and the first of fourteen Type 22 Broadsword-class guided missile frigates, with the early Broadsword-class capable of accommodating two helicopters rather than the usual single helicopter of British escort vessels; twenty-six Leander-class guided missile general purpose frigates and another twenty-one frigates of the Tribal, Rothesay, Salisbury, Leopard, Whitby and Blackwood-classes and including anti-aircraft and aircraft direction ships; two LPD assault ships and six logistics landing ships as well as another fourteen landing ships. The fleet included four Resolution-class SSBN with Polaris missiles and six Swiftsure-class SSNs as well as five Valiant-class and HMS *Dreadnought*, the RN's first nuclear-powered submarine, and the first of seven Trafalgar-class. The landing ships logistics were manned by the Royal Fleet Auxiliary, part of the Merchant Navy, as were the rest of the replenishment ships and tankers.

While the Royal Navy had been reshaping itself into what was primarily an anti-submarine force, when the Argentine invaded the Falkland Islands in 1982, a fleet had to be hastily assembled for the relief of the islands, led by *Hermes* as flagship and supported by *Invincible*, while the force also included the two assault ships, one of which had to be pulled out of reserve. Ships were taken up from trade to support the fleet and provide

The Royal Navy's sole LPH HMS *Ocean*, making a tight turn. The aircraft carrier *Illustrious* has been refitted for the same role, but only one ship will be operational at any one time. (BAE Systems)

such necessities as a hospital ship. Despite the Falklands being 8,345 miles (12,800 km) away from the British Isles and with no suitable bases within unrefueled range, the operation was a success, but this came at a price, with two Sheffield-class destroyers and two Amazon-class frigates lost as well as an RFA-manned landing ship and a merchant ship, the *Atlantic Conveyor*, a converted container ship that had most of the relief force's heavy and medium-lift helicopters aboard. A nuclear-powered fleet submarine, *Conqueror*, sank the Argentine cruiser *General Belgrano*, the first and so far only nuclear-powered submarine to have sunk another ship. The campaign showed the need for fixed-wing naval aviation with success largely due to the Sea Harrier, while the carriers carried a supporting force of RAF Harriers for ground attack duties. It also showed that many ships, especially frigates and destroyers, had a poor anti-aircraft and anti-missile capability.

The campaign followed a programme of defence cuts that would have seen the Royal Navy reduced in strength and with just two aircraft carriers, but while a third carrier was allowed to be retained, it later became the case that just two were fully operational at any one time. It was clear that as well as anti-submarine warfare and protection of home waters, the Royal Navy also needed a strong expeditionary capability.

The end of the Cold War saw further cuts, with the number of escort vessels cut from more than eighty in the early 1960s to fewer than forty, and even this hard-pressed force was then cut to fewer than thirty. To some extent, the cuts were offset by the greater availability of gas turbine-powered vessels, but even so, major warships were not to have an adequate number of escorts in a crisis.

In more recent years, the Royal Navy also took part in the Gulf War for the liberation of Kuwait in 1990-1991, the Kosovo conflict, the Afghanistan Campaign, and the invasion of Iraq in the 2003 Iraq War, with the latter seeing RN warships bombard positions in support of the Al Faw Peninsula landings by Royal Marines. In Iraq, nuclear-powered fleet submarines fired cruise missiles with conventional warheads against targets in Iraq, while the service's mine countermeasures vessels cleared the way for the invasion fleet. In August 2005, the Royal Navy rescued seven Russians stranded in a submarine off the Kamchatka peninsula when its Scorpio 45 remote-controlled mini-sub freed the Russian submarine from the fishing nets and cables that had held it for three days. Incidents such as these show that the service remains a repository of vast experience and capability, the value of which does not always seem to be recognised by policymakers. The Royal Navy was also involved in an incident involving Somali pirates in November 2008, after the pirates tried to capture a civilian vessel.

A Joint Force Harrier unit was established with the RAF after the withdrawal of the Sea Harriers in 2004, leaving the Royal Navy without air defence for the fleet and with the two services sharing three Harrier GR7/GR9 squadrons. *Invincible* was withdrawn and left in a very low level of reserve. Two new landing platform docks, or assault ships, HMS *Albion* and *Bulwark*, joined the fleet while a commando carrier capability remained with the new helicopter carrier *Ocean*.

In late 2010, publication of a Strategic Defence and Security Review finally ended fixed-wing aviation for the Royal Navy until the first of the two Queen Elizabeth-class 'super carriers' of about 66,000 tons displacement enters service from 2016. Originally designed to operate the STOVL Lockheed Martin F-35B, plans to equip one ship to operate the conventional landing F-35C have been abandoned due to mounting costs. Meanwhile, *Ark Royal* has been withdrawn and her sister, the last of the Invincible-class, *Illustrious*, converted to operate as a helicopter carrier and alternate with *Ocean* in this role, with one ship active and the other on extended standby. The two assault ships will also operate in this way. The SDSR also scrapped the RAF's maritime-reconnaissance force. Despite these cuts, in early spring 2011, the British government decided, along with other NATO countries, to intervene in an uprising in Libya, and while much of the

The Bay-class LSD RFA *Lyme Bay* on the river Clyde. The ships of the Royal Fleet Auxiliary are manned by the Merchant Navy, although some have Royal Navy personnel aboard to man weapons systems and operate helicopters. (BAE Systems)

operation has been conducted by the Royal Air Force, the Royal Navy has maintained several ships in the area and assisted in evacuations of civilians from Egypt and Libya. Cruise missiles were fired by submarines and *Ocean* acted as a base for four Army Air Corps Apache helicopters striking against Libyan government targets.

The frigate and destroyer force is being reduced to fewer than twenty ships, with the backbone of the force being six of the new Type 45 air defence destroyer and eleven Type 23 general-purpose frigates, which will be replaced in due course by the new Type 26 frigate. The Type 45s each have VLS Aster 15/Aster 30 SAM, a 114mm gun and accommodation for either a Lynx or a Merlin ASW helicopter, but despite displacing 8,000 tonnes, do not have ASTT or AShM. Type 23s, or Duke-class, frigates, each have Harpoon AShM, VLS Sea Wolf SAM, a Goalkeeper CIWS, two twin ASTT, a 114mm gun and accommodation for either two Lynx or a Merlin ASW helicopter. A small MCMV force is maintained with the Hunt and Sandown-classes. Conventional submarines have been withdrawn and the fleet consists of nuclear-powered vessels, including four Vanguard-class Trident ICBM submarines, each with four torpedo tubes and up to sixteen Trident missiles, while in due course there will also be seven Astute-class fleet or 'hunter-killer submarines, with six torpedo tubes and also equipped with Harpoon AShM and Tomahawk cruise missiles, which will gradually replace the remaining Trafalgar-class submarines, which have five torpedo tubes and are capable of firing Harpoon AShM and Tomahawk cruise missiles. In addition to use of the MCMV ships, there are also three River-class offshore patrol vessels for fisheries protection, while a fourth modified River-class, HMS *Clyde*, is stationed in the Falklands; all of which have a 76mm gun and a helicopter landing platform. A fleet of small unarmed 20m patrol boats is maintained for use by university officer cadet units. Unusually, the Royal Navy's fleet train is provided by the Merchant Navy-manned Royal Fleet Auxiliary, although the larger ships have RN personnel on board as well to operate ASW helicopters and man the SAM missile defences, but even the Royal Fleet Auxiliary has been cut, losing one of its four Bay-class landing support ships. The RFA includes two large auxiliary oiler replenishment, each of 31,565 tonnes displacement, and two auxiliary fleet support (helicopter) of 23,482 tonnes, although all four ships can carry helicopters, as well as an aviation training ship, RFA *Argus*, and a number of smaller ships. The survey fleet is RN-manned and includes HMS *Scott*, 13,500 tonnes, as well as the new and smaller *Echo* and *Enterprise*, which are capable of acting as depot or command ships. Manpower is being cut to 30,000, and eventually to 29,000 by 2016, while the Royal Marine Commando force will be cut by 500 men from its present total strength of more than 6,000 marine, naval and army personnel. Naval aviation currently accounts for 5,520 personnel.

Naval aircraft include four squadrons with Merlin ASW helicopters and two squadrons with Lynx Mk3 ASW helicopters for operations from small ships, while the Sea King HC4 transport helicopter, which equips three squadrons, has been replaced by ex-RAF Merlins. The Royal marines have a helicopter squadron with six Lynx AH Mk7. There are Baron and Conquest aircraft with civil registrations for observer training, while Falcon 20 (civilian-operated) are used for fleet exercises.

Three main bases are operational, with Devonport for the assault ships and helicopter carriers; Portsmouth for the destroyer force and as fleet HQ; and the Clyde Naval Base for nuclear submarines and fisheries protection. Three naval air stations remain at Culdrose, Yeovilton and Prestwick. The main base for training ratings is at HMS *Raleigh*, at Torpoint, and for officers at the Britannia Royal Naval College, Dartmouth.

Despite successive governments attempting to 'withdraw from East of Suez,' the Royal Navy is committed today in the Gulf, as part of the Combined Maritime Force, and in the Gulf of Aden, and with small forces in Bahrain and Oman. The Royal Navy is completing training of the new Iraqi Navy. An escort vessel, an offshore patrol vessel and a nuclear submarine are all present in the waters around the Falklands, while there is also an RN-manned Antarctic patrol ship, HMS *Protector*. A token force is in Gibraltar. The RN also contributes escort vessels to NATO joint forces, mainly in the North Atlantic.

UNITED STATES OF AMERICA

Population: 317.6 million
Land Area: 3,775,602 square miles (9,363,169 sq.km.)
GDP: $14.6tr (£9.48tr), per capita $46,040 (£29,896)
Defence Exp: $712.8bn (£462.9bn)
Service Personnel: 1,563,996 active, plus 871,240 reserves

Today, more than ever, the United States armed forces are the keystone that carries the burden of the defence of the world's democracies. While US defence expenditure has fallen as a proportion of GDP since the end of the Cold War, it is nevertheless much higher than that of any of its NATO allies, and three times that of its next door neighbour, Canada. Active manpower has actually increased over the past six years, although there has been a marked fall in the strength of the reserves.

Is this a glimpse of the future for naval aviation? The nuclear-powered aircraft carrier USS *John C. Stennis* with a deckload of Lockheed Martin F-35Cs. (USN)

All of this is threatened by the massive federal budget deficit and by political uncertainties that may see defence expenditure cut dramatically over the next five years.

During the Cold War, there was the growing realisation that the United States carried more than its fair burden of Europe's defence, but the situation is even worse today and the threat is far more complex. The cynics will suggest that the United States was protecting its overseas investments by contributing so much towards the defence of Europe and its allies in the Pacific and Middle East, and there is no doubt that these countries were also major markets for US exports, but such an imbalance is unhealthy and also leaves the rest of the world's democracies weak and vulnerable to a change in US policy.

One weakness in US defence planning and procurement is the power that Congress has over the annual budget, tackling this in detail unmatched anywhere else. There is no doubt that this is democracy in action, but it does interfere with longer term planning and also makes true participation by the US in collaborative defence projects far more difficult than it should be. The situation is made worse by protectionist attitudes and also by attempts by members of both houses of Congress to protect industry and employment in their own constituencies.

Even within the US armed forces all is not as it might be. The division of maritime responsibilities between the United States Navy and the United States Coast Guard Service, which has been transferred from its original peacetime home in the Department of Transportation to the Department for Homeland Security, cannot but disguise the fact that the USCG is operating an increasingly elderly fleet of ships and aircraft. While it is understandable that the emphasis is on power projection to strengthen the resolve of wavering allies and support those too small to maintain well-balanced armed forces, the need to protect US interests in its own territorial waters remains important, not least with the modern challenges of illegal immigration, arms and drugs smuggling and terrorism. It is also easy to forget that when war actually does break out, control of the USCG is passed to the USN, and surely the service does not want to find that its wartime expansion involves obsolescent ships and aircraft?

There have been moves to bring the air operations of the USN and the United States Marine Corps more closely in line in recent years, and this is to be welcomed, but it must not be an excuse to hamper USMC air operations in favour of the USN. The USMC has an important assault role and needs to remain carrier capable, not repeating the mistakes made at one period of the Pacific War when USMC pilots were not given carrier training. It is also helpful that it retains the capability of conducting aerial reconnaissance and providing fighter defence for the troops on the beaches.

UNITED STATES NAVY AND UNITED STATES MARINES CORPS

Today, the world's most powerful navy backed by a strong US Marine Corps and with the facility to incorporate the US Coast Guard (see below) in wartime, the USN has nevertheless been reduced in size in the years

The San Antonio-class LPD USS *New York*, which includes some 50 tons of steel salvaged and recycled from the World Trade Center twin towers destroyed in the world's worst terrorist atrocity in September 2001. She has accommodation for up to 720 marines. (USN)

since the end of the Cold War and may face further cuts in the foreseeable future. It has already fallen below its post-Cold War target of 600 warships.

The origins of the USN lie in the Continental Navy, which was formed during the American War of Independence, also known as the American Revolutionary War, but which was disbanded shortly after the war ended. It used ships taken up from trade and armed, with initially seven ships used to capture British supply ships, so this figure increased substantially by 13 October 1775, which became the official founding date of the USN. Despite its disbandment, the country's constitution gave Congress the power to 'provide and maintain a navy.' Before long, the activities of the Barbary Pirates in the Mediterranean and in the easternmost stretches of the North Atlantic led to the Naval Act, 1794, which authorised the construction and manning of six frigates.

Before this, for almost a decade, the United States was without a navy and its only armed ships belonged to the US Revenue Cutter Service, the main processor of the US Coast Guard. The first three of the new frigates were commissioned in 1797, the USS *United States*, *Constellation* and *Constitution*.

The first actions for the new ships were in an undeclared running war with France but, in 1812, anger at the interference with American merchant-men by the Royal Navy during the Napoleonic Wars led to the Anglo-American Naval War of 1812. The conflict saw numerous single-ship engagements between the two navies, while British vessels were driven off Lake Erie and Lake Champlain. Despite these successes, the Royal Navy was able to blockade American ports and even land troops on American territory. With the return of peace, the USN concentrated most of its efforts in the Americas, including South America, and maintained a presence in the Atlantic and the Pacific Oceans as well as the Caribbean. Nevertheless, in 1816, a combined British, Dutch and American naval squadron finally suppressed the Barbary pirates, destroying their bases in North Africa.

The war between America and Mexico saw the USN blockading Mexican ports while between 1846 and 1848, the USN deployed the marines from its Pacific Squadron to assist in the capture of California, assisting the Californian Battalion, a locally-raised volunteer force, having captured or destroyed the Mexican fleet in the Gulf of California. Baja California was substantially occupied by landing 12,000 army personnel during one day at Vera Cruz in the USN's first major amphibious operation.

During the American Civil War, 1860-1866, the USN was primarily with the Union forces and stronger than the Confederate Navy, which was unable to break the blockade of Confederate ports. The Battle of Hampton Roads, 1862, saw the USS *Monitor* pitted against the CSS *Virginia* in the world's first engagement between steam-powered ironclads. The outcome was inconclusive.

Despite the obvious importance of sea power during the first century of the United States' existence, after the American Civil War, the USN was neglected and its ships increasingly obsolescent. The situation began to be retrieved in the 1880s, when a major modernisation programme started, so that by 1907, President Theodore Roosevelt was able to order most of the USN's battleships, known as the Great White Fleet, on a fourteen-month circumnavigation of the world to demonstrate that the USN was a true blue water navy. In the years running up to the outbreak of the First World War in Europe, the USN was involved in the first flights from warships, with a flight from a wooden platform built over the bows of a cruiser in 1910, and supported work on maritime-reconnaissance flying boats during the war years. While the United States did not enter the war until 1917, legislation in 1916 authorised a substantial construction programme. Battleships were sent to join the British Grand Fleet in 1917, in which they formed a squadron, while US admirals pressed for a convoy system, mainly on the North Atlantic, where US troop reinforcements were on passage to Europe.

Plans for continued naval expansion after the First World War were limited by the Washington Naval Treaty of 1922, which capped the USN at 525,000 tons, the same as for the United Kingdom, but well ahead of Japan's 315,000 tons, while France and Italy were limited to 175,000 tons apiece. The various categories of warships were also limited both in total tonnage and the maximum size of any single vessel. The USN's total battle-cruiser tonnage was too high and this led to the conversion of the USS *Saratoga* and *Lexington* into aircraft carriers, becoming the largest of their kind when they entered service in the late 1920s. The service's original aircraft carrier, the USS *Langley*, was exempted from the aircraft carrier total tonnage for the USN as she was classified as an experimental vessel. In an attempt to revitalise the economy during the years of the Great Depression, the 'New Deal' package of financing allowed the construction of two more carriers, the USS *Yorktown* and *Enterprise*, so that by 1936 the USN had five aircraft carriers.

As it became clear that the Washington Treaty limitations were being ignored by a number of nations, and especially Japan and Germany, USN expansion resumed and battleship construction restarted. By the outbreak of war in Europe in 1939, the USN had seventeen battleships; six aircraft carriers, as the *Langley* had been reclassified as an aircraft tender, as well as two seaplane tenders and an airship tender; thirty-five cruisers; twenty-five flotilla leaders and 191 destroyers as well as a number of submarine chasers and minelayers; 100 submarines, although many were small; six submarine depot ships; and a substantial number of other support ships and both gunboats and river gunboats.

Even before the US entered the war, by 1941 the USN had started to escort convoys to a mid-ocean handover point, ostensibly to protect neutral shipping in the North Atlantic from German U-boats, while battleships

A Grumman EA-6B Prowler electronic countermeasures aircraft lands aboard the USS *George Washington*. (USN)

were transferred from the Pacific to augment the Atlantic Fleet. The surprise Japanese attack on the US Pacific Fleet's main base at Pearl Harbor on 7 December 1941 brought the US into the Second World War, with Germany declaring war on the United States. This meant that the service was faced with fighting a war on two fronts, the Atlantic and the Pacific. In collaboration with the United States Army Air Force, the USN mounted a surprise attack on the Japanese Home Islands with sixteen B-25 Mitchell bombers flown off the aircraft carrier *Hornet*. Japanese progress was stopped with the Battle of the Coral Sea, 8 May 1942, and by a devastating defeat at the Battle of Midway, 3-7 June 1942. In the Pacific, the theatre was divided in two, with US forces island-hopping towards Japan, and in the southern area, assaults were made by US Army units, while in the north, the assaults were by the US Marine Corps, but the USN was involved in both areas. The action in the Pacific culminated in the Battle of Leyte Gulf, the largest naval battle in history, which marked yet another Japanese defeat as US forces retook the Philippines, and eventually saw USN, USMC and Royal Navy aircraft operating over Japan itself.

A vital, but largely unsung, role was played by the USN's submarines after early problems with torpedoes were resolved and by 1945 the supply lines linking Japan to oil, rubber and food resources in the occupied territories were severed. Towards the end of the war, US submarines were often operational in the Japanese Inland Sea.

In the European theatre, under the 'Lend-Lease Programme', the USN supplied fifty destroyers to enlarge the RN's escort force, where they were known as the Town-class, as well as escort carriers and naval aircraft. In return, the UK allowed US use of bases in the Caribbean, and there was also a measure of 'reverse lend-lease' with the transfer of sonar-equipped frigates and corvettes to the USN.

The USN was also heavily involved in the start of offensive operations in the European theatre, including Operation Torch, the Allied landings in North Africa, followed by landings in Sicily and on mainland Italy, the Normandy landings, or Operation Overlord, in June 1944, and then the landings in the south of France. These all involved close collaboration with other Allied forces, mainly from the UK and the British Empire.

Developments during the war included the escort carrier, initially conversions from merchant ships but later built from the keel upwards with the intention of being capable of conversion back to merchant ships post-war. A shortage of carriers led to the Independence-class light carriers, initially with conversions from Cleveland-class light cruisers although again, the later ships were built from the keel upwards, but this move might have been unnecessary, as the Essex-class fleet carriers soon arrived in large numbers. Landing craft and landing ships were major innovations that made amphibious assaults more likely to be successful. The escort carriers soon proved to be useful for providing air support over beachheads both in the Pacific and in the Mediterranean, and as aircraft transports or repair ships. On the other hand, battleships, for long considered the measure of a fleet's strength and status, were soon relegated to providing heavy bombardment of coastal installations and joining the cruiser force in providing intensive AA cover for the carrier force and landing ships. The United States Marine Corps took the lead in providing carrier-borne air cover, usually from escort carriers, over beachheads, although for a while USMC pilots stopped receiving carrier deck-landing training, but this was a temporary restriction.

By 1943 the USN was larger than the sum of the fleets of the other belligerent nations and, by VJ-Day in August 1945, it had no fewer than 6,768 ships, the world's largest and most powerful navy. In just less than four years of war, the fleet had received eighteen new large aircraft carriers and eight battleships, while destroyers and escort carriers were mass produced, with major structures prefabricated.

Naturally, the usual rapid post-war reduction in the service's strength occurred, with the USN having twenty Essex-class aircraft carriers and eight Independence-class light carriers on 1 July 1945, as well as seventy escort carriers, compared to twelve aircraft carriers, including those of the Okinawa-class developed from the Essex-class, a single light carrier and ten escort carriers. Other types of ship suffered similar reductions. Aircraft numbers dropped over the period from 40,912 to 24,232, with many of these in storage or reserve.

Peace was short-lived as the USN and the RN took much of the brunt of the Korean War, 1950-1953, because the initial rapid advance by North Korean forces into South Korea saw many air stations ashore overrun. The USN was active in supporting the landings at Inchon in 1951, and the USMC transported troops from a carrier to the frontline by helicopter for the first time.

The Korean War and the Berlin Airlift were the opening shots in what became the Cold War, and the USN soon found a role in many parts of the globe, in many cases playing a part in joint forces with other NATO allies while NATO naval bases were established at Guantanamo Bay in Cuba, Rota in Spain, Soudha Bay in Crete and in the Philippines.

Technical advances continued with the helicopter and jet aircraft being introduced to the fleet, while aircraft carriers were fitted with more powerful steam catapults, angled flight decks and mirror landing systems, all British inventions that the USN was quick to introduce to improve performance and safety. The USN was first to introduce nuclear-powered submarines, starting with the USS *Nautilus*, commissioned in 1954 and which in 1958 became the first vessel to complete a submerged transit of the North Pole. The USN and USMC based their post-war strategy on the concept of expeditionary warfare, with carrier battle groups providing the basis of naval deployments.

Rationalisation of US military aviation saw the USN and USMC lose their transport force to the USAF's Military Airlift Command, but responsibility for maritime-reconnaissance, which during the Second World War had been divided between the USN and the USAAF, became a naval function.

While the USN held on to its base at Guantanamo Bay after a Communist revolution swept through Cuba, plans by the Soviet Union to base nuclear-tipped missiles on the island led to a confrontation with the United States in late 1962, during which the USN blockaded the island to stop Soviet shipping bringing the missiles and other military equipment to Cuba.

During the Vietnam War, the USN played a major role and in turn was targeted by North Vietnamese forces, notably when its destroyers were targeted by North Vietnamese patrol boats in the Gulf of Tonkin incident in 1964. Over the next ten years, some fourteen aircraft carriers saw service off the coast of Vietnam at different times, often with their aircraft mounting attacks against targets in North Vietnam in what were known as the Iron Hand sorties. These ships included the first nuclear-powered attack carriers, while many of the older ships dating from the Second World War and the immediate post-war years were reclassified as anti-submarine carriers.

Nuclear-power also led to the development of ballistic missile submarines, initially carrying the Polaris ICBM, which was also supplied to the

The Oliver Hazard Perry frigate USS *Carr*. The USN has substantially reduced its frigate strength in recent years, which could mean a dangerous shortage of escort vessels in a crisis. (USN)

Royal Navy. This meant that the USN joined the USAF in maintaining a nuclear strategic deterrent against attack by the Soviet Union.

By the late 1970s, the USN had four nuclear-powered aircraft carriers including the first three ships of the Nimitz-class, on which the service standardised until well into the twenty-first century, and another eleven conventionally-powered aircraft carriers with four more in reserve. Supporting the carrier groups were nine nuclear-powered guided missile cruisers as well as twenty-one with conventional power while five cruisers with gun armament were in reserve. There were thirty-nine guided missile destroyers, many of them conversions of older ships, as well as thirty Spruance-class guided missile destroyers in service or under construction, as well as another forty-four destroyers, six Brooke-class guided missile frigates and the first of more than seventy Oliver Hazard Perry-class guided missile frigates, and another fifty-eight frigates. Amphibious warfare vessels included two Blue Ridge-class command ships; two Tarawa-class assault ships with three under construction; seven Iwo Jima-class assault ships, which like the Tarawa-class could accommodate helicopters; twenty-seven landing ship docks with another seven in reserve, as well as another thirty landing ships, plus more than 100 landing craft. By this time, the emphasis was on nuclear-powered submarines, with the first four of thirteen Ohio-class SSBN, as well as thirty-one Benjamin Franklin and Lafayette-class, five Ethan Allen and five George Washington-class; the first thirteen of forty Los Angeles-class SSN were in service, and operating with more than sixty of other classes, while there were still ten conventionally-powered submarines. Compared to these numbers, there were relatively few patrol craft, totalling about ten, and the mine countermeasures force consisted of just twenty-five minesweepers and eight boats. More than 100 auxiliaries provided logistics and support as well as salvage, rescue and repair.

After the Shah of Iran was deposed in 1978, tension arose between the new Islamic regime and many Western states, and the USN was involved in an unsuccessful attempt to rescue American diplomats held hostage in the US embassy in Tehran. While outsiders were not involved directly in the war between Iran and Iraq, a naval presence was maintained in the Gulf. The USN took the lead in using naval air power in the operation to remove Iraqi forces from Kuwait in early 1991, an essential addition to the air forces based ashore. It also played a role in the invasion of Afghanistan in 2001, and later in the invasion of Iraq. These campaigns were notable for the use of cruise missiles launched from warships in the Gulf, which had a devastating effect on the target areas.

In recent years, there has been closer integration of the USMC with the USN, especially as regards air power. With the USCG, they have combined to formulate a new maritime strategy known as A Co-operative Strategy for 21st Century Sea Power, which puts the emphasis on prevention of war as much as its conduct. With a shrinking fleet but continued global responsibilities, the strategy also relies on partnerships with other navies, not only within NATO but also with countries such as Australia and New Zealand.

Today, the USN has 336,289 personnel, of whom 6,229 are described as active reservists, while the USMC has 204,056 personnel, including 2,930 active reservists. Including the active reservists, this force is backed by 109,222 reservists in the USN, and the USMC has 109,600 reservists. Of the total USN personnel, 98,588 are engaged in naval aviation, which includes a shore-based force of twelve squadrons operating up to 147 P-3C Orion maritime-reconnaissance aircraft, which will in the future start to be replaced by Boeing P-8Is, while the USMC has 34,700 personnel involved in aviation.

The fleet is built around eleven carrier combat groups, all of which are nuclear-powered and include the USS *Enterprise* plus ten Nimitz-class ships, all of which have Sea Sparrow SAM, and carry about seventy aircraft with a typical air group consisting of fifty-five F/A-18 Hornet fighters with an air-to-surface strike capability; four EA-6B Prowler electronic warfare aircraft; four E-2C Hawkeye AEW aircraft; four SH-60F Seahawk ASW helicopters and two HH-60 Seahawk SAR helicopters, while carrier

A shot from the destroyer USS *Chafee* of underway replenishment at sea. The USN was the pioneer of the abeam method of replenishment. (USN)

onboard delivery uses C-2A Greyhound transports. A twelfth aircraft carrier is in reserve. There are twenty-two nuclear-powered Ticonderoga-class guided missile cruisers with the Aegis command and control or 'command and decision' system, which co-ordinates sensors and firepower, with Harpoon AShM, Mk41 VLS SAM and also capable of launching Tomahawk cruise missiles, and also armed with two 127mm guns, and which can accommodate two SH-60B Seahawk ASW helicopters, and which are being upgraded to include Evolved Sea Sparrow SAM missiles. There are fifty-nine guided missile destroyers, all of the Arleigh Burke-class, but of these, thirty-one are Flight IIA ships with accommodation for two Sea-hawk ASW helicopters and another twenty-eight are Flight I/II ships with a helicopter landing platform and which may be replaced by additional Flight IIA ships under construction. These ships also have Aegis missiles and Harpoon AShM, Mk 41 VLS, ASROC anti-submarine missiles and can carry Tomahawk cruise missiles as well as having two triple ASTT and are armed with a 127mm gun. There are twenty-two frigates, of which twenty are the remaining Oliver Hazard Perry-class ships after many have been sold abroad in recent years, and which have a 76mm gun, two triple ASTT and accommodation for two Seahawk helicopters, but another nine of these ships are in reserve. The remaining two ships are the first of up to twenty Freedom-class and up to twelve Independence-class ships (the latter, a trimaran design), officially described as 'littoral defence vessels' and are smaller than frigates in most modern navies, but both have accommodation for a Seahawk helicopter or up to three Firescout UAV, and have Phalanx CIWS as well as RAH-116 RAM. These ships have small core crews of about forty to fifty personnel, and high surface speeds.

Submarines have an important place in the modern USN, which no longer operates conventional submarines. There are fourteen Ohio-class SSBN, each with up to twenty-four Trident ballistic missiles, augmented by another four Ohio-class boats modified to carry up to 154 Tomahawk cruise missiles. A total of fifty-three tactical nuclear-powered submarines includes twenty Los Angeles-class, each with four torpedo tubes and capable of launching Harpoon AShM, while another twenty-three improved Los Angeles-class also have four torpedo tubes each and can launch Sea Arrow HWT or Harpoon AShM and up to twelve Tomahawk cruise

The LHD USS *Makin Island* with a deck-load of helicopters. (USN)

missiles. In addition, there are three Seawolf-class boats with eight torpedo tubes able to launch up to forty-five Tomahawk cruise missiles or Harpoon AShM or Sea Arrow HWT, and seven Virginia-class with four torpedo tubes and a vertical launch missile system. Additional boats of this class are under construction.

Expeditionary warfare requires major amphibious ships, of which the most modern are five San Antonio-class LPD, with five more under construction, capable of carrying a CH-53E Sea Stallion or two CH-46 Sea Knight helicopters or a MV-22 Osprey VTOL transport as well as landing craft and up to 720 troops. The additional San Antonio-class ships may replace the four Austin-class LPDs, which can carry six CH-46E Sea Knight, two landing craft and up to forty tanks or 788 troops. There are eight Wasp-class LHD, each with Sea Sparrow SAM, and capable of carrying five AV-8B Harrier II FGA, forty-two CH-46E Sea Knight and six SH-60B Seahawk helicopters, up to sixty tanks and 1,890 troops. LHAs include two Tarawa-class with RIM-116 SAM, and with accommodation for six AV-8B Harrier II FGA, twelve CH-46E Sea Knight and nine CH-53 Sea Stallion helicopters, four landing craft, 100 tanks and up to 1,900 troops. There are four Harpers Ferry-class LSD with RIM-116 SAM, a helicopter landing

The USS *Independence*, one of two types of littoral combat ships that will enter service over the next few years, mainly to protect the coastline and coastal waters of the United States. The design has been criticised for lacking sufficient defensive armament in a hostile zone. (USN)

The Virginia-class nuclear-powered attack submarine USS *Texas* alongside a depot ship. (USN)

platform and accommodation for two landing craft, forty tanks and 500 troops, as well as eight Whidbey Island-class LSD also with RIM-116 SAM, a helicopter landing platform and accommodation for two landing craft, forty tanks and 500 troops. These are augmented by almost 300 landing craft of various kinds. Providing command facilities on amphibious operations are two Blue Ridge-class command ships, which are also capable of carrying five landing craft and 700 troops, while there is a helicopter landing platform.

Although there are twenty-eight patrol craft, many of these are non-operational or in reserve, as are many of the twenty-four MCMV.

There are almost 1,000 combat aircraft, of which the most numerous is the F/A-18 Hornet and Super Hornet, with some 800 aircraft.

Logistics and support ships include five replenishment ships, plus a substantial Military Sealift Command with seventy-four logistics and support ships and thirty-five sealift ships, some of which are on long-term charter.

Officer training is at Annapolis, Maryland, while the major bases are Newport News on the Atlantic, San Diego and Pearl Harbor in the Pacific, and Guantanamo Bay in Cuba. Overseas bases are at Rota in Spain, Naples in Italy, and Soudha Bay in Crete, while there are also command and communications facilities in a number of locations, including Australia.

The organisation comprises the United States Fleet Forces Command; United States Pacific Fleet; United States Naval Forces Central Command; United States Naval Forces Europe; Naval Network Warfare Command; Navy Reserve, United States Naval Special Warfare Command; Operational Test and Evaluation Force; and Military Sealift Command. Below this there are seven active fleets, each numbered, with the Second, Third, Fifth, Sixth, Seventh Fleet and Tenth Fleets each led by a three-star vice admiral, and the Fourth Fleet, whose operational area is off Central and South America, is led by a rear admiral. The First Fleet had been re-designated Third Fleet in early 1973.

It is possible that in the near future the number of aircraft carriers and carrier groups may be cut from eleven ships to nine as the country struggles to balance its budget deficit.

UNITED STATES COAST GUARD SERVICE

Although the modern United States Coast Guard dates from 1915, the service can trace its roots to the United States Revenue Cutter Service established by the Department of the Treasury on 4 August 1790. Until 1798, when the United States Navy was re-established, it was the country's only maritime force and its main duty was to stop smuggling, but from the beginning, rescue was also a function. Its presence during the early period in the history of the US has led some to give the service the name of the 'First Fleet', but this has never been officially recognised.

In 1915, the Revenue Cutter Service merged with the United States Life-Saving Service, creating the USCG. It took over the US Lighthouse Service in 1939 and, in 1942, the Bureau of Marine Inspection and Navigation followed. During the Second World War, the USCG came under the command and control of the USN, but reverted to Treasury control post-war, having served in both the Atlantic and Pacific theatres during the war years. The service was transferred to the Department of Transportation in 1967, but in 2002 was transferred again to the Department of Home-land Security, formed following the terrorist attacks in New York and Washington of 11 September 2001.

Today, the USCG has 43,598 uniformed personnel and another 7,659 civilian employees. It is the primary search and rescue organisation for the United States as well as undertaking EEZ duties and operating patrols to prevent illegal immigration and terrorist infiltration. It has two area com-mands, the Pacific, based on Alameda, California, and the Atlantic, based on Portsmouth, Virginia, and below these commands are nine districts, four in the Pacific and five in the Atlantic. There are 160 'warships', armed and known as cutters, of which the largest, the twenty-eight ships of the Alex Haley, Famous, Hamilton and Legend-classes, can carry helicopters. These ships are supported by ninety-two logistics and support vessels, including two used for training. Aviation is an important function, including twenty-seven HC-130H/J Hercules, with maritime patrol by twenty-six HU-25A/B/C/D Guardian aircraft, while there are 125 SAR helicopters, including thirty-five HH-60 Jayhawk and ninety HH-65 Dauphin II. In addition, there are a number of training and light transport aircraft.

URUGUAY

Population: 3.4 million
Land Area: 72,172 square miles (186,925 sq.km.)
GDP: $41.1bn (£26.7bn), per capita $12,196 (£7,919)
Defence Exp: $431m (£279.8m)
Service Personnel: 24,621 active, plus 818 paramilitary

NATIONAL NAVY OF URUGUAY

The National Navy of Uruguay (*Armada Nacional del Uruguay*, ANdU) traces its origins to the time before the state existed when, in 1817, a Spanish general was given a letter of marque to plunder Buenosairean shipping. He established a privateer force that at one time amounted to fifty armed schooners. The country became a province of Brazil in 1820, and it was not until after an uprising that the country became independent in 1825. The country spent most of the nineteenth century in unrest in which the Navy could play little part, although a small fleet was maintained.

The service's first purpose-built warships arrived in 1884, with a gunboat assembled in Uruguay, while another was bought from Austria-Hungary, and in 1886 these were joined by an ex-French *Marine Nationale* gunboat. The following year, a British-built cruiser was added and a British-built gunboat was commissioned in 1889. After several false starts in the late nineteenth century, a training academy opened in 1907.

Modernisation and expansion continued in the early years of the twentieth century. Uruguay was neutral during the First World War. Afterwards, an air arm was founded in 1920, the *Aviación Naval*, although this remained a small land-based force. The 1920s were a period of reduced funding and cutbacks, during which the efficiency of the ANdU was badly affected. In 1934, the service became autonomous after having been effectively controlled by the army. In 1935, three patrol craft built in Italy were commissioned, served for thirty years, and were then recommissioned back into service in the 1990s.

By 1939, the Navy had just four ships, including the elderly cruiser *Uruguay*, built in Germany in 1910, and the three Italian-built patrol craft already mentioned.

Although Uruguay was officially neutral until early 1945, it was involved early in the war when the German *Panzerschiff Graf Spee* sought refuge in Montevideo harbour after the Battle of the River Plate and before being scuttled. Convoys were escorted in Uruguayan waters and the USN supplied a frigate as well as a number of aircraft for maritime patrols.

Post-war, Uruguay joined the Organisation of American States in 1948 and became eligible for US military aid. This included the supply of destroyers and frigates in 1952 and 1953 as well as Grumman Avenger torpedo bombers. Three coastguard launches were received later in the decade, while the capability of the fleet was enhanced by the addition of an oiler. The 1960s saw Grumman Tracker ASW aircraft enter service as well as additional naval vessels, while a marine corps was established in 1972.

By the late 1970s, the service had a total of 4,000 personnel, with three ex-USN frigates, two corvettes and two German-built Type 209 submarines, as well as patrol craft, landing ships and auxiliaries, while a small number of Tracker ASW aircraft remained with three transport aircraft and a handful of trainers, plus four small helicopters. In 1981, three new patrol boats were commissioned, followed by frigates, also from France. When the Warsaw Pact ended, a number of former East German MCMV were bought, and the US supplied new cutters for the Coast Guard.

Today, the ANdU has 5,403 personnel, of whom 1,800 are Coast Guard members and 211 are engaged in naval aviation, while another 450 are marines. The fleet includes two Portuguese-built frigates of the Uruguay-class, each with two 100mm guns and two triple ASTT. A variety of eighteen patrol and coastal vessels is operated, including three 15 de Noviembre-class (French Vigilante-class) and two Colonia-class (USCG Cape-class), while there are three ex-East German MCMV. There are three landing ships, and the fleet of seven logistics and support ships includes an oiler and a support ship.

Aircraft include a flight with Beech 200Ts and BAe Jetstream, with trainers and six Bo-105M helicopters, and for transport there is a Wessex (S-58) helicopter and a Ecureuil light helicopter.

The main base is at Montevideo, with a second base at Fray Bentos and a river base at Rio Negro.

VENEZUELA

Population: 29 million
Land Area: 352,143 square miles (912,050 sq.km.)
GDP: $381bn (£247bn), per capita $13,113 (£8,514)
Defence Exp: $3.33bn (£2.16bn)
Service Personnel: 115,000 active, plus 8,000 reserves and 23,500 paramilitary
    National Guard

BOLIVARIAN NATIONAL ARMADA OF VENEZUELA

The Bolivarian National Armada of Venezuela (*Armada Nacional Bolivari-ana de Venezuela*) is so called because of the winning of independence from Spain in 1821 by forces led by Simon Bolivar, although the country was united with neighbouring Colombia and did not become independent until 1830. Nevertheless, the service dates its formation from 1811 and the creation of a force to assist the rebels in the fight for independence from Spain. By 1813 a fleet of fourteen ships had been assembled, although its first significant naval battle was that on Lake Maracaibo in July 1823.

Once Venezuela had attained independence, financial problems led to the fleet being reduced, and it was not until 1845 that new ships began to be introduced and conversion from sail to steam started. Nevertheless, the rest of the nineteenth century saw continuing political instability and insurrection in the country that hampered the development of the Navy's full potential. The situation improved during the early years of the twentieth century when the Navy received a number of modern ships, including a cruiser and a number of gun boats and patrol craft. Shipbuilding also began in the country. These ships were augmented by the purchase of vessels withdrawn by other navies during the 1920s and early 1930s. New ships were bought from Italy shortly before the outbreak of the Second World War and, although officially neutral, Venezuela allowed US forces to use bases in the country and benefitted from US military aid, including four submarine hunters. In 1943, a marine corps was formed.

Post-war, Venezuela joined the Organisation of American States in 1948, and qualified for further US assistance. Amongst the first ships provided were seven wartime corvettes and an ex-USN LST. Up until this period the navy had been controlled by the army, but autonomy was gained by 1950.

The 1950s saw considerable expansion and modernisation. New destroyer leaders were commissioned from British yards in 1953 and 1954, followed by light destroyers from Italian yards. By the end of the decade, these had been joined by French-built transports and US-built patrol craft. It was not until the early 1970s that two submarines were transferred from the USN, followed by new submarines from Germany.

By the late 1970s the service had more than 8,000 men and included three destroyers and four Almirante Clement-class frigates, while six Lupo-class frigates were on order from Italy. In addition to ten patrol craft, there were also two ex-USN Guppy-class submarines and two German Type 209 submarines. A force of six amphibious ships included an LST, while a strong force of auxiliaries and logistics ships supported the fighting fleet. Aircraft included Tracker ASW aircraft and Albatross amphibians for SAR, as well as three C-47 Dakota transports, six Agusta-Bell AB-212 ASW helicopters and two Bell 47J training helicopters.

In recent years, new ships have come from a variety of sources, including South Korea, but the country has moved leftwards in recent years with the election of a new government and was the first in the Americas to hold naval exercises with the Russian Navy when ships of the Northern Fleet visited the Caribbean in 2008. It is likely that in the future Venezuela will look to Russia or even Communist China for her naval requirements.

Today the Bolivarian National Armada of Venezuela has 17,500 personnel, of whom 3,200 are conscripts serving up to thirty months, although conscription is by selection and the period varies, with 7,000 of the total being marines and 500 engaged in naval aviation. There are six Mariscal Sucre-class (modified Lupo-class) frigates, each with Ottomat AShM, Aspide SAM, two triple ASTT and a 127mm gun, as well as accommodation for an AB-212 ASW helicopter. There are three British-built missile boats with Ottomat AShM and three British-built patrol craft with a 76mm gun. Amphibious forces include four ex-Russian Capana-class capable of carrying twelve tanks and 200 troops as well as three landing craft. Logistics and supply ships include a replenishment tanker capable of handing a helicopter, and five others.

The main bases are at Puerto Caballo, Caracas and Punto Fijo.

VIETNAM

Population: 89 million
Land Area: 129,607 square miles (335,724 sq.km.)
GDP: $105bn (£67.8bn), per capita $1,178 (£760)
Defence Exp: $2.41bn (£1.55bn)
Service Personnel: 482,000 active, plus 5,000,000 reserves, with 40,000 para-
  military

VIETNAM PEOPLE'S NAVY

Vietnam was originally part of French Indo-China and following French withdrawal in 1954, the country was divided into North and South Vietnam. The country was reunited in 1976, after the United States withdrew from South Vietnam. For most of the period between 1954 and 1976, backed by the Soviet Union, the North infiltrated troops into South Vietnam, which was backed by the United States.

In 1955, the Vietnam People's Navy (VPN) was established to control the country's territorial waters and also patrol the many inland water-ways. Although most of the war involved ground and air forces, the VPN targeted US warships, primarily destroyers, with the most famous incident being when patrol boats attacked the USS *Maddox* in the Gulf of Tonkin on 2 and 4 August 1964. This was dismissed by the North Vietnamese at the time as a fabrication, but the official VPN account since confirms that the destroyer was attacked. Less dramatic, the VPN maintained a seaborne version of the famous Ho Chi Minh Trail supply route, using ships usually disguised as trawlers to carry supplies for the Communist ground forces in the South. While the VPN used seized former South Vietnamese ships to land troops on the Spratly Islands in 1976, the Chinese seized the Paracel Islands, which had formerly been South Vietnamese territory. Vietnam also claims the Paracel Islands, although none of its forces are stationed there.

The fall of South Vietnam provided the VPN with the means to expand from a force of about forty patrol boats and junks to a fleet with two frigates, about 100 patrol craft and fifty or so ships for amphibious warfare, including an ex-USN LST. Taking advantage of its new acquisitions, the VPN formed a detachment of marines.

Today the VPN has some 40,000 personnel, of whom about 27,000 are marines. The most recent additions to the fleet have been two Soviet-built Gepard-class frigates, which may have 'Switchblade' AShM, 'Gecko' SAM, five single ASTT, two 30mm CIWS and a 76mm gun, which arrived in 2011. There are also five ex-Soviet Petya II/III frigates with quintuple or triple ASTT, RBU 6000/2500 rocket launchers and 4 76mm guns, while two older frigates may have been deleted or reduced to training duties. The larger offshore patrol boats include seven Soviet-supplied Tarantul-class, some of which have P-15 Termit ('Styx') AShM, while others have the 'Switchblade' AShM, but all have 'Grail' SAM and a 76mm gun. There are another forty patrol boats, although the serviceability of some of these is doubtful, as well as thirteen MCMV. There are just two small submarines supplied by North Korea, each with two torpedo tubes. There are three LST and three LSM, as well as thirty landing craft and twenty-five auxiliaries, including two floating docks.

The main bases are at Hanoi, Ho Chi Minh City, Da Nang, Cam Ranh Bay, Ha Tou, Haiphong and Can Tho.

YEMEN

Population: 24.3 million
Land Area: 184,289 square miles (486,524 sq.km.)
GDP: $30.7bn (£19.9bn), per capita $1,264 (£820)
Defence Exp: $2.02bn (£1.3bn)
Service Personnel: 66,700 active, plus 71,200 paramilitary

YEMEN NAVY

The Yemen Navy was formed in 1990 after the merger of North and South Yemen, the latter being the former British mandated Aden Protectorate. The country has a problem with smuggling, especially of arms, and this problem has grown since, with much of the country unstable and governed by local warlords with Islamic terrorist allegiances. It is a coastal or 'brown water' force and does not participate in international operations against Somali pirates or in protection of merchant shipping, despite the country's important strategic location.

Today, the YN has 1,700 personnel. It has a patrol craft, the *Tarantul*, whose operational status in doubtful, but officially has 'Styx' AShM. There are another nineteen patrol boats, of which thirteen are Hounan-class fitted with 'Styx' AShM but, again, their operational status is doubtful. There is a former Soviet MCMV, an LSM and three landing craft.

The main bases are at Aden and Hodeida, but there are a number of minor bases.

BIBLIOGRAPHY

Chesnau, Roger, *Aircraft Carriers of the World, 1914 to the Present*, Arms & Armour Press, London, 1992.

Gardiner, Robert (Ed), *Conway's All The World's Fighting Ships, 1906-1921*, Conway Maritime Press, London, 1985.

Ireland, Bernard, *Jane's Naval History of World War II*, HarperCollins, London, 1998.

Le Fleming, H.M., *Warships of World War I*, Ian Allan, London, 1970.

O'Hara, Vincent P., Dickson, W. David, Worth, Richard, *On Seas Contested – The Seven Great Navies of the Second World War*, Naval Institute Press, Annapolis, 2010.

Preston, Antony, *Aircraft Carriers*, Bison Books, London, 1979.

Destroyers, Hamlyn Books, London, 1977.

Wragg, David, *Second World War Carrier Campaigns*, Pen & Sword, Barnsley, 2004.